Christian Feminist Theology

D0470561

IB

CHRISTIAN
feminist
THEOLOGY

A CONSTRUCTIVE INTERPRETATION

DENISE L. CARMODY

BLACKWELL
Oxford UK & Cambridge USA

First published 1995
2 4 6 8 10 9 7 5 3 1

Blackwell Publishers Inc.
238 Main Street
Cambridge, Massachusetts 02142, USA

Blackwell Publishers Ltd
108 Cowley Road
Oxford OX4 1JF
UK

Library of Congress Cataloging-in-Publication Data
Carmody, Denise Lardner, 1935–
    Christian feminist theology : a constructive interpretation /
Denise Lardner Carmody.
        p.   cm.
    Includes index.
    ISBN 1–55786–586–8 (alk. paper). —ISBN 1–55786–587–6 (pbk. :
alk. paper)
    1. Feminist theology.   I. Title.
BT83.C365   1995
230'.082– –dc20   95–14743
                                                                        CIP

British Library Cataloguing in Publication Data

A CIP catalogue record for this book is available from the British Library.

Typeset in Meridien on 11/13.5 pt by CentraCet Limited, Cambridge
Printed in Great Britain by T. J. Press Ltd, Padstow, Cornwall

This book is printed on acid-free paper.

Contents

Preface   ix

1   Introduction   1

Constructive Christian Feminism   1
Theology   6

2   Foundations   12

The Search for Justice   12
The Search for Meaning   17
The Search for Beauty   21
The Search for Love   25
The Great Choice: Despair or Hope   30
What Women Can Hope   34

3   Revelation and Tradition   40

Revelation   40
Scripture   45
Tradition   49
Church History   55
World Religions   61
Feminist Revisions   66

4   Creation: Nature and Ecology 72

How the World Was Born 72
How the World Is Maintained 76
The Signs of God in Nature 82
The Place of Human Beings in the World 88
Ecology as a Religious Issue 91
Diminishing Dominion 95

5   Ecclesiology: Society and Politics 102

A Vision of Community 102
Social, Structural Sin 107
Christian Feminism and Power 113
Sacraments as Acts of Christ's Body 119
The Social Location of Redemption 126
Women in the Church 133

6   Anthropology: the Self Sick and Healthy 139

Finding Oneself in God 139
A Christian Feminist View of Love 144
The Self as a Social Relation 148
The Sins that Shackle the Self 153
Faith and the Life-cycle of Women 159
Prayer as the Ultimate Freedom 166

7   Theology: God So Far and Yet So Near 173

God So Far: Thinking Correctly about Transcendence 173
God So Near: Thinking Correctly about Immanence 178
Jesus: the Wisdom of God in Flesh 182
Jesus: the Suffering of God 187
The Trinity: God as Father and Mother 192
The Trinity: God as Inclusive Spirit 199

8   Practice: Ethics and Spirituality 206

A Christian Feminist View of Ethics 206
Community as an Ethical Touchstone 211

Love as the Power of Persuasion   216
Women and Scandalous Poverty   220
Christian Feminism and Sexual Ethics   225
Ethics and Spirituality: the Case of Ecology   230
Conversion: Prayer and Social Justice   234

9 Conclusion   242

The Harmony of "Christian" and "Feminist"   242
The Mutual Challenge of "Christian" and "Feminist"   247
Theology as a Lyrical Calling   252
Holiness as a Realistic Goal   257

Index   263

For Bernadette Proulx

PREFACE

This book is an overview of traditional Christian theology, written for college undergraduates and developed in the light of moderate present-day feminist sensibilities. As such, it combines two allegiances. The first is to the faith handed down through the Christian centuries – repeated, interpreted, brought up to date, reformed, practiced at the altar and in the workplace. In my usage, the designation "traditional" is a badge of honor. I want to pass along to students a representative specimen of how the mainstream of the Christian population (which is now the largest religious body in the world, numbering about 1.87 billion according to the 1994 Encyclopaedia Britannica *Book of the Year*) have thought about God, the world, and themselves – about "reality." Certainly, I want to make this traditional theology relevant to present-day concerns, but I do not want to offer anything merely modish, ephemeral, or idiosyncratic. That is not the sort of theology that traditional Christians believe renders well the gospel, the glad tidings, in which their forebears have delighted for nearly twenty centuries. That is not the sort of theology that takes the Bible as the regular starting point for Christian theological reflection. Certainly, we ought to use the Bible critically, with a properly sophisticated mind. But we cannot make another source more central without departing from the traditional mainstream.

This book is also "constructive," meaning integrated, organic, systematic. I am presenting the traditional major topics of Christian theology in what I hope is an orderly, connected fashion, so as to make them emerge as a coherent worldview. Constructive theology is not a survey of current trends. It may draw on a variety of sources, recent or classical, but it labors to work them into a consistent, harmonious statement of the whole of Christian faith. In such a statement, the various parts or doctrines depend on one another and support one another mutually. As in a building, there is a floor, supporting walls, and a roof, all of which work together to make a whole. The construct here ought to leave the reader who works through it patiently with a solid first sense of the whole of traditional Christian doctrine, the full edifice.

Finally, perhaps it bears noting that this is *a* constructive layout. Just as different architects design different buildings, so do different constructive theologians design different orderings of the major components of traditional faith. Nonetheless, the theologians with whom I am allying myself all depend on the common Christian faith (creed) long handed down, and they all subscribe to the classical Augustinian–Anselmian description of theology as "faith seeking understanding." When we labor at constructive Christian theology, none of us traditionalists works in "religious studies," where faith should not call the tunes. All of us desire to render afresh the venerable teachings that first solicited our commitment regarding Jesus and then developed in each subsequent Christian generation.

My second allegiance in this work of traditional, constructive Christian theology for college undergraduates is to the current movement of women to gain recognition of their full equality with men in the possession of human nature. In this sense, I write as a "feminist," though hardly as a radical or separatist one. For I believe that feminists ought to be as concerned about claiming equal access to common human qualities as about showing what has been distinctive in women's experience. We ought to realize that the "existentials" of the human condition (finitude, death, sin, reason, work, love, prayer) determine more of our ultimate, religious meaning than the differences that gender develops.

This means that my understanding of a traditional, historically mainstream Christian theology makes it much more applicable to the needs and hopes of women than not. It means that I believe that women have as much reason as men, as much emotion, as much mortality, as much sin, as much holiness, and as much calling from God to live full, fruitful lives. For example, I believe that Jesus directed his message to women as much as to men. When Jesus preached about the Kingdom of God he did not restrict it to men, as such scenes in the gospels as his instructing the Samaritan woman (John 4) show. Certainly, the gender of the woman shaped how Jesus interacted with her, as did her being a Samaritan. But in my view, and the view of what I take to be the historical mainstream, these particulars mattered less to Jesus, were more accidental, than the substantial fact that the woman was a human being in great need of God. Three models of recent constructive theology that I consider cognate to my own on this score, and that have encouraged me in my development of this textbook, are Elizabeth Johnson's *She Who Is*, Catherine LaCugna's *God for Us*, and Sallie McFague's *Models of God*.

Despite its conviction that women are as human as men, as much shaped by the common existentials of the human condition and as much addressed by religious prophets such as Jesus, the moderate feminism to which I feel loyal does not shrink from criticizing the many ways in which, throughout the history of the Christian church, women have not been treated as the equals of men in aptness for religious instruction, for serving as ministers of the gospel and leaders of the church, and for influencing how the gospel ought to be translated for given epochs, cultures, or geographical locales. What feminists call "patriarchy" and think of pejoratively has defaulted on the radical equality latent in the gospel of Jesus, often sinfully. The rule by men that has prevailed in most of the Christian churches in most historical periods has worked to the neglect of women's rights, freedoms, and joys.

Women have been the second sex in most times and places of Christian history, just as they have been in most of world history overall. The Christian church has not distinguished itself as the champion of women's rights as it would have had it been holier – better attuned to the Spirit of its Master. In this failing the church has been all too human, as it has been all too human when dealing with matters of racial justice, economic justice, respect for the natural environment, respect for indigenous cultures, and respect for sexual minorities. Certainly, many Christians have led reforms that have raised the awareness of their contemporaries and brought better education, medical care, working conditions, and the like for the underclasses. But too often the Christian church has been so aligned with the status quo, the blocs of those holding economic, political, and cultural power in the Western nations, that churchpeople have perpetuated, even deepened, sinful, oppressive social structures.

While I hold no brief for the brands of feminism that repudiate the Christian gospel as a whole, or that fan among women a hatred for men, I do associate myself with what I take to be a broad, populist movement among feminists (male as well as female) who now think that women have often gotten a raw deal. This thought naturally prompts another thought: such injustice has to stop, both outside the churches and inside. Inasmuch as traditional Christian theology has abetted injustice toward women or colluded with a sexist depreciation of women, traditional Christian theology needs a reform, an overhaul. In calling this text a constructive *feminist* Christian theology I want to indicate my desire to contribute to such an overhaul, my intent to advance such a reform.

Practically, then, I want students to find in this book an exposition of Christian faith that is (a) loyal to what the mainstream of believers – the majority of the Orthodox, Catholic, Protestant and Evangelical members – consider their treasure and birthright, and (b) loyal to the desire of tens of millions of women to receive a better representation, a fuller justice, in both the speculative and the practical aspects of such a traditional Christian faith. I want to be moderate in my faith: generally acceptable to the 80 percent of Christians who are neither wild radicals nor mossbacked conservatives. I also want to be moderate in my feminism: generally acceptable to the 80 percent of women who neither hate men nor are blind to the injustices that women have suffered from patriarchal institutions, the Church included emphatically. This moderation renders what I think the realities of Christian faith, the realities of the human condition, the actual feelings of most women, and the actual good of most women and men dictate.

Finally, may I say that such moderation (striving for balance, concern not to err by either excess or deficiency) is also what twenty-five years of teaching college undergraduates (thousands of students, in eight different colleges) and writing more than a dozen textbooks for college courses have convinced me is most appropriate. What ecologists call the "commons" of the natural world has its analogue in theology. God is a "commons," as is the salvation that Christ offers and the flourishing of the human species through justice and love.

To refuse to elaborate one's theology or ethics in the light of this commons, preferring the shadows of partisanship or political (linguistic, conceptual, behavioral) correctness, is to make idols, heresies, and feckless combines doomed to failure. In my view, it is to be stupid and sinful, because it is to be unwilling to let the Spirit of God stretch one through her demanding love of the whole – all the earth, all the earth's people. So I ask you, my readers, for one boon: be hard on your stupidity and sinfulness, your narcissistic partialisms; and, if you read this on a good day, be merciful toward mine. Thank you.

My thanks go out to Alison Mudditt of Blackwell Publishers for inviting me to undertake this project, and to my husband, John Carmody, for working it through with me.

Chapter 1

INTRODUCTION

Constructive Christian Feminism

We embark on a work of construction, an enterprise of building. What are we setting out to construct, what is our building for, to house, to serve? We are setting out to construct a view of the world, of reality, indebted to, faithful to, in the service of, two principal sources or inspirations. The first is traditional, orthodox Christian faith. The second is moderate feminism, understood as "a commitment to the complete equality of women with men in the possession of humanity." Let us begin by elaborating this description and reflecting on the compatibility of the two principal sources or inspirations that it entails.

Traditional, orthodox Christian faith is the following of Jesus that has gone forward, marching through history for most of the past 2000 years, in the mainstream churches. If we date the life of Jesus to roughly the first forty years of what we now call the Christian era (AD or CE), then for nearly 1960 years followers, disciples, have structured their lives, constructed the world of the meanings by which they have interpreted their human condition, by reference to Jesus. All who have called him "Lord" and made him their most precious treasure have acted in this way. "Faith" is precisely this action, this treasuring, this living by reference to Jesus as the key interpretation of what is most important in life, of where we come from and where we are going, of how we can more nearly become what we long to become in our best moments, of how we can endure the sufferings that seem to afflict all human beings, including the sufferings entailed in our certain deaths.

I emphasize that the Christian faith at play in this book is traditional and orthodox. "Tradition" is what people "hand on." It goes from one generation to the next, both formally and informally. Formally, a people's teachers instruct the younger generation explicitly, through classes of some sort, initiations, apprenticeships. Informally, the mainstream of the community reminds the membership as a whole of what they should believe, treasure, assume about the shape of reality, through the processes, the ordinary interactions, of daily life.

There is nothing peculiar to Christianity in my description of tradition to this point. One can find a fine example of everything mentioned so far in a good book on Jewish life in the Eastern European *shtetl* in the twentieth century prior to the Second World War.[1] Everywhere, traditional cultures have handed on, reworked, applied, updated, retrieved, reformed, and generally kept going their central convictions through the ordinary, largely unconscious, social dynamics that have constituted their cultures. In the measure that their cultures have been homogeneous, closer to uniform in their central convictions than pluriform or divided, traditional peoples have tended to be nearly unaware that their social dynamics might have been very different. How they have lived, what they have believed, has seemed almost as natural as the patterns of the sun and the rain, as the regular ways of the animals.

It is virtually impossible for a citizen of a present-day, modern Western culture to live in as traditional a fashion as I have just described. Indeed, what we mean by "modern" is in conflict with "traditional," inasmuch as modernity (for our purposes, beginning in the European West in the sixteenth century, with the takeover by the Reformation and the Renaissance) ushered in a new era of consciousness, because it split the relatively seamless sense of tradition and faith that had obtained prior to such epochal events as the Reformation, the Renaissance, and, in the eighteenth century, the Enlightenment.

In actual historical fact, of course, no human century or era has ever lacked diversity or challenge or at least a creative minority of the population who sensed the frailty, the contingency, of the cultural assumptions that the majority wanted, sometimes nearly desperately, to the point of psychic distress, to make appear as natural as the rising and setting of the sun or the flow of the seasons. But modernity certainly broke with the pace of prior centuries, where change seemed slower and cultural assumptions less assaulted. In fact, modernity eventually placed diversity, pluralism, and so skepticism and doubt close to the heart of its "enterprise," its wholesale exploration of new physical and cultural frontiers. Modernity is where human beings became much more aware of their diversity than they had been previously, and also much more aware that they themselves create much of their meaning. Previously, human beings had felt deeply immersed in a nature obviously more powerful than they. In modernity, first through the rise of empirical natural science and then through philosophical reflection, human beings began to face the fact, both exciting and frightening, that they themselves construct, create, huge portions of their meaning – what their time under the sun will signify.

So, when I say that the Christian faith at work, under investigation, entering into the construction that we are attempting, is "traditional," I really mean that it is a modern, or post-modern (post-Second World War) version of what in prior, pre-modern ages apparently flowed along considerably less self-consciously than has been possible since the Reformation, the Renaissance, the Enlightenment, and the other capital cultural events that separate our present era of Western Christian history from what prevailed 500 or so years ago, at the dawn of the sixteenth century. I also mean that a few capital convictions (such as that in Jesus the Christ one finds a complete humanity fully united with, joined to, but not mixed confusedly with a complete divinity: one person, two natures) continue to prevail in this constructive venture, giving the Christian faith that I am building in league with a feminist allegiance its basic shape.

(The two other capital traditional convictions that I should single out, at this juncture, are that (a) the Christian God is a Trinitarian community customarily named "Father-Son-Spirit," and that (b) "Grace," which is both the deathless life of this communitarian God and that God's particular helps for human beings, has been revealed in the life, the historical story, of Jesus the Christ to have prevailed over "Sin," understood as everything that opposes such a life. Moreover, the prevailing of grace over sin makes human existence a comedy, in the profound sense of a dramatic success, rather than a tragedy.)

These doctrinal convictions are further indications of what I mean by the word "orthodox." "Orthodoxy" is "right opinion" and/or "right praise." It is what the mainstream churches, assemblies of disciples of Christ, and gatherings of the followers of Jesus for social life, worship, instruction in faith, political action, and other functions natural to communities of human beings have, sometimes with precision, more often in rough-and-ready fashion, considered to be sound, traditional, customary, reasonable, faithful to the understandings, allegiances, and values of their parents and grandparents, as well as to the commitments of other Christian communities, near and far both historically and geographically.

"Orthodox" faith is catholic, held by the many, ordinary rather than special or idiosyncratic. While it admits room for local diversity and individual interpretation, it prefers to stress the commonweal, the life of the whole rather than that of the part. Orthodox Christians run the danger of becoming mossbacked, conservative in a pejorative sense, rigid psychologically as well as intellectually. On the other hand, they are the great preservers of the tradition, the strong glue against fissiparous protests and sectarianism. To their mind, to what they consider right Christian opinion and praise, God hates heresy and schism, usually, though not always, attributing them to pride, singularity, individuals puffing themselves up and forgetting their immense debts to prior ages, and forgetting as well the utter necessity that individuals finally bow to those holding legitimate authority in the community, if that community, that church, is to survive.

So much for a first suggestion of the traditionally Christian character of our enterprise. The full suggestion, presentation, and rendering will unfold relatively leisurely through the chapters that follow. Let me now elaborate the sense of "feminism" at work in these pages. Just as I desire to present a Christian faith that is faithful to the mainstream, the median tradition that has come down through the past two millennia, so I desire to present a balanced, mature, moderate or median feminism. I am not a disciple of any feminist theory or movement that advocates the superiority of women to men, any more than I can accept any philosophical or theological anthropology (view of human nature) that subordinates women to men as inferior. Observation, historical study, cultural analysis, and years of probing Christian faith have convinced me that the sexes are fully equal in their possession of humanity, both its flaws and its graces.

Moreover, I cannot accept separatist views that would take the sexes apart. I believe that females and males, women and men, are coordinated to one another, both obviously, as a simple fact, brutal as well as lovely, built into our bodies, absolutely necessary for reproduction, and more subtly, through the endless cultural varieties of romance, conflict, comfort, misunderstanding, laughter, and tears. Few things, realities, or phenomena seem to me doubted less properly than the basic heterosexuality, male–femaleness, female–maleness, of "humanity." From the elementary fact that children get half their chromosomes from their mother and half from their father to the perhaps more intriguing fact that females have created half of human history, simply by being present everywhere that our species has made meaning, with minds and hearts that said yes and no, I assume and postulate, that we, women and men, have a conjoint destiny – that the "image of God" that Genesis (1:27) says we carry comes from God's having created humanity as two-sexed, male–female.

Without denying that 5–10 percent of human beings appear to have a homosexual orientation, I believe that both a balanced feminism and a traditional, orthodox Christian faith depend on making the heterosexuality of the 90–95 percent majority normative. In my view, both evolutionary biology and the creative will of the Christian God determine that women and men should usually live together, though the ways in which we may do this are endless, ideally depending more on our creative imaginations than on any rigid biological, social, or religious constraints.

Why should we have to champion the perhaps obvious equality of women in the possession of humanity (embodiment, reason, emotion, the image of God) and so speak of a constructive traditional Christian faith that is "feminist"? Principally because of both the historical influence of "patriarchy" (the apparent predominance of men over women in shaping social consciousness and culture) and the recognition nowadays that patriarchy has often rendered women second-class citizens, victims of injustice and discrimination. Any healthy Christian faith or human spirituality (pursuit of idealistic living) has to abhor injustice and fight it. Inasmuch, then, as our time, our cultural moment in Western countries at the end of the second millennium AD, finds a widespread conviction that patriarchy has twisted the lives of many women (and also of many men) out of joint, those healthy in conscience find themselves opposing patriarchy: thinking, and ideally acting, as feminists, as champions of the full equality of women with men in the possession of human nature, and so as foes of "sexism" – any claim or practice that denies this full equality. The first reason for accepting "Christian" as a proper predicate for "feminism" is the obvious kinship of its traditional convictions about justice with the passion of moderate feminists to restore the female half of the race to its rightful equality with the male half.

Theology

Our title calls this book a constructive Christian feminist *theology*. It will be useful at the outset to meditate briefly on the significance of this peculiar word, as I hope it has been useful to meditate on the significance of the words "constructive," "traditional," "orthodox," "Christian," "feminist," and "patriarchy." The philosopher Ludwig Wittgenstein reminded us that the limits of our language are the limits of our world. If we can get our language straight, and make it maximally imaginative, we can experience worlds of meaning full of sense, beauty, and the open-endedness that we do well to call hope. If we can un-limit some of the terms that we customarily employ, when we deal with religion, we can begin to realize how rich our traditions of faith actually are – and how full of wisdom concerning the best ways to live, think, and try to feel in the future.

"Theology" is an especially rich word, because it bears on the ultimate mystery of human existence, God (*Theos*). The most common traditional definition of Christian theology, developed for Western Christianity in the patristic era and clarified among the medievals, is *fides quaerens intellectum*: "faith seeking understanding." Faith comes first. People make a commitment, or semi-consciously, semi-deliberately, semi-responsibly accept and appropriate the commitment of their community, to Christ as the pearl of great price, the personal treasure on whom to set their hearts. Then, in a second moment and move, they put their minds to work on this commit-ment-already-in-place, seeking to generate what understanding they can. One might say that first the Christian goes into the church, kneels, and prays – acts like an ordinary believer. Then the Christian reflects, tries to understand why such actions seem natural, even beautiful, thereby becoming "theological."

The word *Theos* shapes this reflection, this potentially disciplined effort to understand what one believes, because this effort quickly focuses on the source, the main referent, of the religious practice that has preceded it. For Christians, that source and main referent can be nothing other than the divine mystery itself, because Jesus referred his entire teaching and practice to his "Father," the form in which the divine mystery, the traditional Lord of Jewish faith, piety, and practice, appeared to him.[2] Faithful followers of Jesus are therefore bound to find the search for the meaning of Christian faith leading them onto the same boundless track, the same limitless mystery of creation and destiny, beginning and beyond, that Jesus and prior Christians have traditionally called their "God" (the Father).

If theology has any valid reason-to-be, if there is in the sweep of reality that the human mind can survey any such limitless mystery as that which beguiled Jesus' heart, then theology is both inevitable and crucial. It is inevitable, because we human beings have an itch to understand, a congenital, probably evolutionarily necessary, ambition to map the world in which we live, so as to orient ourselves both physically and spiritually. For this reason, Aristotle laid it down that all people by nature desire to know. Reason, the active search to understand, is what characterizes our kind, separating us from the other animals. We are the species, the evolutionary unit, that has a *logos*: word, reason, mind. Certainly, we also make tools characterist-ically, manipulate symbols, possess opposable thumbs, and are feath-erless bipeds. One can even observe usefully that we are incarnate spirits, median or "synthetic" beings, located midway in the Great Chain of Being, a little less than the angels, a little more than the great apes. All of these traditional descriptions of human specificity are interesting, illuminating.

However, the most crucial thing about us, and the one that gives all other specific descriptions their source and rationale, is the fact that we women and men have minds and hearts oriented to meaning and capable of creating it. And because, as we probe this most crucial thing, we find that we cannot separate it from the mysteriousness, the ineluctible excess or too-fullness, of our situation, of the world in which we find ourselves placed, we have one day to confront the word "God," which is the most customary and famous name that our kind has hung over such too-fullness, such too-much-for-us-ness. On that day, we can realize that theology is natural to the human mind, indeed that there is no human mind, no elevation toward the light of understanding, apart from this mysteriousness that eventually turns out to be limitless.

Finally, on a later day, when we begin to become properly sophisticated about all these factors, and so at least glimpse their inextricable correlation, we can see that the mysteriousness, God, is truly holy, since by the word "holy" we mean what is most real, basic, primitive, original – most the source rather than the effect, the font rather than the derivative. Nothing is more basic or generative than the divine mystery. The divine mystery makes the human mind much more than the human mind makes the divine mystery. There is no human mind without the limitless horizon that we call God. We only get meaning, only have the mental space that our metaphors require for their play, only receive the spiritual oxygen that our brains need for their life-sustaining symbols, from God, the infinite horizon that makes possible all the definitions that constitute human meaning.

Without God, the unfenced whole, we could not fence in the constituents of our necessarily partial worlds of business and science, art and politics, family life and sports. We could not be able to define, or specify, or delimit, particular terms, problems, analyses, and solutions as we must do, if we are to make our way, largely piecemeal, through our days, our jobs, our towns. God is the backdrop against which all our play, drama and outstanding action occurs. God is the silent spiritual context, universe, in whose midst, from whose encouragement (to put them in the light), we give at least inner voice to our stories, the narratives that gather our days into a life.

Theology is the effort to understand God, and our faithful relations to God, as best we can – with all the help that our traditions can provide. Theology is humble, when it knows its business, because the mysteriousness of God, and so the inevitable failure of our efforts to understand, is so obvious that it threatens to overwhelm us. Traditional Christian theology is full of cautionary reminders about the need for this humility. The more widely you read in traditional Christian theology, especially in its patristic sources, the more likely you are to come across phrases such as "If you understand, it has not been God," and "Whatever we say about God, no matter how true, what we say is more unlike God than like." God is always greater (*semper major*).

If our minds exalt us, God is greater. If our minds depress us, discourage us, threaten us with despair, God is greater. Neither exaltation nor discouragement limits what God can be, what God can do for us, how God always holds both the priority and the final say. If our hearts condemn us, God is greater, and so may forgive us, restore us, wipe away every tear from our eye. We are wrong, idolaters of sorts, to wander into culs-de-sac of hopelessness, dead ends where we are sure that the confusions of life offer no way out. Equally, we are wrong to wander into foolish optimisms, let alone prideful certainties that we know the will of God, or that the angels of God have inscribed our names in the book of life with ink indelibly gold.

God answers only to God. God remains God, regardless of how we twist or turn. The audacity of Christian faith is the faith, hope, and love it draws from the sacramental life of Jesus the Christ to trust that God's answer to God, God's unmoveable sovereignty, is good, blessed, for us human beings. Christian theology draws from this audacity, which it grounds in its acceptance of the resurrection of full meaning and hope in the raising of Jesus from the grave, its courage to continue tracking the divine mystery, braving the divine wilderness, trusting that, when asked for bread, the Father or Mother will not hand over a stone.[3]

In this book, our theology will be constructive, Christian, and feminist. We shall be trying to build an understanding of traditional, orthodox Christian faith that displays the "ecology," the tissue or web of conceptual connections, characteristic of a living organism, a "building" of the order that the Pauline New Testament figure of the "Body" of Christ and the Johannine figure of the vine-and-branches call to mind. The chapters that we develop will be traditional, in that one can find their material contents in most ordinary textbooks of Christian theology. Indeed, in many ordinary textbooks one can find a sequence much like that followed here: (a) foundational issues (where the search to understand faith comes from, what anchors it in human experience); (b) revelation and tradition; (c) creation; (d) ecclesiology (issues regarding the Church, the Christian community); (e) anthropology (issues regarding human nature); (f) theology proper (the nature of the Christian God); and (g) the practice of Christian faith (ethics).

If our ecological construction, our spinning of a web of reflections about the divine mystery that Jesus presents to us, goes well, by the end we shall have gained considerable light, as well as a considerable reminder that God always remains dark, in the sense of too bright for our limited, dull minds to grasp except very partially.

Finally, it bears repeating that our constructive Christian theology will be feminist, in the sense of being born out of a commitment to the full equality of women with men in the possession of the human nature defined and addressed by God. I write this book feeling invited to ponder the peculiar, in many ways hitherto neglected, stimuli to reflection, to richer understanding of faith, glimmering in the religious experience, the praxis, of Christian women. For example, with a few exceptions creditable to Protestant sources, the traditional, orthodox theology of the mainstream churches has done little with family life, the care of children, and even conjugal sexuality, though all have offered hundreds of millions of women, and men, legions of hints about the nature of God, the implications of the teaching of Jesus about God, the ways and means of the grace of God, of the saving divine life that believers hope with all their hearts is moving in their depths, carrying them into rich meaning, even into eternal life.

Had more women been welcome in the patristic catechetical schools and medieval universities where traditional Christian theology took shape, later ages might have received in all the chapters of its ordinary textbooks materials stemming from such domestic experiences, concerns, occasions of grace. Often, that might have humanized theology greatly, making God seem warmer, closer, easier to trust and love, than tended to be the case. In short, it might have made the Christian God seem as much Mother as Father, Sister as Brother, gentle and graceful as strong and just.

Be that as it might have been, in a different past, there is no good reason why we should not attempt to make some proper equivalent of it appear in our day, when feminism has become a potent cultural factor. Indeed, there are many good reasons for thinking that those of us drawn to such an enterprise, intrigued by the prospect of exploring the divine mystery anew from the perspective of feminist appreciations of Christian orthodoxy, have the obligation, as well as the exciting opportunity, to get on with it, for the beauty that it holds out, the enrichment of faith that it just might create. Consequently, I'm glad to be under way.[4]

Study Questions

1 Write a short paragraph explaining your preliminary understanding of the words "Christian," "feminist," and "constructive."
2 Develop a preliminary definition for the word "theology," and then describe how theology changes if we modify it with the adjectives "Christian," "feminist," and "constructive."

Notes

1 Mark Zborowski and Elizabeth Herzog, *Life Is with People* (Schocken Books, New York, 1962).
2 Bernard Cooke, *God's Beloved* (Trinity Press International, Philadelphia, 1992).
3 Elisabeth Schüssler Fiorenza, *Bread Not Stone* (Beacon Press, Boston, 1984).
4 As general background, see Arvind Sharma (ed.), *Today's Woman in World Religion* (State University of New York Press, Albany, 1994) and Ursula King (ed.), *Religion and Gender* (Blackwell, Oxford, 1995). Also useful is Joann Wolski and Walter E. Conn (eds), *Horizons on Catholic Feminist Theology* (Georgetown University Press, Washington, DC, 1992). I am grateful to the editors for dedicating this book to my husband John and me.

Chapter 2

FOUNDATIONS

The Search for Justice

We have described feminism as a search for justice – a commitment to the full equality of women with men in the possession of humanity. Justice is the situation that obtains when people receive and give fairly, get and provide what is right, due, fitting. Justice makes for balance, equity, proportion. It keeps things, relationships, and systems in joint, keeps them from getting out of kilter. Spurred by a Christian understanding of how God draws us human beings forward, into fuller appreciations of the divine mystery that holds out our richest fulfillment, I believe that a strong search for justice is in fact a religious (ultimate, sacred) quest. This seems clear, for instance, in the passionate resistance of Daw Aung San Sun Kyi, the delicate woman who won the 1991 Nobel Peace Prize, to the military government of Myanmar (formerly Burma).

Mrs Aung San Sun Kyi comes by her political commitments from her father, Aung San, who led Burma to independence from Britain in 1948. Placed under house arrest in the summer of 1989 for leading a democratic movement, she draws strength from a sign bearing a saying of her father: "You cannot use martial law as an excuse for injustice." If the saying was true during the Burmese struggle for independence, and so shamed the British, it remains equally true today, to the shame of those who have jailed Mrs Aung San Sun Kyi merely for speaking out against their dictatorship.

The corruption of the military dictators shows in their complete disregard for the will of the people of Myanmar:

> Her [Mrs Aung San Sun Kyi's party], the National League for Democracy, won a landslide victory in the May 1990 general election while she was detained. The military government refused to recognize the results and arrested most of the party's leaders under a law intended to protect the nation from the "dangers from the subversive elements." She has never been on trial.[1]

In addition to the example of her father, Buddhist wisdom has kept Mrs Aung San Sun Kyi going:

> "When I first went out campaigning, a very, very old abbot – he was over 90 – gave me two bits of advice," she said. "The first was that to get happiness, you have to invest in suffering. The second is that if you want to indulge in honest politics, you've got to be prepared to be reviled and attacked. He was right."[2]

What creates so fine a spirit as this, willing to suffer great deprivation to fight for social justice? Where does the strength, the conviction, the determination come from? Usually, people signal for such determination cannot say, at least fully. Usually, their determination, their commitment, is virtually identical with their conscience, their moral self, and so they cannot think of themselves as feeling or acting otherwise. For Mrs Aung Sun San Kyi to be dedicated to the liberation of her people from dictatorship to democratic self-determination is simply for her to be herself – to act upon the perceptions that come to her, the evaluations she makes spontaneously, as she observes life around her, participates in her local culture. It is so clear to her that the military leaders are oppressively wrong, abusive and self-serving that she has no choice except to oppose them. She could no more call their rule right than she could say the sun rises in the west or the moon has nothing to do with the tides.

Inasmuch as history suggests that most human beings have lived in times that seemed to them out of joint, most human beings have searched for justice, a better political climate and equation than they were being served. The majority probably have not seen the problems as clearly as heroes such as Mrs Aung San Sun Kyi, but most human beings have been well aware that social life ought to have been better, fairer, than it was.

More or less bravely, explicitly, and effectively, many human beings in each generation have tried to make social life better, fairer. They have tried to tell the truth, and so to name the lies distorting their cultural climate. They have tried to help the poor, lift up the downtrodden, heal the sick. And, normally, they would do these things undramatically, in a low key, because they thought of such deeds, such helpfulness, as merely what any good person would do, what any good neighbor would extend.

In fact, though, it is by no means obvious that it is natural and unexceptional for one human being to help another at cost. Even when we can make a good case for the evolutionary benefits in cooperation, we have to note that a great many human beings are slow to practice it. Even slower are they, we human beings as a bloc, to practice altruism – taking the needs of the other, especially the other suffering from injustice, as more important than our own wants. Generosity is sufficiently rare to make the generous stand out. A passion for justice is sufficiently remarkable to distinguish a person manifesting it as exceptional, perhaps even holy.

Thus, nowadays we tend to regard Mohandas Gandhi, the leader of the movement that freed India from British rule in 1948, and Martin Luther King Jr, the leader of the Civil Rights Movement in the United States during the early 1960s, as holy men, even martyrs (inasmuch as they were murdered for their leadership). Similarly, many people now regard Mrs Aung San Sun Kyi, and her Guatema-lan counterpart, the 1992 Nobel Peace Laureate Rigoberta Menchu, as holy women, saints, fearing that they too will become martyrs.

Inasmuch as they show us the best in human nature, what any of us might become, were we struck by a psychological miracle and enabled to live at the peak of our potential, putting aside all our debilitating self-concern, fear, and division, saints make plain the holiness of the searches for justice, meaning, beauty, and love that we examine in this chapter (as indications of what founds or grounds the life of Christian faith). Justice is a name, a concept, a symbol, an ideal that we can never drop, relegate to a world of fantasy that makes no claim on us, without forfeiting something crucial to our basic humanity. Consequently, justice is a straight corridor marching us toward the mystery of God, the fully untrammeled reality that our spirits intend, pursue, in the measure that they are creative, hungry for meaning, repulsed by injustice.

"God" is the whole of meaning, truth, goodness, beauty, justice. Mrs Aung San Sun Kyi might prefer the Buddhist word "nirvana," but in using it her spirit would intend, pursue, the same ultimacy that Christians pursue as "God." The structure of her pursuit of social justice is recognizably the same as the structure of the pursuits of social justice that formed the lives of Gandhi and King. Similarly, though the details of their biographies differ considerably, the passions of Daw Aung San Sun Kyi and Rigoberta Menchu mark them as spiritual sisters, two of a dissident kind. It is this structure, this cast of the human spirit, that suggests why ventures such as Christian theology as a whole, even much smaller ventures such as our work here on *a* constructive Christian feminist theology, arise in history so constantly, though hardly inevitably.

Injustice creates pain. Throwing things, relationships, out of kilter, it rubs people raw, giving them the emotional or spiritual equivalents of displaced joints – separated shoulders, dislocated hips. Aware of such pain, people try to remove it. They struggle to get their joints, their social relations, back in place. They seek healing, a return from disorder to order and harmony. They, we, do this instinctively, from a sense that pain is wrong, that health, normalcy, is not painful, but rather is pleasant, in a modest, largely unselfconscious way. When our stomach is normal, healthy, we do not notice it, are not throwing down chalky substances to settle its upsets and dilute its sour acids. When our minds are clear and our emotions are tranquil, we worry little about migraines, suffer little anxiety that we may lose our job.

This means, of course, that both health and sickness, both justice and injustice, are two-edged swords. If health and justice stem more from good biological or historical fortune than from any active labors on our part, our sense of their significance may be shallow. We may be sleeping our way through them, rather than passing through with quickened spirits and sensing the great things at issue. Similarly, if injustice, causing suffering physical or mental, isolated or politico-social, heightens our awareness that a great deal is wrong with the world, injustice can become a significant benefactor.

The old abbot who told Mrs Aung San Sun Kyi that she had to invest in suffering if she wanted to get happiness was working along at least a variant of this spiritual seam. Following Gautama, the

Buddha, he knew that all life is suffering, inasmuch as no life that we experience in time, through our bodies, gives us complete satisfaction or happiness. Until we come to grips with this foundational fact, we are deluded and live in illusion. When we do come to grips with it, we prepare ourselves to hear, begin to grasp, the solution that the Buddha offered to the problem, the omnipresence, of suffering. We create at least a first store of the quiet we need if we are to register the overtones in the Buddha's teaching that we can remove suffering by removing desire – by ceasing to care in wrong ways about what happens to us.

When we accomplish, or receive as a gift, the conversion, the change of mind and heart, that the Buddha described as ceasing to care in wrong ways about what happens to us, or that Jesus had in mind when he urged his disciples to put their faith in God, his Father, we enter into a new relationship with justice. Freed of many of our attachments to failed or dysfunctional social patterns (such as patriarchy, as feminists perceive it), we learn a little, in the depths of our being, about a harmony, a right order, that does not fail, indeed that cannot fail, as long as we have minds that give us light.

Certainly, the *recognition* that many things ought to be different is but the beginning of the political responsibility that widespread suffering and the example of the activist saints press us to accept. Until we have *acted* on our convictions, taken up our share of the organizing and protest and work necessary to make "justice" more than an interior comfort, we are not on the same team, not even in the same league, as a Mrs Aung San Sun Kyi or a Rigoberta Menchu. Nonetheless, as early as the recognition that many things ought to be different we can start to appreciate the need for, the rightness of, human admiration of "God," even human worship of "God." Why? Because even so early we can know, at least intuitively, that only "God" can provide the full justice that we crave, and so that "God" only leaves us when we leave our own humanity, the cravings that drive us toward holiness.

We never find in history, any actual city or town, the fine, round measure of justice, pressed down and overflowing, that our spirits know, constitutionally, ought to be. We can enjoy good patches, seasons of peace, but they never remain secure. Moreover, our reach always exceeds our grasp: we want justice to flower ever more fully, for ever more people who are now trodden down. Inevitably, therefore, we look outside of history, perhaps turning biblical images of justice this way and that, as though what God gives the rational human spirit to hope for has already to be present in the plain rationality, the simple intellectual light, by which alone any of us becomes aware of any thing significantly human. Spooned over in images to nourish the heart, such a biblical measure can deliver a foretaste of God – an anticipation sufficient to sustain our spirits.

Second, beyond the compensatory, redemptive aspects of "justice" that our spirits find as they work along the foundations of what makes us human appear transcendent aspects – intimations that the source of creation, the divine mystery experienced as being or reality without beginning or end, limit or flaw, includes (or in many ways simply is) a justice, a beauty, a fulfillment far beyond what we can imagine. In Pauline terms (1 Corinthians 2:9), no eye has seen this fulfillment, no ear heard it, the human heart has never conceived it adequately. In general theological terms, this transcendence is the godness of God, the in-finity that gives our entire human situation its casting. Experiencing God, being drawn toward a justice worthy of heaven, we change. Less and less do we think of ourselves as put-upon, suffering creatures. More and more we feel grateful for a dazzling birthright: a chance to share in God's own life. Can all this be implied in a simple move of our spirits toward fair sexual dealing, honest elections, adequate housing for poor people, proper punishment of thugs? Watch the movements of your own spirit and see.

The Search for Meaning

At the end of the second Christian millennium, few crises seem more radical than the manifest disruption of nature's basic ecology. Consequently, nowadays few searches for meaning – an understanding able to grasp the principal causes and redress their worst effects – draw people into more basic questions about the character of the natural world, the kind of creation God is running (if God is), than the search to rehabilitate the earth's ecosystem. It is *à la mode*, then, for Elizabeth A. Johnson to begin her 1993 Madeleva Lecture in Spirituality with a section on ecocide – the killing of the planetary environment. Noting the likeness of her recital of dismal recent happenings to a biblical lament, Johnson chants elegiacally:

> We are poisoning our life-support systems of soil, water, and air, with toxic waste such as fumes, chemicals, sewage, detergents, pesticides, and radioactivity. . . . Through burning, logging, or industrial showers of acid rain we are destroying the earth's forests, ruining the trees that create and purify the air we breathe. . . . Largely through the chemicals used in refrigerators, air conditioners, and several industrial processes that serve the life-styles of the rich nations, we have torn a hole in the protective ozone layer that shields life on earth from the ultraviolet rays of the sun. . . . Our great oceans are littered with plastic and laced with sewage. . . . We are turning fertile soil into deserts through insensitive agricultural methods, losing roughly eighteen billion tons of topsoil every year. . . . From the beginning of the human race to the turn of the first Christian millennium (1000 AD), human population grew to approximately one-quarter billion people. By 2000 AD the number will be six and a quarter billion people; by 2050 AD, eleven billion.[3]

Johnson proceeds to analyze this laying waste to nature as a species of rape. A stereotypically male will to power is abusing physical nature much as violent men have always abused vulnerable women. Prior to recent biological understanding, and the effect of the technologies developed in the northern nations during the past fifty years, humanity could think of nature as sovereign – always in control, never at risk. That has changed, and we shall not reverse the horrible patterns stemming from such change until we adopt a new attitude. For Johnson, the proper new attitude is feminist: cooperation rather than domination; prizing connections, relationships, more than autonomies. Any profound protection of nature, liberation of nature from human abuse, will go hand in hand with the acceptance of women's ways (of being, knowing, and doing) into an influence, a potency, at least equal to that of men. So sayeth this prophet.

Elizabeth Johnson is trying to understand the meaning of the current ecological crisis. By training and motivation, she can immerse herself in reams of data, follow trains of argument, and make connections. In her Madeleva Lecture, the connections include what her insights (for example, about the coincidence of the abuse of nature with the abuse of women) imply for feminist spirituality. In other works, other thinkers are concerned with other data, arguments, connections. Common to all such works, though, is the search to understand. Just as we can move so profoundly into a practical search for justice that we can find lineaments of the divine mystery, we can move so profoundly into other searches for understanding, other intellectual or moral quests, that "God" appears in the midst of our spirituality, our searching, as the ground of all understanding.

It is easier to speak of searches for understanding in the first person singular than in the first person plural, because the consciousness at issue, the awareness, is more contained. Nonetheless, communities do form around common searches for meaning, and religious communities (synagogues, churches, mosques) depend on conjoined efforts to keep the good news that launched them alive and well through latter days. We can also speak of a team of scientists ("The Lab of X") pursuing the structure of a key gene or a new retrovirus, with the implication that many minds are sharing a great search. We can even generalize from the enormous impact of modern science to the statement that few forces are more powerful than humanity's now organized, disciplined, controlled passion to understand.

Whether the human passion to understand blazes toward beauty (reality clarified) or the removal of suffering, it is a refining fire. Indeed, humane theologians can realize that physical science is often a quite pure form of religion, inasmuch as "religion" connotes being bound only to what is so – true, real, normative for human intelligence. The "God" of mature religion, both Christian and non-Christian, consecrates all searches bound only by what is so. Yes, at points that we shall examine carefully, Christian language has traditionally turned paradoxical, even anti-intellectual, in an effort to handle the intrinsic irrationality of sin. But the mainstream of Christian faith and theology has supported reason, locating "God" in the human mind (as well as the human heart), and thinking that every advance in the understanding of creation ought to advance humanity's will to worship the source of creation, the reason why there is something rather than nothing.

Suppose we had no ardent will to understand the world (natural, social, personal, religious) in which we found ourselves. Suppose we were content to cope, in makeshift fashion, with counting-pebbles and caves. Or, suppose that, with Karl Marx, we became convinced that understanding was (relatively) beside the point and social change was the overwhelming imperative. If any of these things happened in us, or our Lab, or our religious community, the image of God would fade. Whether it would be better to call such a fading a tarnishing or a dimming is an interesting question, but the gist would remain, regardless of the name we chose. As soon as human beings give up trying to understand – the natural world, their culture, their selves, their Creator – they give up trying to be their best, to fulfill their potential. We can sympathize with the fatigue, usually more moral than physical, that tends to cause such giving up. But we cannot face squarely, responsibly, any giving up on the search to understand without fearing that we have come upon a suicide.

Human beings are more themselves when they keep struggling to understand the world, less themselves when they give up. Experience is bound to teach them that both struggling and giving up have their proper times, their appropriate seasons. But once we get beyond the physical implications (death comes to us all, and a good death accedes to a proper moment), we experience a challenging solicitation by the divine mystery.[4]

Just as people passionate to clean up slums or emergency rooms or orphanages seldom stay for the long haul unless this passion has become a balm for their spirit, so people passionate to understand AIDS, or the destruction of the rain forests, or the shape of the classical Platonic mind (where the "beyond" of God first came to analytical clarity), keep going because of their quest itself. In the very search, the plain yet powerful moving of their minds and hearts, they "feel" that they are *en route* to where they most want to be, most ought to be.

It is well for human beings to be at table, with satisfying food, drink, and companionship. It is well for human beings to be at play, with laughter and imagination. It is probably better for human beings to be at wonder, study, contemplation, eventually worship. Searching to understand is probably more human than eating pizza or playing golf. Reason probably tells us more than our belly.

Just as being at table pleasurably need not interfere with playing well, so neither eating nor playing need interfere with contemplation. Equally, contemplation need not interfere with action, politics, getting things done. There are different occupations of the human spirit, but we need not make them antagonistic. We can make them complementary, and in "balanced" lives we do. Still, even when unbalanced, overly intense, the drive to understand is a wondrous image of God, an especially energetic icon.

Even before contemplation starts to make the immensity of creation clear, inculcating humility and devastating any naive expectation that one day we shall understand completely, contemplatives – students formed by their searches, enraptured by meaning or justice – have pledged their hearts. Understanding has become a love. What they want to understand, nature or the divine mystery, has become a lover. What happens in their intercourse with nature or the divine mystery makes scientists and theologians fertile. Anything that they can say might be, significantly, is worth their perusal. For anything that might be, significantly, is a light of God awaiting confirmation, a telex of God expecting a reply. We cannot give ourselves to the search for full meaning, both what might be and what surely is, without referring, however tacitly, to God. We ought not to credit with maturity, the self-knowledge of an adult, any form of the search for meaning, scientific or artistic, that does not recognize this reference – is not aware that alpha and omega never come clear.[5]

The Search for Beauty

Just as the human spirit moves toward justice as a homeland long sought, and moves toward meaning as the air it breathes, so the human spirit moves toward beauty as the fire of its sun. The beauty in question is, of course, as incarnational, as much enfleshed, as has been the justice and meaning we have surveyed. Mrs Aung San Sun Kyi lives in a particular country at a particular time. Her political witness is nothing angelistic, unbound to her body or her nation or the earth. Elizabeth Johnson gives her lecture to a specific audience on a specific night. Though what she has to say about the patterns of ecological devastation might appear in a German lecture, or a French, in fact she speaks the American English of a native New Yorker, and she has to gather her data before her lecture is printed. Justice and meaning must submit to significant restraints, if they are to be human. The same human spirit that can move transcendently beyond any particular axis of space and time always belongs to a given individual wholly rooted in a given such axis. This strikes you as paradoxical? Good, you are paying attention.

So, the physical beauty that we associate with painting, music, sculpture and other arts – the physical colors, forms, sounds – falls into our foundational inquiry, our opening search for the theological significance of characteristically human searches, as much as a more cerebral or spiritual beauty might: the elegance of a perfect equation, the integrity of a saint. In any case where we use the word "beauty" appropriately, the mind and heart of a human onlooker, a participant observer of our kind, draw nourishment from sensible data, ride material metaphors toward a heavenly Jerusalem, where silence can rule for half an hour (Revelation 8:1).

Religious speech is often poetic, because often it wants to entice, allure, draw to stop-mouthed attention a listener inclined to rattle on. If whatever we say about God, no matter how true, is more unlike than like what divinity is in itself, it must follow that any glimpse of God, no matter how satisfying, is but a sliver off God's mirror. The beauty of God involved in the rise of our human spirits toward light, color, and pleasing form has to go outside these created containers, stand in itself, and be for us more simply, now and then vouchsafing the thrill that caused Parmenides to cry out, "Is!" The is of God is stunning. The being of God is beautiful – light and life and love.

Creatures, expressions of God, can tease us with this beauty. The cherry tree back by the garage still stands, linking the visitor to her childhood. In May it will again be gloriously, in colors and blossoms now real only in memory. Still, memory can be vivid enough, kindly enough, to preserve records of the excitement the cherry tree first caused decades ago in a child's mind. And, come May, the visitor may realize she is still a child, as the colors and blossoms again pour joy into her vessels, again make her gape.

This joy, this gaping, this wonder, this delight at having been made for delight is the best part of aesthetics. It is nothing superficial, satisfied with passing fashion or gloss. It is something deep in the soul, stirred most directly by oceans and mountains, borne on the wind like an Irish linen. Equally, it is a matter of conversion, being turned around toward the light, just as authentic searches for justice and meaning are. One must repent of one's prior indulgence of trash and accept a new beauty, a good news, that is non-profit. One must realize, in fear and trembling, that God is beautiful, all that soul desires, and so very dangerous.

We find conversion such as this, realization such as this, in the mystics. Though most have gone through hard times, when they felt God had abandoned them, and a few try to blink away the pain and ugliness in creation, the majority of mystics, East and West, thrive by the thrill of God's beauty. Now and then, light or harmony so seizes their spirit that darkness, evil, even suffering, seem penultimate, perhaps (for many Easterners) illusory. Where sin abounds, sadly and manifestly, grace abounds the more – because, for the moment, beauty is manifest to be unrestrained. The tides move so majestically that the mystic cannot doubt the majesty of God. The lace at the base of the tree is so delicate that God must be very fine. Neither of these beauties denies the beauty of a powerful storm, a quick predator, a volcanic plume. But both work their allure closer to the cave, where the still small spirit canonized in the appearance of God to the prophet Elijah (1 Kings 19:9–14) tames the mystic's terror. Both remind us that the core of mystical experience can be a union so simple it wants no thunder and lightning, indeed no images or words.

We want beauty, even when we are not mystical and remain little aware. So on the fire escape of a terrible ghetto apartment a flower pot remains. In the battered face of an alcoholic a quirk of light brings back a favored child. Are these tricks of the senses, or a legerdemain of the soul? Why do the best of our times, the times when we are most acute, thrust beauty at us like a razor blade, make us long again to be dull? When we set our hearts on beauty, want glory in God and the world, we open ourselves to extra trouble. It is hard enough to survive, day by day, the normal slings and arrows. To want sparkling waters and freckled kids is to bare one's bosom, offer one's throat to the knife. Yet who could begin to appreciate creation, the lissome play of the mites, and not want on and on? Who could feel, however fleetingly, the gratuity of rocks and trees, and not hope that they came down from a prodigal Father (God) of Lights (James 1:17)?

In a foundational religious consciousness, where the soul most loves to move forward into the divine mystery, "beauty" is more a feature of any well-wrought phenomenon, natural or cultural, than something found mainly in museums. Consider, for instance, the following potentially prosaic, actually poetic, bit of astrophysical and evolutionary science:

> "Every atom of iron in our blood would not have been there had it not been produced in some galactic explosion billions of years ago and eventually condensed to form the iron in the crust of the earth from which we have emerged." Chemically, humanity is all of a piece with the cosmos. The same is true of our genes. Molecular biology shows that the same four bases make up the DNA of almost all living things. The genetic structure of cells in our bodies is remarkably similar to the cells of other creatures, bacteria, grasses, fish, horses, the great gray whales. We have all evolved from common ancestors and are kin in this shared, unbroken genetic history.[6]

I first read this description sitting in my car, taking a little quiet and sun between classes. Reflected in my mirror was the limestone facade of the University Methodist Church. My imagination tipped, and I saw the limestone emerging in the cosmic process that first produced carbon, oxygen, and the other fundamentals. The hardness of it, the sheer facticity, made me gasp. There is nothing obvious about the stone of our churches, offices, homes. There is no necessity that the ribs of the earth should in any place be limestone. Where did this dense, brute, silent stuff come from? How does it happen that we human beings share the world with it, have it on offer to us as raw material?

My questions were ontological, concerned with the being of the stone in the mirror. They were also aesthetic, dazzled by the beauty of the streaks of brown, beguiled by the ridges. The ridges took me out of myself, as did the questions about creation, the rise of something from nothing. The ridges made me ecstatic – a pilgrim stepping out of her ordinary dullness, taking the hand of a muse she could hope would be religious, a latter-day Virgil. This ecstasis is worth probing.

I could only travel to the stone, its more challenging suggestions of meaning and beauty, by forgetting the small scene in the mirror. When I came to the abyss of creation, the dark fault from which the cosmic hardness emerged, I was imagining beyond anything I had ever seen or could know empirically. Like a pioneer of non-Euclidean geometry, I was affirming and denying simultaneously. The shape and reality that lured me both were and were not familiar, ordinary, sure to be found on most neighborhood blocks. The physical anchor of the ecstatic imagining was University Methodist Church, but the engine of the exercise, the fuel of the joy, was the beguilement of my mind and heart, my soul. I lingered with the imagery, acceded to the ecstasis, because it was beautiful. It was not beautiful because I had made it. Rather, it invited me into a beauty born with the stars. When I said a proper thank you, I felt sure that the muse had indeed been religious. For the moment, I was also sure that, at their moment in creation, all the angels sang together, and the morning star shouted for joy.

The Search for Love

A Native American lawyer sits in the kitchen of a woman in her thirties, the mother of an Indian child:

> "A lawyer? I never would have guessed a lawyer."
>
> "Well, thanks, I guess. I work in an office that does a lot of work for the Cherokee Nation. That's what I want to talk with you about. Turtle's adoption might not be valid."
>
> Taylor's cup stops an inch from her lips, and for nearly half a minute she does not appear to breathe. Then she puts down the cup. "I've been through all this already. The social worker said I needed adoption papers, so I went to Oklahoma City and I got papers. If you want to see, I'll go get them."
>
> "I've already looked at the records. That's the problem. It wasn't done right. There's a law that gives the tribes the final say over custody of our own children. It's called the Indian Child Welfare Act. Congress passed it in 1978 because so many Indian kids were being separated from their families and put into non-Indian homes."
>
> "I don't understand what that has to do with me."
>
> "It's nothing against you personally, but the law is crucial. What we've been through is a wholesale removal."
>
> "Well, that's the past."
>
> "This is not General Custer. I'm talking about as recently as the seventies, when you and I were in high school. A third of all our kids were still being taken from their families and adopted into white houses. One out of three."

Taylor's eyes are strangely enlarged. "My home doesn't have anything to do with your tragedy," she says. She gets up and stands at the window, looking out.

"I don't mean to scare you," Annawake says quietly. "But I want you to have some background on the problem. We need to make sure our laws are respected."

Taylor turns around and faces Annawake, her hair wheeling. "I didn't take Turtle from any family, she was dumped on me. *Dumped.* She'd already lost her family, and she'd been hurt in ways I can't even start to tell you without crying. Sexual ways. Your people let her fall through the cracks and she was in bad trouble. She couldn't talk, she didn't walk, she had the personality of – I don't know what. A bruised apple. Nobody wanted her." Taylor's hands are shaking. She crosses her arms in front of her chest and slumps forward a little in the manner of a woman heavily pregnant.

Annawake sits still.

"And now that she's a cute little adorable child and gets famous and goes on television, now you want her back."

"This has nothing to do with Turtle being on television. Except that it brought her to our attention." Annawake looks away and thinks about her tone. Lawyer words will not win any cases in this kitchen. She is not so far from Oklahoma. "Please don't panic. I'm only telling you that your adoption papers may not be valid because you didn't get approval from the tribe. You need that. It might be a good idea to get it."

"And what if they won't give it?"

Annawake can't think of the right answer to that question.

Taylor demands, "How can you possibly think this is in Turtle's best interest?"

"How can you think it's good for a tribe to lose its children?" Annawake is startled by her own anger – she has shot without aiming first. Taylor is shaking her head back and forth, back and forth.

"I'm sorry. I can't understand you. Turtle is my daughter. If you walked in here and asked me to cut off my hand for a good cause, I might think about it. But you don't get Turtle."

"There's the child's best interest and the tribe's best interest, and I'm trying to think about both things."

"Horseshit." Taylor turns away, facing the window.[7]

Turtle got her name from the tenacity with which she clung to Taylor's hand in the first weeks at her new home. She seemed terrified that this new adult would also abandon her, or perhaps subject her to new abuse. Taylor accepted Turtle only because she could not say no to a child. She let the birth-mother dump Turtle on her, rather than subject Turtle to another abandonment. But what began as an act of conscience, a generous response to the vulnerability of a child, has become a fierce love. This little girl is now her daughter. Regardless of what any lawyers, tribal or white, say, they're not getting Turtle.

Annawake is young, naive, self-righteous. She has lost her twin brother through adoption, and her heart aches. She cannot see Turtle as the center of any decision. She is too angry at the pathetic status of her tribe. So she lumps Taylor with adoptive parents who have in fact taken advantage of Cherokee poverty, drunkenness, and self-loathing. The only warning she takes, more through an animal registering of hostility than through an intellectual sympathy, is that she has made Taylor an enemy. Perhaps later Annawake will know more about love.

Christian theology ought never to wander far from the Johannine conviction (1 John 4:8) that God is love. Love is the best explanation for creation (God wants to share the divine bliss). Love is the best explanation for redemption (at the behest of the Father, Jesus lays down his life for his friends). And love is the most divine, transforming force in human experience – the best evidence that the Spirit of God moves in our spirits, often with sighs too deep for words. So what passes back and forth between Turtle and Taylor, as Turtle clings to Taylor's hand, is an epitome of the most central Christian theology. In her need, Turtle stands for all of bruised, battered humanity, everyone that time has used badly. In her generosity, which soon also becomes a need, Taylor stands for the goodness we want to associate with God but often find suffering, in tragedy, making this hard for us to do. Taylor's thumb can cramp, from the strength of Turtle's grip. Why doesn't Annawake see this? How can she miss two live lovers, or prefer to them her law?

The search for love tends to be painful, even more painful than the searches for justice, meaning, and beauty. The love of God poured forth in people's hearts by the Holy Spirit (Romans 5:5) is an Archimedean lever, but few of the saints received it before their hearts were broken. In the beginning, need tends to predominate in human love, or superficial satisfaction. In the middle, people notice the impurity of their loves, the narcissism and egocentricity. Only at the end, in full maturity, does love appear godlike, and the good of the beloved clearly take priority over the pleasure of the lover. Taylor is impressive precisely because so much of her love focuses on what is good for Turtle. Annawake is dangerous because forces drive her that she does not recognize. Indeed, she is in danger of becoming an ideologue.

An ideologue cares for ideas, paper convictions, more than round realities, what is happening to people of flesh and bone. An ideologue wants to win arguments, rectify by words a lop-sided world. As ideology takes hold of a soul, that soul loses its honesty. Losing its honesty, it cannot love in good conscience, must always be slanting the data. The love we ought to want, the love that makes us an image of God, is the desire and delight of an open soul, a person pursuing the light. How might Annawake become such a person? Not by abandoning her conviction that her tribe ought to hang on to its children and bring them up proud. Rather by taming this conviction, so that it does not ride roughshod over other imperatives, passions, clusters of experience that cry out to be recognized. What does it profit a tribe to reclaim a child at the expense of the child's happiness? What does it profit a lawyer to ignore the abuse that a child suffered from its first people, and so to ignore that people's forfeit, morally, of its parental rights? Until an individual or a tribe owns up to the actual realities shaping a situation, neither can command full respect. Equally, neither can love well. Love only thrives deeply, lastingly, when it submits to the light. God is light, in whom there is no darkness at all. God is love: benevolence flowing out, creativity willing to suffer for her offspring.

When we come across people who love the light and lay down their lives for their offspring, we come across what all of us ought to want to be. Do we also come across what any of us could be, had we ordinary courage? Where does the love that makes "image of God" a plausible theological description of human nature come from? How much in such love is gratuitous, a free gift of God poured out according to no human programs, and how much is a matter of human choice, will, and achievement? Why is Taylor so dedicated to Turtle? What made her willing to open her heart and let Turtle become her treasure? It is too easy to say that Taylor is expressing a natural maternal instinct previously frustrated. The actual reality is more complicated and mysterious than that. Turtle's natural mother abandoned her, while Taylor had a full life before Turtle's coming. In fact, we cannot understand the best of human loves. They come when they do, take the shape that they do, less because we choreograph them than because we wander, seemingly by chance, into a peculiar network, a given local cobweb, of effects and causes.

Hindus and Buddhists tend to speak of such a network as *karma*. Christians do not. Christians tend to speak of how their loves go, what nourishes their hearts and what makes their hearts explode, as providential. "Providence" is the oversight of God. The Christian sense that God is the single, comprehensive source of creation leads easily to providence. If God has fashioned the world from nothingness, and has kept it in being through all its evolutionary developments, then it makes sense to speak of a divine plan, guidance, provision. Speaking this way is anthropomorphic (treating God as though divinity were a human being), but so is virtually all other speech about God or ultimate reality. A partial being is trying to describe a whole, foundational Being. Not only is the partial being bound to fail, it is also bound to use its own limited experience as the basic point of reference.

The search for love, as Turtle and Taylor show it, stands out among the references that human beings tend to make. When people think about God, try to feel their way forward, their regular instinct is to extrapolate from what in their own lives is best and brightest. So God becomes an artist (creative worker), a scientist (master of the patterns of the natural world), and a healer (both physical and spiritual). God also becomes a lover – the romantic partner, spouse, parent, sibling, friend, even child that our human passions encourage us to create. If a friend or spouse has been good to us, how more so God? If a romantic lover has stirred our blood, how much more the God beguiling the mystics?

So it goes, this analogical imagination, working from pristine, primitive human experiences toward a glimpse of the nature of God. It must affirm, deny, and then reaffirm at a higher order. God is love, but not exactly what human beings call love, rather love at a fuller measure, level, and purity. We can take our searches for love as invitations from God to become creative and redemptive, and we can be confident that now and then our searches touch the divine heart. But this confidence ought to remain blank, dark, patient. To what our touching the divine heart will lead lies hidden in God's mystery, God's providence. God is love, and those who abide in love abide in God, but they only learn the more intimate implications of the capital terms ("God," "love," "abiding") by experiencing them. They, we, can only sense the bond of love between Creator and creature by suffering. The pot never measures up to the potter. Always there is some mismatch. We are the pots, not the potter. The love of God crucial to the world is God's gift of divine life, not our puny responses.

The Great Choice: Despair or Hope

We have been working at the foundations of the human spirit, examining some of the searches, the quests, what the classical Greeks might call the *zeteses*, that suggest in dynamic form to what being human ought to lead. Analyzing the passion of a Daw Aung Sang Sun Kyi for justice, the struggles of an Elizabeth Johnson to understand the current crisis in the earth's ecosystems, any person's possible rapture before the adamant beauty of creation, and the love between a fictional mother and a child, we have found something indomitable in the human spirit, something it cannot deny or give away without attempting suicide.

We human beings have an orientation toward the light, a call as primitive as our bone marrow to move after meaning, toward holiness, into the deserts and jungles of God. Built into our beings, constitutional, is a restlessness of mind and heart, a sense of being spiritually a displaced person. Making this restlessness revelatory, Saint Augustine said that any of us would only rest properly when safe in the arms of God. Making it definitive, I have cast what it means to be human, the principal obligation in any of our lives, as an active agreement that light and love are our measure. Indeed, I think that we have to struggle mightily, perversely, unnaturally to deny that our love of the light, our experience of being drawn toward a Whole for which from the beginning our partiality has made us long, is the signature of our maker across our souls.

However, while years of thinking about the implications of our foundational searches have convinced me that Tertullian was right, that the soul *is* naturally Christian, I must admit that those who do not reach this conviction have many data to which they can point. Whether we consider the international news, which in recent memory has featured great wrong-doing in Bosnia, Somalia, Mexico, South Africa, India, and Tibet (to name only a few superstars), or the local news, full for women of such wrongs as rape, beating, incest, prostitution, pornography, disproportionate poverty, illiteracy, and depression, any representative reports of how human beings are doing business nowadays, what sorts of history we are making, would put even Pollyanna down deep in the dumps. Reinhold Niebuhr once said that original sin is the one empirically verified Christian doctrine. Reinhold Niebuhr was no idiot.

Still, people who have read more than six good books know, or at least suspect, that much in any person's overall estimate of human history, past or present, or of human nature, its goodness or evil, depends on that person's point of view. The data – military, political, environmental, sexual, racial, economic, psychological – do not compel either optimistic or pessimistic findings. Is the overall ghetto poverty to count for more than the flowerpot on one fire escape? Surely yes, but the flowerpot, despite its seeming so small and lonely, raises a cautionary finger. Conversely, what is the significance of the fact that the majority in most cultures are not criminals, love their children, are willing to work fairly hard? This fact, if such it is, does not block out the murders, abuses of their children, and laziness that we can find in any large population, but how the silent majority lives, and what estimates of the goodness of being human such living projects, should weigh more heavily than how the destructive minority comports itself.

Ultimately, we all choose, in the depths of conscience, our horizon. We all establish, more or less knowingly, the interpretational framework we impose on the data that come to us through the years. Happy are we if we realize what framework we are using and allow those data to correct it on occasion. Even more happy are we if we can go into the future honestly with hope. The great choice when it comes to interpretational horizons is whether we shall hope or despair. "Despair" is simply refusing to hope, rejecting hope (Latin *spes*) as unrealistic. Genuine despair is rare, but profoundly moving. Less rare, but still startling, is a mature hope, balanced and blessed with self-knowledge.

The rightness of hope comes from the uncertainty, the open-endedness, of the future. Bad things may happen in the future, tomorrow or next year. There are reasons, data, for fearing the future and steeling ourselves. But good things may happen, too. The reasons for fearing the future are historical: bad things have happened, often, in the past. The reasons for leaning into the future with hope are also historical: good things have happened in the past, often, if we have been fortunate. It seems the part of mental health to focus more on such good things than on bad things. It seems the posture more likely to give us energy, to help us hoist the loads that tomorrow and next year may entail.

Take two people in their fifties, the parents of a boy ending his college years and a girl ending her years of high school. The parents have managed to do well by the children for twenty years. The children have responded generously, using their educational opportunities well. Certainly, these parents can look out the window and see a world terrifying in its disease (for example, AIDS), its crime (for example, drugs), its hardness of heart (for example, the starving of millions of children). But only by ignoring the good things that have happened in their own home, with their own children, can the parents let the terrors of the world overwhelm them, so that they judge human existence to be a trial more than an opportunity. The parents would be foolish to think that no evil could ever claw at their children, but they would be even more foolish to discourage their children from hoping for a long and good life, rich in love and useful work.

Now consider a man, also in his fifties, who has received a diagnosis of terminal cancer. He has much to ponder, many reasons for wondering whether nature, life, God are not careless or deeply flawed. He also has the chance to ponder the significance of premature death, bodily suffering, and the flight of some acquaintances he had thought were friends. His cancer can bring his life, his hope, to a halt, as though pushing him into an alley sealed with a brick wall. Or the very mysteriousness of his cancer – epitomized in the unanswerable question, "Why me?" – can break the significance of all human life open, inviting the man to look at death as a summing up and transition. The man may even realize that what he makes of his diagnosis, how he chooses to understand this bad news, is more important in the long run than anything his doctors have told him.

In the long run, all people die. What the man with terminal cancer faces now, all his friends will have to face eventually. Whether soon or many years on, all his friends will enter the last phase of their life, when it is clear that they are going to die. A death that we consider premature, in terms of the average lifespan, is simply a death that has come sooner than, by the actuarial tables, we might expect. A terminal cancer diagnosed in one's fifties would not be extraordinary if diagnosed fifteen years later. The intrinsic mortality of human flesh has a range of ways in which it can show itself, but they all reduce to the same hard question: how can we mean anything significant, if death withers us all to dust?

We can mean something significant, if death need not turn our imaginations and spirits to dust. We can stand out from the rest of mortal nature if we can point to stories of resurrection and immortality. At the roots of the story of the New Testament lie Jewish stories of resurrection and Greek stories of immortality. They do not prove that we shall arise from death with new, undying bodies, or that the spiritual part of us, the spark in our clod, cannot decompose. But they do remind us that through all generations some people have found the future unpredictable, all the more so when they have seen it as the advent of a divine mystery.

For Christian theologians, the divine mystery, God in God's own form, razes all barriers, making the future thoroughly undetermined. Inasmuch as our time, our years, flow into the future, we ought not to indulge the illusion that we can imagine how they will go. They will go as new combinations of causes shunt them, and as God, the ringmaster of all causes, decides. The children now finishing their schooling will make good or bad marriages, have lucky or ill health, in ways and through means that their parents certainly cannot control and probably cannot imagine. The man afflicted with terminal cancer will survive longer than the median term for all who get his disease, or he will not. In the present, at this moment, he cannot know, and he need not. It is enough that he has today, with its front windows opening on tomorrow. It is enough that in time future he may lie down at night grateful, at the end of a useful day.

As long as the future allows us to imagine good, deeply humane happenings, our choice for hope or despair ought to be simple. Unless we are twisted or disabled by spiritual disease, we have to opt for hope. The simple fact, the imperative reality, is that tomorrow may be a good day. If we ignore this fact, flee from this reality, we twist our conscience badly. Certainly, people can come into situations where the goodness of tomorrow seems unlikely. At the end of life, when sickness has become king, it can seem better to end today. But most days are not plausibly our last, and before our last day we can make up our mind about the significance of all the days we have been given. If in that process we find any evidence that our deaths may, like the death of Jesus, be an experience of passover, "last" becomes a relative, even hopeful, term.

Just maybe our death will show itself to have been necessary, and along with it our sufferings. To get to where we have come, we may have "had" (the *dei* important in Luke) to walk this peculiar, painful pathway. But since over the hill, around a bend not yet visible, the pathway may deliver us to an eastern shore, where the sun is about to rise over warm endless waters, we can keep walking onward, letting ourselves become more and more excited that soon we shall learn what has been building since our first breath.

What Women Can Hope

Anything generically human, with the basic equipment, comes into the legacy of women as much as the legacy of men. So women can hope to pass over at death into a new, fulfilling existence, just as much as men can. The same is true of any and all of the other hopes that human embodiment, restlessness to know, and hunger to love create. Women can hope to find the material world a source of nourishment, both bodily and spiritual. They can hope for good tastes, smells, vistas, music, caresses. Books to nourish their minds, friends to gladden their hearts, churches to encourage their prayers – these are further examples. Women can hope to find at the end of their lives that their time has been fertile in children, good deeds, maturation toward wisdom, even a modest holiness. They can hope to have endured the sufferings that biology, circumstances, and their own weaknesses have laid upon them. They can hope, trust, that God will have kept faith with them and seen them through.

None of these hopes, so encouraging to contemplate, is specific to either women or men. Each derives from something generically human. And, in fact, through countless generations women have hoped for these good things, sometimes expressly, perhaps more often tacitly. If we had more records of what women of prior centuries said when they prayed, or of what they thought at midnight, lying in the dark, we would know more about their hopes. Less would be tacit. But we have enough records, and enough other indications of the full humanity of women, to argue persuasively that women have usually looked to the future for good things and so kept themselves going.

Are there things peculiarly women's own, distinctively feminine, that we ought to add to the generically human list? That is our question for the rest of this section. I believe that there can be – that if women recognize what the next decades of human history may conceive, they can carry reasonable hopes that their half of the species will fare better than it has through most past decades.

For example, women can now hope reasonably, with some data to give spring to their leap, that patriarchy, rule by men, will decrease, subside, and become less noxious. Reversing such a coin, women can hope, positively, that their cultures will admit their voices, their ways, to an official influence more equal to men's than has been true in the past. The coin is a compound hope, for the reduction of a force feminists consider negative and the concomitant increase of a force feminists consider positive, but it simply extends some current perceptions. Inasmuch as patriarchy is on the defensive, forced to respond to charges that it has inflicted much damage, much injustice, on both women and mother nature, feminists can hope that a tide is running with them. Inasmuch as patriarchy remains entrenched, digging itself in deeper and deeper, feminists have to hope beyond anything visible, trusting in the rightness of the demise of patriarchy, the goodness of the fall of sexism, the courage of women to continue fighting.

Women should not be ruled by men, just as men should not be ruled by women. Equal in their humanity, constituted so that only together do they show the world an image of God, women and men ought not to speak or think of rule in any sense that would make one the inferior of the other. Rather, their speech, their imagery, their directive hopes ought to be of cooperation, mutual delight, holding hands, laughing and crying together. They ought to think of living together as sisters and brothers, friends and friends, lovers and lovers. They should say, both to one another and in the mirror: We can be allies, rather than enemies. In Latin countries, we can be *compadres*, in Australia mates. With peace to the cynics and yellow journalists, we need not be foes, battling sex from the cradle. By the grace of God, the softening and bettering that comes from living with Christ, we can turn our differences into mutual supplements.

Women can also hope that the God coming on the horizon will be feminine as much as masculine. To buttress such a desire, they can look to traditional cultures, such as those of India, or they can ruminate about naming the ultimate mystery Mother as legitimately as Father. In India the Mahadevi, the Great Mother, is as powerful as any male god. In sound theological rumination, God only has sex "supereminently," so "female" is as divine as "male." However they choose to firm up their hope that the lover and joy of their soul will be as like to them as to men, feminist theologians ought to ruminate so as to help both women and men pray with more elan, more intrigue, to a God as beautifully feminine as handsomely masculine.

Let us return to the "supereminently" (*supereminenter*) of the previous paragraph. For traditional Christian theologians, this word came into play at the third of three stages of predication – at the end of an inquiry into how we ought to describe God. The first stage was (and still is) positive: God has, is like, anything, everything, good in a creature, good in what God has made. So, God is intelligent, graceful, beautiful, faithful, nurturing, as women can be. But (second stage), God is not intelligent, graceful, beautiful, faithful, nurturing, whatever, *precisely as* women (or men, or perhaps dolphins) can be. Why? Because all the good attributes, the positive qualities, of these creatures (these expressions of God's desire to communicate the divine being and bliss) are limited. God is not limited. Therefore, (third stage), the intelligence, grace, beauty, fidelity, nurturing, whatever that we predicate of God exists in God uniquely, in a way that is proper only to God. For lack of a better name, theologians have called this way "supereminently:" to a degree, in a fashion, suiting the unlimited divine being and bliss.

So, to say that God is feminine is, when our speech is proper, to say that God is both like and unlike the women, the females, the femininity that we experience every day. Femininity exists in God, is an expression, an outflow, of the divine nature, supereminently – in a unique way that befits the (perfect, unlimited, all-powerful, and so forth) divine being. In my opinion, this predication *supereminenter* does *not* dilute the femininity or beauty or other-attribute-under-discussion. God is *more* feminine, beautiful, whatever, than the instances we meet in space and time, not less. Everything in God is more, as long as such moreness, such "majority," is positive. So, if by "mothering" we mean something positive, an attribute to praise, then God is more mothering, more motherly, than the best of our human female parents.

What might this sort of imagination, this way of reasoning from our human constitution as images of God to what God is in him-her-itself, imply for women's future dealings with God? It might imply, first, more freedom to deal with God as our hearts prompt than patriarchal religious authorities have wanted to grant us in the past. Seldom if ever in the past did such authorities say explicitly that feminine imagery for God was inappropriate or undesirable or heretical. Usually, either they did not even consider such imagery (for example, "mother" or "sister" or "female lover"), never even imagined that it might be relevant to the prayer and ethics of ordinary Christians, or the theology of the patriarchs was sophisticated enough to make the sex of God, like the beauty or the goodness of God, an analogous term and so in itself not a problem.

Now, if we seize the opportunity offered us in the present historical moment to think about God apart from patriarchal biases – even, occasionally, against patriarchal biases – we can say some interesting things. For example, we can say that, as fully spiritual, not having (apart from the Incarnation) a body, God is beyond the brute biology of sex. Yet, as having supereminently any positive attribute that we can draw from the created realm, even without a body God possesses any good quality that flows from human sexuality. Further, any such good quality predicable of God would exist in the divine nature or be expressed in the divine activity analogously, when compared to human instances. It would be both like and unlike such human instances. So, for example, God would be nourishing, receptive, or any other good thing that one might consider characteristic of women in a way that was richer, fuller, than the human instances – in a way that did not suffer as they did from finitude or sinfulness.

With this understood, so that all our theological speech and reasoning became radically analogical (metaphorical, sacramental, through and through), any Christians might picture God, speak to

God, look for God, from a feminist perspective. If the equality of women with men in the possession of human nature prompted them, any might ask God to be for them, toward them, like the most understanding of mothers, the most loyal of sisters, the most winsome, seductive, beautiful of female lovers. They might imagine the work of God in creation as a gestation, or an education carried out in the home, or a weaving together of disparate yet complementary strands.

Women can hope to contribute to, even to shape decisively, future theological inquiry and creative research such as this. They can hope to hasten the day when their fellow Christians, or any other people of faith, speak about God inclusively, in ways that embrace female imagery, metaphors drawn from women's lives, as much as male. In a church for Sunday worship, they can hope to find in the sanctioned prayerbooks, the prescribed liturgies, and the customs of the given congregation language that distributes imagery for God evenhandedly, as though in God, as in the Christ of Galatians 3:28, there were no Jew or Greek, slave or free person, male or female. Sex would be irrelevant, because the crux of future, non-patriarchal Christian existence would be a faith, hope, and love stemming from the male–femaleness of the human icon for God. Yet sex would also be central, because every actual, historical human existence, living icon, is either male or female – because sex comes with every human body.

Women can hope that this sort of theological rumination will make them as valid icons of God, as revelatory images, as men. In sober estimate, they may have to counsel one another to patience, realizing that many patriarchal characteristics of the Christian mainstream are likely to die hard. But feminists have on their side the *sensus fidelium* (common Christian instinct) that God is beyond any sexual limitations and so may be dealt with as either male or female. Equally, they have the freedom of the children of God, the mature Christian conscience, to approach God in any way, with any imagery or conceptualization, that respects both the divine otherness (holiness) and the core of Christian tradition. From such freedom, they may hope to deal well with their Father of lights, their Mother of religious invention, the foundation of their whole lives.[8]

Study Questions

1 How significant is the human search for justice?
2 How does the human search for meaning differ from the search for justice? Which is more significant?
3 How widespread is the search for beauty in your own neighborhood, your circle of friends, your soul?
4 In the light of the design of this chapter, comment on the following line from a once-popular song: "Love is just a four letter word."
5 What evidence do you find for the proposition that despair is rare, hope is connatural to human beings?
6 What do you think that women may, or ought to, hope will emerge from the current feminist critiques of culture and religion?

Notes

1 Philip Shanon, "Detained Burmese laureate speaks out to US visitors," *The New York Times*, February 15 (1994), pp. A1, 6.
2 Ibid., p. A6.
3 Elizabeth A. Johnson, *Women, Earth, and Creator Spirit* (Paulist Press, New York, 1993), pp. 5–6.
4 See Sherwin B. Nuland, *How We Die* (Alfred A. Knopf, New York, 1994).
5 See Eric Voegelin, "Reason: the classic experience," in his *Collected Works, vol. 12* (Louisiana State University Press, Baton Rouge, 1990), pp. 265–91.
6 Johnson, *Women, Earth, and Creator Spirit*, pp. 34–5, quoting at the outset from Arthur Peacocke, "Theology and science today," in Ted Peters (ed.), *Cosmos as Creation* (Abingdon, Nashville, TN, 1989), p. 32.
7 Barbara Kingsolver, *Pigs in Heaven* (HarperCollins, New York, 1993), pp. 75–6.
8 For an indication of religious (mystical) *experience* of God as the foundation, indeed the virtual entirety, of all being and life, see Bernadette Roberts, *The Experience of No-self* (State University of New York Press, Albany, 1993), pp. 32–3. On the religious experience of Third World women, especially their experience of injustice, see Ursula King (ed.), *Feminist Theology from the Third World* (SPCK, London/Orbis, Maryknoll, NY, 1994).

Chapter 3

REVELATION AND TRADITION

Revelation

In the previous chapter we dealt with some of the foundational experiences to which Christian theologians can point, from which Christian theologians can draw, when they want to establish the centrality of God, the divine mystery, in the struggle of human beings to become fully human. In the present chapter we take up the first of six topics that any representative constructive Christian theology has to handle. We should note at this juncture that some theologians would reverse the order of our chapters 2 and 3. For them, revelation and tradition ought to come before any consideration of the foundations in human nature of the search for God, of the quest of theology to understand faith in God.

I respect this point of view, but I have found that beginning with plain human experience, things that one may at least plausibly offer to any people as readings of the drives, the searches, structuring their own minds and hearts, is more effective. It is ecumenical, in the broad sense of wanting to be in dialogue with people outside one's own confessional tradition. By its stress on experience it is akin to most feminist constructive work, which makes experience a watch-word. Finally, though certainly my Christian faith primes me to find what I claim to find in the human search for justice or meaning or beauty or love, my finding wants to stand on its own, as an invitation to any readers, Christian or not, to reflect on the movements of their spirits and determine what are the most important vectors, where the pressing forward, the "intentionality," seems to want to take them. Therefore, I began with some fundamental human desires, hopes, passions, and then moved to such issues, critical for this book, as the choice between hope and despair, the matter of what women may hope – where the desires of women may go today with reason and grace.

We may think of revelation as a response of God, by God, to the desires that structure our human hearts. Thinking of revelation in this way need not short change the initiative or gratuity with which God acts – need not signal a failure in our religious make-up that leaves our gratitude thin. I believe that God made us to want divinity as our fulfillment, and so I believe that God's revelation is a response of God to God. If we say that human nature is a question, a dramatic inquiry, we can say that God both prompts the question and implies that divinity – he himself, she herself, it itself – is the most appropriate answer.

Thinking in this way, playing with this construction, we can imagine ourselves, what we are as human beings, the stories of our lives, as part of a divine conversation. We come in in the middle, *in medias res*, and we leave before the end, so we never catch the full drift, are always waiting for Godot. But we can catch some of the drift, apparently more than Samuel Beckett, if we let ourselves trust that our lives do have meaning, and that the great creedal symbols, rituals, books and other loci of Christian wisdom can mediate "salvation:" healing that overcomes our alienation from God.

God speaks moment by moment through "creation," the making of both the natural world and the worlds of human cultures. For Christians God also speaks in a cluster of privileged moments, texts, rituals, at the center of which stands Jesus the Christ. Jesus the Christ, the Messiah, is the crux of revelation, as Christians understand it. If revelation is the disclosure by God of what God is, what God wants for us, and what God wants from us, then Jesus the Christ is the richest of the metaphors, the analogical meanings, that God has used for such disclosure. Muslims feel similarly about the Koran, the revelation given to Muhammad. There, they believe, is the most definitive word of God, the fullest declaration of Allah.

Inasmuch as God has disclosed a great deal about both the divine nature and human destiny in the way that God has made human beings, we can say that God gives us, reveals, the key questions that

ought to structure our lives: Where can we find rest for our restless
hearts? Where can we find the justice, meaning, beauty, and love
that we want, often passionately, but never find, at least in lasting
and adequate measure, in the space-and-time of our earthly sojourn?

Inasmuch as God offers the histories of Israel and the early
Christian community as canonical, normative accounts of how God
has revealed further aspects of both what God is and what God wants
in our regard, these histories become further instances of revelation.
In the next section, we deal with "Scripture," a good traditional word
for such canonical, normative accounts of God's ways with us, God's
purposes for us. Here let us concentrate on the process, the dynamics,
through which, Christians (and perhaps other theists) believe, the
divine mystery makes available (really, though not always plainly)
more of itself than we can discern in nature alone – either physical
nature (the universe, with stress on its preponderantly nonhuman
parts and character) or human nature (as read apart from Christian
faith).

In the first chapter of the gospel according to Luke we find several
instances of revelation, the most famous of which is the "annunciation" to the Jewish girl Mary by the angel Gabriel that she is to
become the mother of an extraordinary child (Luke 1:26–38). God
sends Gabriel to Nazareth, where Mary lives. Mary is a virgin
betrothed to Joseph, a man whose bloodline relates him to King
David. Gabriel greets Mary by telling her that God favors her. The
experience of dealing with the angel and hearing about God's favor
troubles Mary, but Gabriel tells her not to be afraid: she will conceive
a son, to be named Jesus, who will be "great, and will be called the
son of the Most High, and the Lord God will give to him the throne
of his father David and he will reign over the house of Jacob forever
and of his kingdom there will be no end" (1:32–3). Mary boggles at
this, because she has had no sexual relations, but Gabriel assures her
that "the Holy Spirit will come upon you, and the power of the Most
High will overshadow you; therefore the child to be born will be
called holy, the Son of God" (1:35–6).

This is a scene that has drawn numerous painters. What is
revelatory about it? First, there is the information supposedly given
to Mary. If we take the text as an accurate account of something that
Mary experienced before the birth of Jesus, then we are witnessing a
dramatic disclosure by God, through Gabriel, of a miracle-soon-to-

occur. Second, there is the disclosure, left in the text (which has since become "scripture" for Christians), of how God began the drama of salvation enacted in the life, death, and resurrection of Jesus. Third, there are the disclosures that people experience when using such scriptures for either common worship or private contemplation.

Most scholars think that scriptures such as Luke are less eyewitness historical accounts than literary-theological creations. The "truth" that they convey does not contradict what happened, in this case to Mary, but whether it represents what happened to Mary precisely as it happened is not certain. More certain is the solid Christian conviction that Luke, like other books of the New Testament, conveys in trustworthy fashion the basic realities, historical and religious, of the life of Jesus. Further, through that trustworthy conveyance, Luke has always offered to Christian believers a canonical (regulative, orthodox) version of how the Christian divinity comports itself – good news on which the followers of Christ have been able to rely.

The value one places on revelation such as this depends, of course, on one's need for, one's appreciation of, such good news – one's indifference toward the gospel or delight in it. If we interpret "salvation" broadly and deeply enough, we can argue that the characterization of Jesus by Gabriel has a wide import. The child that Mary is to conceive will be a ruler, an anointed leader, for the great benefit of all his Jewish people. Later, when Gentiles have entered the church, his rule, his messiahship, will shift somewhat, so that it embraces more than Jews. Indeed, the genealogy that Luke gives at the end of its "infancy narrative" (3:38) takes Jesus back to Adam, the father of all human beings. What Mary is hearing bears on the healing, the radical cure, that God has offered to all human beings. Jesus both illumines the action of grace, God's favor, in all people's lives and serves as the axis of the history of that action. He is for Christians the privileged metaphor, the best of interpretations, and also the most important agent. As such, he is revelation and salvation in one.

This is a "strong" exegesis of the annunciation, but one congenial to the Christian mainstream. Read with a developed Christian faith, what Luke presents as happening to Mary could not be more momentous. Divinity is announcing its intention to take flesh, become fully human. The incarnational character distinctive of the Christian God is assembling itself. Ever since the appearance of Luke and the other gospels, Christians have had this revelation available in textual, narrative form. Certainly, that form is paler than what happened to Mary, only words on a page, images passing from mind to mind. Nonetheless, regularly those words and images have mediated the Word – the revelation of God that enlightens human minds toward wisdom, warms human hearts toward love.

Inasmuch as this narrative of the annunciation has become part of the gospel, the Christian master-story, it is an ingredient in *the* tale by which Christians judge all other stories of how God operates and how human beings ought to respond. In the process, Mary has come to serve as a model Christian. Her response to the overtures of God, the revelations by God, has set the standard for the other Christian saints. Only Jesus himself has been more central, more important, in modeling how any of us ought to respond to God.

And this revelation of exemplary Christian discipleship, like the revelations of exemplary Muslim discipleship that Muslims find in Muhammad and the Muslim saints, shows us that the primary mode of God's disclosures of the divine nature and will has to be through human flesh. Nothing can be nearer to us, more directly our human own, than the enspirited flesh that marks us from shortly after our conception. When the Word of God takes flesh from Mary, the core of the Christian message draws near. Ever after, Christian believers have had available a God as approachable, as vulnerable, as an infant, and a role model as affecting as a teenage unwed mother.

Those are striking "revelations" indeed. If we can step back from the habituation that years of unthinking Christmas rituals have thrown over our imaginations, we may sense the newness, even the scandal, that the story of Jesus, the revelatory good news his followers found, thrust into Middle Eastern history nearly two thousand years ago. Then, with such a sense, we may look for confirmations and denials that God does in fact act incarnationally, as one of us, in the lives we can observe in our own neighborhoods. In other words, we may test the supposed revelation offered us in the annunciation – see whether what Mary saw, heard, took to heart is indeed credible and salvific.[1]

Scripture

Throughout human time, people who have not had writing have kept their records in memory (or such innovative systems as several peoples' knots).[2] The people who have had writing have developed scriptures – writings they considered sacred, revelatory, privileged, canonical. Each of these words suggests a different aspect of what scriptures have been throughout human history, though all such aspects overlap, even coalesce.

For a writing to be "sacred," it must deal with, lead readers into, ultimate realities – the divinity or buddha nature that the people in question most reveres. For a writing to be "revelatory," it must disclose such sacredness, be credibly the speech, self-expression, and will of God, the ultimate. Scriptures are privileged writings, because no other writings have more authority, hold more central or higher ground. Last, scriptures are "canonical" inasmuch as they provide the measure, ruler, or norm for both other religious writings and what the given people holds as proper doctrine, worship, and ethics.

East Asian collections of scriptures tend to be enormous. The Buddhist canon (approved collection) called the *Tripitaka*, the canon of Hindu scriptures (*Vedas*), and the Taoist canon, for example, stretch to thousands of pages. For Islam, the Koran suffices. Judaism gives several denotations to its key word Torah (Guidance, Instruction, Law), the narrowest of which is the first five books of the Hebrew Bible. Tanak, the entire Hebrew Bible, qualifies as Torah in mainstream readings, and the Hebrew Bible is the most popular Jewish referent of "scripture." The Talmud, collecting rabbinic commentaries on both scripture and prior esteemed commentaries, comes under the broad umbrella of Torah, as does oral tradition.

For Christians, scripture is only two collections of writings, the Old Testament and the New Testament. The Old Testament varies only slightly from the Jewish Bible, such variance being due in part to the Old Testament's being based on a Greek version (the Septuagint) more than on the Hebrew. The New Testament, whose three main parts are the synoptic materials (Matthew, Mark, and Luke-Acts), the Pauline letters, and the Johannine materials (gospel, epistles, Revelation in some groupings), consists of memories, theological interpretations, moral admonitions, and other testimonials generated by Christian communities after the death and resurrection of Jesus. Most of these materials came into being before the end of the first century, and all assume faith that Jesus was the Messiah and is the best source of salvation.

The Christian Bible, both testaments, is the wellspring of traditional theology. What the early Christian thinkers considered to be scripture guided their efforts to understand their faith. Certainly, what they experienced in common worship also guided their work as catechists and theologians, but much of Christian worship has always been scriptural: readings from the Christian Bible, prayers based on Psalms or striking New Testament passages.

Neither the Old Testament nor the New Testament is a tidy collection. Both include disparate materials, some of which appear, at least initially, to be odd bedfellows for others. How, for example, does one relate an Old Testament legal text such as Leviticus to Job? What is the connection in the New Testament between Acts and Revelation?

Theologians can work out connections, and mature Christian believers of any stripe can find all such writings helpful. But one of the first lessons to be learned about Christian scripture is that the presently canonical collection (many other works circulated in the early centuries but did not gain entry to what became the Christian Bible) was formed eclectically. If a writing had gained a good reputation (because many Christian communities considered it both a valid expression of Christian faith and a solid help for Christian living), such that one could argue that it had legitimacy or approval by the catholic (universal) church, it was a candidate for scriptural status. Only in the fourth century did today's collection of New Testament books become standard, but the synoptic gospels, Pauline letters, Johannine literature, and other materials of the present New Testament had by then been long revered (had in practice been treated as scripture).

When people take up a writing that they consider scriptural, they invest it with their faith. It is not an ordinary piece of literature. Still, churches vary in the way that they understand the revealed character of a scriptural book. Most churches in the Christian mainstream, however, consider scripture to be the Word of God and so attribute some sort of authorship, revelation, to God. Equally, churches of moderate outlook tend to attribute some sort of authorship to the human writers who set the words down. Many biblical scholars concentrate principally, even solely, on the human authorship, informing themselves about the historical period, religious beliefs, and literary features of the biblical work that they are studying. Only a few Christians take the Bible to be the Word of God literally, inflexibly, as though it came down bound in leather from a cloud. Most let the metaphor "Word" address them with its full richness, and so with some ambiguity.

For ordinary believers, sometimes in contrast to theologians investigating the nature of scripture, the godness of the Bible, its authorship by God, is more practical than speculative. If they find in the Bible a light, a warmth, a support that they find nowhere else, such believers tend to consider the Bible unique – a book more directly from God, holier, than any other. The devotional use of the Bible, in contrast to the academic study of the Bible, tends to be slow and personal. It is interested in religious nourishment, not objective facts or textual analysis.

All three of the main branches of Christianity – Protestant, Roman Catholic, and Eastern Orthodox – have sponsored what the medieval Latins called *lectio divina* (divine reading). This is using the Bible (and, by extension, other religious books) slowly, as befits a source of revelation. The objective is not to gain information but to find consolation, comfort, strength to persevere. Tacitly, implicitly, many Christians through the ages who used the Bible in this way assumed that it was the speech of God. God had put in the Bible a perennial message, such that in any age one could find a challenge to repent and change one's ways, a promise of grace and forgiveness. They wanted to experience that challenge and promise once again.

Outsiders have to work hard to understand this devotional mentality of many traditional Christians, as outsiders have to work hard to understand the devotional use of the Koran in Islam or of Torah in Judaism. They have to imagine themselves sitting before the text alongside pious believers and feeling, as such believers do, that God has inspired these pages and wants to inspire those who read them.

No doubt, the psychology of *lectio divina* includes a prejudgment that scripture contains words of eternal life. For the pious Christian, God has made available in scripture guidance sufficient to mediate salvation. There is no way to falsify the teaching laid out in the New Testament. The pious reader grants God a blank check, reads scripture docilely. Because of such a mentality, a given page of scripture can turn a life around. That was true, for instance, of Saint Augustine, whose autobiographical legend says that he found his way to conversion by hearing a heavenly voice tell him to take up scripture and read.

In the final section of this chapter we shall deal with feminist revisions of past views of the topics we have treated here. We may say at this juncture, however, that the Bible seems to strike mainstream Christians and feminists alike as both patriarchal and subversive of patriarchy. That is to say, the general cultural assumptions behind most of the biblical texts are patriarchal. Men expect to rule the institutions by which the biblical societies do business, and men tend to depict divinity in male terms. Women are lesser official powers in such societies, and lesser players in their theologies. Frequently, in fact, women are marginal to the argument, the mental energy, of the biblical texts, and sometimes women are disparaged. In some layers of the Old Testament the authors seem to consider women the property of men (first of their fathers, then of their husbands), while some of the New Testament imagery makes wives submissive to their husbands and woman the weaker vessel.

On the other hand, strong women appear in both testaments (Eve, Sarah, Deborah, Mary, Magdalene), and the biblical theme that God sides with the poor, beautifies the outcast, can imply a special benediction for women. The prayer ("Magnificat") that Mary utters after being greeted by her kinswoman Elizabeth (Luke 1:46–55) is the outcry of a strong woman. The appearance of the risen Christ to Mary Magdalene leads to her commission as "the apostle to the apostles" – she tells the other leading disciples that Jesus is alive. When Paul says (Galatians 3:28) that in Christ there is neither male nor female, he makes sexual equality, core feminism, part of the birthright of evangelical Christians (all who base themselves on the good news in the Christian scriptures). When readers note that women are present at both the teaching of Jesus and his table, they sense that for him the gospel implied a clean break with the divisions introduced by sex and class. Women and the poor had as much claim on Jesus, as many rights before Jesus, as men and the wealthy.

Inasmuch as patriarchies insist on divisions based on sex and class, the gospel opposes them, wants to subvert them. All this is congenial, indeed consoling, to most Christian feminists. Thus, while scripture may not be a simple blessing, women who use it in good conscience as a source of liberation can find a wealth of grace.

Tradition

Tradition is handing on, passing down. It is what an older generation offers a younger, the heritage that the younger generation has the right to expect. Revelation passes down, gets handed on – for example, inasmuch as older disciples tell younger ones what Jesus said, what Jesus seemed to be, how Jesus asked his followers to live. Scripture is a mode and species of tradition, inasmuch as it makes available in permanent, privileged form what Christians have believed are the most important disclosures of God – the ones most crucial for the salvation of all human beings.

So the terms we find theologians using, when they start to examine the primary ways that Christian faith takes on its distinctive character, overlap and depend on one another. The opposition, perhaps even antagonism, between scripture and tradition that arose in some periods of church history (most notably in the wake of the Protestant Reformation) now seems to ecumenical Christians facile and false. Scripture came from the early Christian churches and formed all the later ones. People find in scripture the meanings that their generation, their link in the chain of tradition, needs, is primed to discover, but scripture also stands free of the needs of any particular group, refusing to be co-opted. As free in this way, scripture becomes the norm for the churches, the mirror in which they can see how closely they resemble the earliest disciples.

Anthropologists sometimes distinguish between higher culture and "the little tradition." For Orthodox Judaism, mastery of the Talmud has been the passport to esteem in the higher culture. Because in past centuries women usually could not study the Talmud, were not allowed, women had little access to higher Jewish culture. On the other hand, women had a great, perhaps even a preponderant, influence on the little tradition. Their role in absorbing folk tales, insisting on family rituals, learning the lore for healing ordinary aches and pains, preparing bodies for burial, and, above all, socializing children made Jewish mothers powerful influences. They ruled the ebb and flow of the home, and the home rivaled the *shul* (study hall) in practical influence.

For traditional Christianity, similar patterns prevailed. Few women had access to higher religious learning. In both Roman Catholicism and Eastern Orthodoxy women could not be ordained as priests. Therefore, they could not hold the offices or gain the political power by which the churches in those two traditions did business. An option for the monastic life, living as a nun, broadened the vocational possibilities of Christian women beyond those (wife and mother, single person) available to Jewish women. (Judaism has had no monastic life to speak of.) Nonetheless, the higher culture of Christianity sponsored few women as creative artists, scientists, church leaders, physicians, musicians, or theologians.

Still, Christian women tended to determine how faith went forward in the home, while nuns shaped much of primary education and nursing, at least in modern times, when religious orders gained approval to work in the world, as well as pray in seclusion. So Christian women shaped the folk tales, informal catechetics, prayers to the saints and Virgin Mary, reading of the Bible, and other aspects of devotional Christianity that we ought to place in the little tradition, just as Jewish women directed the little tradition among their people. The most crucial influence of women in both religious traditions, of course, came from their holding primary responsibility, in terms of daily care, for the children. Christian women were, *de facto*, the primary agents of the socialization of children into Christian ways of thought and practice. As such, their influence was enormous, even though higher Christian culture, tradition at the top, tended to underestimate their capacities.

The Protestant Reformation of the sixteenth century, which raised the status of laypeople generally, opened some doors to church leadership for women, but Luther, Calvin, Zwingli, and the other leaders were far from being feminists. Patriarchy prevailed in most Protestant churches for centuries, largely because those churches read the Bible as understanding women to be the second sex.

Let us take up this question – whether in Christian tradition women are the second sex, in some way inevitably lesser than men – as a way of tackling the difficult but crucial question of how we can determine whether a tradition is authentic. By "authentic" I mean faithful to the original message that launched it. I also mean compatible with our human instincts at their best – when we want to acknowledge what is so and do what is right.

Among the major sources of the deprecating reading of female nature that numerous Christians have claimed to find in the Bible are the depiction of Eve and the depiction of Mary, the mother of Jesus. Both depictions are complex, but each has prompted patriarchal commentators to deprecate female human nature.

For many of the church fathers (Augustine, Tertullian, and Chrysostom stand out), Eve is a "type" of female nature. She is characteristically feminine in seducing Adam to sin. The serpent works the fall of the human race by playing on her weakness – her curiosity, her desire to be like God. Adam is more a dupe than a responsible agent. He wants to avoid trouble at home so he gives in to Eve's desires.

Interpreting the "original" sin of Adam and Eve, Augustine wants to have Eve as the villain in two ways. On the one hand, humanity only falls, from intimacy with God to disfavor, when Adam disobeys. The disobedience of Eve is not so decisive, because Adam is the head of the race, the one who determines its future. Eve is an instrument, the original womb that procreation required, more than a mother equal to Adam the first father. On the other hand, Eve is more corrupt than Adam, weaker, more liable to give in to temptation. She has drawn Adam down to her level, where they both disobey God, through her wiles. The delight that Adam takes in her, when God gives her to him as a companion, is dangerous. Her sensual attractiveness easily drags him down from the heights of reason where he ought to dwell – where, apart from Eve, he would dwell. So do women distract, even destroy men, generation after generation. (Augustine had huge problems with chastity, the control of sexual appetites, and often his theology reflects his biography. For instance, he thought that original sin passes from parents to children through sexual intercourse, and that every act of coition not undertaken solely in order to procreate is sinful.)

Is Augustine faithful to Christian tradition on the matter of sex? Is what he (by consensus the most influential Latin father) teaches an unadorned development of the gospel? Many later theologians, both women and men, think that Augustine is not fully healthy, sound, on sex. By implication, they think that even the best Christian minds can go wonky now and then, and that therefore later readers, or disciples, have to sift critically what Augustine says, what the Christian tradition says overall.

The treatment of Eve that makes her a type, a template of unredeemed female human nature, tends to regard Mary, the Mother of Jesus, as an antitype – the new, redeemed, regenerated woman who moves in grace rather than sin. Where Eve was disobedient, Mary was obedient. The words attributed to her at the annunciation – "Be it done unto me according to thy word" – stand before all disciples, but especially women, as the way to win God's heart. Mary was also chaste, conceiving Jesus without human agency and remaining a virgin throughout her life. That is how orthodox Christianity has tended to regard her.

Christian piety in Greek, Russian, Syriac, and Roman Catholic circles has lauded Mary as the Queen of Heaven and *theotokos* (bearer of God). No praise has seemed too lofty. Roman Catholics have spoken of the "immaculate conception" of Mary, sealing her antitypical relationship to Eve by declaring that Mary never suffered the taints and debilities of original sin that have warped the lives of all other human beings (Jesus excepted). If Eve calls to mind the fall and original sin, Mary calls to mind the grace of redemption – the new creation that Jesus the Christ effected in rising from the dead.

While Marian piety can be quite moving, feminists tend to ask how helpful it has been to have as a role model a woman who becomes a mother while remaining a virgin. That is not a trick that other women can bring off. And while there are signs that Mary was a strong woman, with a mind of her own, the patriarchal reading of Mary as the most docile of disciples has tended to reinforce the timidity of pious Christian women in face of a masculine God and a male power structure. Too often in Christian history, the hard physical details of Mary's life have receded and a mythological being has taken center stage. Mary has become the Queen of Heaven, the Star of the Sea, and a dozen other ornate wonders. The faithful have thought that she was the Sorrowful Mother, who had suffered more keenly than any other human being (Jesus excepted again), since her refined sensibility had to endure the death of her son, the Son of God. Perhaps out of her refinement through suffering, Mary also, winningly, has been thought to welcome sinners (people wounding themselves haplessly) and present their petitions to her son, who could refuse her nothing.

Volleyed back and forth between Mary and Eve, traditional Christian women tended to find themselves both overly praised and overly blamed. They tended to hear that they were "naturally" more religious than men, more sensitive, more spiritual, more docile – like Mary. They also tended to hear that they were more carnal than men, weaker, less rational, more emotional, and more prone to sin – like Eve. They were pure as virgins, but also corrupt as whores. What they seldom heard themselves called, seldom found themselves treated as, was: the equals of men in ordinary, representative, normative humanity – neither great saints nor great sinners, simply people, ordinary apples of God's eye.

When theologians try to estimate the authenticity of the mainstream Christian churches' traditional depiction of women, they have to note well the patriarchal biases responsible for this relegation of women to the margins and establishment of men, masculine human nature, as the median and norm. In fact, all with eyes to see know that women have been as numerous as men throughout Christian history, and that how women have received the gospel that men have taken the lead in preaching has determined a great deal of its impact. When they find the tradition wanting, askew, regarding women, to what may such theologians refer? If, for example, Augustine seems unreliable on sex, too harsh to represent Christian charity, too puritanical to represent common sense, what is more reliable?

An important principle for the interpretation of the Christian scriptures is that they have to be read in the round, taken as a whole, so that one book can balance another. We can extend this principle to Christian tradition as a whole. Regarding women, the round, whole reading is both encouraging and disturbing. Encouragingly, the tradition, taken as though it were a single great river (in fact, it is formed of many streams), says that women are as fit for discipleship, salvation, and glory (life with God in heaven) as men. Women have as good a chance of becoming saints as men. Female human nature is as essential as male to our race's being made in the image and likeness of God. God loves women as much as men, God is as much female as male, and Jesus counted several women (Martha and Mary stand out) among his closest friends.

Disturbingly, even when read in the round Christian tradition, from its scriptural foundations to the present, shows many patriarchal biases. On the whole, women *have* been the second sex, less preferable than men at birth, less honored by higher Christian culture, offered many fewer opportunities for leadership in either the church or civil society. The language of theology, worship, and church documents has, by today's standards, been sexist. The practice of many of the churches has been equally sexist, because the men at the helm often have not discarded, have not even restrained, their prejudices against women. These prejudices could be ordinary scars from the battle between the sexes, inevitable because of our differences. Or they could be deeper disturbances, fueled by an enthusiastic reading of an Augustine, or by too full a reception of Hellenistic dualism, which tended to split the human being into body and soul and then align women with the body and disparage the rationality of the female soul. (Thomas Aquinas, for example, said that a woman was a misbegotten man – a process of gestation gone wrong.)

To combat inauthenticities (sins against Christian charity and ordinary fairness or common sense) such as this in a tradition, one has to find at the source better beginnings and then argue that in the historical aftermath of its good beginning the tradition lost its way and became less good. In the case of the traditional Christian treatment of women, the better beginnings available at the source boil down to the practice of Jesus – his treatment of Martha, Mary, the Samaritan woman (John 4), his even-handed use in his parables of examples from women's circles of experience (baking bread, sweeping the house) as much as men's. One probably could not call Jesus a feminist, if that term had to mean an explicit, political commitment to championing women's full entry into socio-cultural equality with men. Jesus did not admit women into the college of the twelve, his cadet corps of disciples. But he did preach a good news, and give a ministerial (servant) example, that in principle made women the equals of men. He did love the fidelity of women, as he loved the fidelity of men, and he must have been impressed that at the end, on Golgotha, when all of the twelve except John had fled, several women remained, braving significant scorn and danger, fearless because of their love.

In addition to clashing with the preaching and example of Jesus, a sexist (viciously patriarchal) reading of Christian tradition clashes with our human intuitions at their best. It offends, repels, the honest, fair-minded person to think that people should be deprecated or denied ordinary opportunities because of their sex, color, or other secondary characteristics. Such prejudicial, unfair treatment sends out a rank odor, makes the alert and goodhearted observer recoil.

For, in real life, down on the empirical ground, fair observers think that a woman brighter than a man, more creative, ought to have more say than he, because of her greater intrinsic authority. Analogously, so should a woman who has more experience, or appears to be holier, or enjoys more respect in the community at large, be chosen as its leader. In other words, a subprinciple of merit drives the great principle of equal opportunity and fair employment in Christian ethics. The freedom of the children of God ought to mean the freedom to choose as leaders the people best qualified, without regard to sex or race or class. Inasmuch as many churches have denied this freedom, shutting out the gifts, the charisms of women, they have sinned against the Holy Spirit, from whom such gifts come.

Combined, an analysis of (a) how Jesus depicted women, and (b) a fully admirable, truly humane intuition of sexual equality sketch a powerful call for the reform of Christian tradition regarding the dignity and rights of women. Nowadays Christian feminists are well into the task of working out the details of such a reform, and because the task takes them to basic questions about how to interpret revelation, scripture, tradition, and other central aspects of their faith, their feminist reforms have been generating some new, exciting theologies.[3]

Church History

In what Karl Rahner disparaged as "average theology," church history has little theological clout. Few average theologians look to church history as a living font, a laboratory of grace. Few average church historians display much theological sophistication – ability to interpret the movements of God through time or interest in doing this. Our tack will not be average.

I am interested in the history of the Christian community for what it tells us about life with God, not for its antiquarian features, its curios. Taken with such an interest, church history suggests that women have found God, been romanced by God, at least as much as men. They have been the beneficiaries of revelation, scripture, and tradition sufficiently to have enjoyed fully the graces of Christian faith and to have suffered its pains. How, then, does church history look, when one's horizon is the construction of a Christian feminist theology? What are the themes and periods that stand out?

The most crucial period, clearly, is the time of Jesus, on which the New Testament draws. Had there been no Jesus of Nazareth, there would be no Christianity. What Jesus preached, what he did and suffered, what he was – these are the paving stones that set the Christian way. Occasionally commentators debate whether Jesus meant to found a church, establish a religion. The debate seems to overlook some obvious facts. If we take the New Testament (our only source) as a credible witness, Jesus preached with the intention of announcing the reign of God. He healed people, as a sign of the power drawn near in that reign. He instructed a small group of intimate disciples, who carried the symbolism of the twelve tribes of Israel, as though they were seedlings for a renewed people of God. He asked for faith, in himself as well as his Father. He died for his work, his convictions, his own faith, and he rose in tribute to the Father's ratification of his way, to the unbreakable bond between himself and the deathless Creator. In all this, Jesus built for the future, provided for the years and generations to come.

Certainly, later generations of Christians developed the intentions of Jesus considerably, and not all their developments were judicious. The Protestant slogan that the church always needs reform (*semper reformanda*) is an apt gloss on Christian history. But if Christians stop believing that the life, teaching, healing, death, and resurrection of Jesus is the axis of history, the navel of a new creation, they have broken faith with the first generations. Those who saw Jesus in the flesh, and the first generations to which they handed over what they had seen, had no doubt that Jesus had been the focus, the sacrament, of the most momentous act in history. God had in Jesus established a new creation, an order of grace and divine life, that took human destiny, indeed the destiny of the entire cosmos, onto a new plane. All creation had been in labor, groaning for deliverance. For the foundational era of Christian history, the constitutional period that created the church, all creation was delivered of its conceptus, offered its deliverance, in the event, the person-and-history, of Jesus of Nazareth, the Christ of God.

If we say that virtually all of the New Testament existed in something close to the present form of its books by the end of the first century (an exception may be some Johannine materials), then the first century is the slab, the ground, on which to construct a viable church history. What happened to the currents set free in the first century? How did the headwaters fare downstream?

Two developments are worth underscoring, granted our task of constructing a Christian feminist theology. The first is the clarification in the succeeding three and a half centuries of what Christians ought to believe about God and Christ. The second is the dulling of the originally sharp egalitarianism, which had dire consequences for women.

As Christians debated with Jews and pagan Gentiles, they developed their conviction that Jesus was the nodal point, the hub, of history. With Jews the debates tended to focus on whether Jesus was the Messiah, the fulfillment of Jewish expectations regarding a leader anointed by God to deliver his people from bondage. These expectations were poetic as much as historical, religious as much as political. In an era of Roman occupation, for example, they could take the form of wishing for a champion to throw the rascals, the bullies, the oppressors from Rome out. The first Christians were Jews who thought that Jesus was the Messiah, had fulfilled the expectations rooted in the Hebrew scriptures. The Jews who refused to accept Jesus thought that he was not the Messiah, had not fulfilled those expectations.

In their debates with pagan Gentiles, many of whom participated in "mystery religions" that offered promises of salvation (life after death), the early Christian apologists tended to argue that Jesus offered a wisdom and healing power superior to that of the gods venerated in the mystery religions. When they dealt with well-educated Gentiles, the apologists sometimes spoke well of Plato, Aristotle, Plotinus, and other Greek lovers of wisdom, to the end of making Jesus the fulfillment of what the best pagan wisdom had glimpsed.

In both debates, Jesus appeared as the fulfillment of human hopes. Things long stirring in the human breast could find in him their rest, consummation, validation. The experience of Jesus in their midst at worship, wherever two or three or more of them gathered in his name, and available in the Christian scriptures, when one took them up with a ready heart, convinced the early Christians that their theme of fulfillment was valid. In church councils at Nicaea in 325 and Chalcedon in 451, assemblies of bishops (heads of geographical regions) stipulated that Jesus was fully human and fully divine (one "person" in two "natures"), and that the Christian God was a trinity of Father, Son, and Holy Spirit (three "persons" in one "nature").

Scholars debate the precise overtones of the capital terms "person" and "nature," and historians note that the stipulations of the bishops that became the orthodox position suffered through much controversy. Arians, Nestorians, Monophysites – the list of naysayers, refuseniks, was considerable. The party that won the day (that of Athanasius at Nicaea, that inspired by Cyril of Alexandria at Chalcedon) branded such naysayers heretics, saying that their misunderstanding of traditional faith debased it, putting in jeopardy its power to mediate salvation and divine life.

So, on the capital doctrinal question of how disciples ought to understand the being of their Lord, by the middle of the fifth century the Christian churches had fought their way to a first, rather messy solution. On the capital political question of how members of the churches were to regard one another, what disciples were to do with the egalitarian ways of Jesus the preacher, Jesus the dinner host, the tactics or practical solution that the churches had evolved by the time of Chalcedon were equally clear and equally messy.

On the one hand, they had established such formidable controls as: a line of bishops thought to be in succession from the original twelve, the inner circle that Jesus himself had trained; a canon of scriptures, laying out which writings held pride of place as coming from the apostolic generation and presenting Christian faith in its purest forms; a system of sacramental rituals, among which baptism and the eucharist (Lord's Supper) were the most important, and by which disciples could celebrate their faith and pace themselves through both the human life-cycle (birth, adulthood, marriage, commission for church service, death) and the annual seasons, the cycles of nature; and a monastic life, first developed in the deserts of Egypt and Syria, that offered a way for both men and women to pursue God, holiness, with few distractions.

On the other hand, these developments, which ensured the survival of the Christian communities, reflected the church's accommodations to life in the world, even privilege as the religion favored by some of the Roman emperors (Constantine, early in the fourth century, boosted Christianity into imperial favor; both before and after that, Christians were liable to persecution as aberrant, dangerous members of the Roman Empire). One interpretation of the monastic movement sees it as a protest against the accommodations of the church.

From the time of the "pastoral epistles" (1 and 2 Timothy, Titus) and the epistles attributed to Peter, early Christians had shown a cooling of their original expectation that Jesus would soon return, in glory, to bring the history of salvation to its climax. Settling in for a longer stay, such Christians tended to accept many of the mores, the social customs, of their surroundings. Because frequently those mores were not egalitarian as Jesus seems to have been, socio-economic class and sex became bases for distinction. Within the community love was supposed to soften any differences, but masters could continue to possess slaves, and husbands could continue to dominate wives.

These were rights, practices, that men of power assumed almost unthinkingly in the Hellenistic and other cultures with which early Christianity interacted. But their infiltration into the politics, the social life, of the Christian churches meant a strong dose of patriarchy. Added to the strong dose that Jewish Christians had inherited from Judaism, the Gentile patriarchy sealed the fate of both women and social deviants. No longer would they enjoy the freedom, the free zone, apparent in the practice of Jesus. By the time that it settled into the favor offered it by Constantine, the church had largely spiritualized such freedom. It was supposed to flourish in people's hearts, even though "outside," in their social lives, the church did distinguish between Gentile and Jew, slave and free, women and men.

Similarly, the welcome of "sinners" so prominent in the ministry of Jesus became complicated, because the rules, moral and legal, of the church proliferated and deviance could seem to threaten the stability of the Christian community. Prophetic voices that challenged the Christian system tended to be unwelcome. "Orthodoxy" in faith and practice, doctrine and morals, became more rigid than it had been originally, and less tied to worship (where contact with the living God tends to relativize all formulas).

A pattern of retaining enough of the prophetic, radically new vision and power of Jesus to maintain faith with him, yet accommodating enough to the surrounding cultural milieu to blunt many of the sharp edges of the original gospel, has continued throughout church history. The patristic era (roughly, centuries two through five), the medieval era, the era of reform, and the modern era played variations on this theme. Christians were both in the world and out of the world, resident in heaven. They were both sinners and people graced with forgiveness, divine life. They were equal in needing God for salvation, but their churches depended on a variety of gifts, many of which had to be set in order, submitted to a (patriarchal) instinct to make hierarchies. Until modern times the classical both/and of the councils of Nicaea and Chalcedon determined that Jesus would be both fully human and fully divine, and that the Christian God would be both fully one and fully three. The high or sacramental Christology of Nicaea and Chalcedon, along with the conciliar trinitarian theology of God, found its clearest New Testament basis in John, but both there and in the other New Testament texts disputatious minds could multiply problems. So in many generations of church history opponents of orthodoxy, heretics, have arisen, sometimes largely to cause turmoil, sometimes to provoke salutary reforms.

Regarding socio-political life in the churches, only with the recent coming of "the women's movement" has patriarchy received a stiff challenge. The majority of the Christian churches have for nineteen hundred years been quite authoritarian, and quite convinced that men ought to take precedence over women. Christian views of slavery, race, the poor, and other potential challenges to the hierarchies, the status quo, in which given churches found themselves, have varied through the centuries, enough prophetic vigor arising to keep the pristine gospel aglimmering, but also enough indenture to worldly regimes obtaining to prevent radical reforms, clean sweeps that would abolish socio-economic classes and the debilitating effects of sexual inequality.

These are the main lines, the key theological issues that, for our present purposes, I see running through the main periods of church history: New Testament, patristic, medieval, reformation, and modern. Certainly, in each era faith, impressions of Jesus and God, and institutional forms shifted significantly.[4] But until quite recently there was in Christian circles no serious challenge to either the twofoldness of Jesus (fully human and fully divine) or the persistence of classes within the church (most notably the rule of women by men and, in both Roman Catholicism and Eastern Orthodoxy, the rule of laity by clergy).

A key question nowadays is what a postmodern consciousness, aware of the relativity that history suggests, ought to make of Jesus and his community. Feminism, the study of non-Christian religions, and analyses of historical existence (our human being in time) have all become significant factors in the Christian effort to answer this question.[5]

World Religions

Ought the world religions to serve Christian theologians as a source of revelation, a repertoire of instructive traditions? Should feminist theologians regard the world religions as the friends of women or the enemies? We begin our reflections with these questions.

The "world religions" are those traditions that have shaped large numbers of people in many different cultures. Usually, Judaism, Christianity, and Islam predominate in discussions of "Western" (originally Near Eastern) world religions, while Hinduism, Buddhism, Confucianism, and Taoism head the Eastern (Asian) list. One may enter qualifications and caveats about several of these traditions: Jews have always been a small population, numbering nowadays around 20 million; Hinduism has remained mainly the religious culture of Indians, though as Indians have moved to other countries, so has Hinduism; Confucianism and Taoism have been inter-national (more precisely, more-than-Asian) only inasmuch as Chinese people have moved to many different lands. Few Europeans or Africans have become Taoists or Confucians. These, however, are minor qualifications. The three great families of world religions, as measured by the populations they have enrolled and the cultural depth they have achieved, are the Abrahamic (Judaism, Christianity, Islam), the Indian (Hinduism, Buddhism), and the Chinese (Confucianism, Taoism; an adapted Buddhism has also been influential in China, Japan, Vietnam, Korea, and the other East Asian countries).

To single out these three families, or these seven traditions, is not to deny that everywhere human beings have been religious. Virtually all tribal peoples, living in small-scale societies, have been religious, most frequently in an oral (non-literate) and shamanistic mode. According to Mircea Eliade, the dean of the past generation of historians of religion, a shaman is a specialist in archaic techniques for ecstasy.[6] The shaman heals sick members of the tribe, serves as an intermediary with the gods (who have sent famine, or sickness, or tribal strife, or good fortune), guides the dead to the land of rest, and often keeps the store of tribal traditions (myths, rituals, memories of movements and heroes past).

Shamans do most of this business by traveling out of ordinary consciousness. They enter an altered state, by dancing, singing, fasting, going into solitude (sensory deprivation), taking drugs (tobacco, peyote), and other techniques. They are familiar with the spirits of animals, whom they ask for help, and they fight against wicked spirits and the witch-doctors, the evil shamans, who send them. The great majority of native Americans, Africans, and Australians have done business, been religious, in a shamanistic mode. So have the traditional Europeans and Asians who lived close to their people, at the level of folk religion and the little tradition. For example, in Germany, Ireland, and the Slavic lands, shamanic leaders, ecstatics, were major powers, prior to the coming of Christianity (and sometimes afterwards). In Africa north of the Sahara, a similar situation obtained prior to the coming of Islam (and sometimes afterwards). In Korea, China, Japan, and other Asian countries, shamanism has continued to fuel the religion of the peasants, despite the predominance of Confucianism, Taoism, or Buddhism in the higher culture. In India to this day, many rituals for healing and blessing mix a Hindu dressing with shamanistic trances.

I prefer to understand "world religions" as the full span of human traffic with ultimate reality – oral as well as literate traditions. While the seven great religions that I have singled out deserve special treatment, we neglect the lesser traditions to our loss. One can also make a case that such sophisticated small religions as Jainism, Zoroastrianism (Parsis), Sikhism, and Bahai, which have been "small" insofar as they have enrolled relatively few adherents (though still millions), deserve study and indicate still other ways that human beings have pursued holiness – still other evidences of the nearly endless variety of human creativity in religious matters.

The wealth of religious pathways that human beings have constructed through the millennia testifies to the inherent hunger of our kind for meaning. Faced with the inevitable mysteriousness of their lives, human beings seem bound to imagine ways the world might have begun, reasons for living honestly and lovingly rather than selfishly. The sources of theology that we studied in chapter 2 take on further depth and color when we go to India or China with an open mind, primed to see in native religious ways legitimate searches for God. So do the patterns of patriarchal dominance of women by men. If nearly always and everywhere human beings have been religious, almost always and everywhere they have been patriarchal about their religion, giving precedence to the rule and judgment of men. Judaism and Islam merit this description as much as Christianity does. Hinduism and Buddhism have been patriarchal, as has Confucianism. Taoism has championed feminine ways, but somewhat stereotypically, as symbols for the indirect way that the Tao (Way) operates, and with little effective challenge to a Confucian social structure.

There is no major world religion in which women have been the social or political equals of men. Small-scale societies, whether very ancient or very recent, tend to have economies in which women are as important as men. This, in turn, tends to give women the right to their own religious ways – ceremonies (for example, for birth, the menarche, menopause), women's societies (which often run such ceremonies and impart feminine lore), myths, and models of holiness. The work of the late Marija Gimbutas witnesses to the likelihood that prehistoric Europeans venerated a Great Goddess,[7] and in many oral cultures, whether at the stage of hunting-and-gathering or of agriculture, female divinities (especially Mother Earth) balance male (for example, Father Sky).

A generous Christian theology of grace takes everything good in a culture as an indication of the presence of the one God. In doing this it is merely extending an impulse of the apostle Paul: "Finally, brethren, whatever is true, whatever is honorable, whatever is just, whatever is pure, whatever is lovely, whatever is gracious, if there is any excellence, if there is anything worthy of praise, think about these things" (Philippians 4:8). One cannot say that Paul was envisioning the whole of human history and culture, but one can say that today, in our planetary culture, his impulse is precisely the large-heartedness that makes Christianity most attractive.

The Christian church has not always exhibited large-heartedness. Often it has sought political power and lost sight of its ministerial nature – its commission from its founder not to rule but to serve. A prayer of the Dutch poet Huub Oosterhuis displays the humility that both recognizing past failures and resolving to do better in the future can inculcate:

> Reform your church, and give her the courage to be, to follow you and do your word. May she cease in her attempts to dominate men [people]. May she make no more demands and claim no more privileges, but only try to contribute to men's happiness. May she neither repel nor exclude anyone by the words she uses or the ideas she has, but be open to everyone who seeks to live a happy and creative life. Help us to remember, God, that we were sent only to spread your grace in all humility, because we have been accepted by you and always need forgiveness.[8]

God is the source of grace, not the church in its human agency. If signs of grace appear outside the discernible borders of the church, Christians cannot in good conscience ignore them or deprecate them. Holiness is holiness, regardless of the robes it wears, the Doctrine/ Dharma it preaches. There are Jews, Muslims, Hindus, Buddhists and members of other religions who manifestly are good, wise, self-sacrificing, courageous, passionate for justice, enraptured by the divine mystery – in a word, holy. As much as their Christian counterparts, they testify to the ways and nature of the one God. Not to admit their testimony is to try to constrain revelation, scripture, and tradition immorally. It is to set one's small human will against the clear action of God.

The apostle Peter met this situation in the form of the action of the Holy Spirit among unbaptized Gentiles. His response should set the pattern that latter-day disciples follow:

> And Peter opened his mouth and said: "Truly I perceive that God shows no partiality, but in every nation any one who fears him and

does what is right is acceptable to him".... While Peter was still saying this, the Holy Spirit fell on all who heard the word. And the believers from among the circumcised [Jews] who came with Peter were amazed, because the gift of the Holy Spirit had been poured out even on the Gentiles [non-Jews, uncircumcised]. For they heard them speaking in tongues and extolling God. Then Peter declared, "Can anyone forbid water for baptizing these people who have received the Holy Spirit just as we have?' And he commanded them to be baptized in the name of Jesus Christ. (Acts 10:34–5, 44–8)

Among the many possible applications of this generous attitude is the one that would consider the gifts of women, their actual religious performances, as the basis for evaluating their potential as leaders, holders of authority, teachers and figures of wisdom. Using such an empirical criterion would oppose the blanket, sex-based criterion that the patriarchal churches tend to use. In Roman Catholicism and Eastern Orthodoxy, for example, no woman, no matter how learned or wise or holy, can be ordained to the priesthood, let alone become a bishop (a member of the college that actually rules the church). Nowadays, the burden of proof falls on any such blanket, sex-based criterion to defend itself against the charge of sexism. If discriminating against people because of the color of their skin is the sin of racism, then discriminating against people because of their sex is the sin of sexism. The patriarchal churches have been slow to admit this logic. Frequently they have preached well to the outside world but refused to reform their own houses. For this reason, they have with many women lost credibility.

Noting the patriarchal biases, the sins of sexism, that stand out in all the world religions, Christian feminists are likely to feel ambivalent. On the one hand, they have to lament the worldwide, centuries-long injustices done to their sisters. On the other hand, they can realize that Christianity imposes no special depreciation of women. Rather, it is part of a general pattern, a regular disorder. By stressing the Christian reasons for considering women the full equals of men in the possession of humanity, Christian feminists can often shame friends of patriarchy into acknowledging the need for change. Actually making substantial changes is a further step, but acknowledgment is a beginning.

Feminist Revisions

In all major areas of Christian theology nowadays, feminists are proposing revisions designed to remove the baleful effects of traditional patriarchy and accommodate the insights of women. Negatively, they want to excise malignancies from the past. Positively, they want the church, and humanity at large, to benefit more explicitly from the contributions of the half of the race that experiences God in a female body, through the roles of wife and mother, sister and feminine friend. These desires have created some imaginative revisions of the traditional Christian views of revelation, scripture, tradition, church history, God, sin, and other cardinal elements of the creed. Let us indicate a few of them.

For the doctrines of God and revelation, such Christian feminist theologians as Elizabeth Johnson and Sallie McFague stand out. Early in her constructive work on "the mystery of God in feminist theological discourse," Johnson explains as follows her stated purpose of connecting feminist and classical wisdom:

> My aim in what follows is to speak a good word about the mystery of God recognizable within the contours of Christian faith that will serve the emancipatory praxis of women and men, to the benefit of all creation, both human beings and the earth. In so doing, I draw on the new language of Christian feminist theology as well as on the traditional language of scripture and classical theology, all of which codify religious insights. By Christian feminist theology I mean a reflection on God and all things in the light of God that stands consciously in the company of all the world's women, explicitly prizing their genuine humanity while uncovering and criticizing its persistent violation in sexism, itself an omnipresent paradigm of unjust relationships.[9]

First, Johnson wants to write a book, construct a theology, about God, who is intrinsically mysterious, that Christians will recognize as referring to their deity (and knowledgeable outsiders will agree). Second, she wants her work to serve, be useful to, the "emancipatory praxis" of (a) both sexes, and (b) all creation, both human and non-human. "Emancipatory praxis" is ways of living, of acting upon one's deepest convictions, that liberate both the individual agent and the other people with whom she or he engages. Usually this praxis will entail public, political action and witness – a being in the world, before others, both friends and foes, that puts one's faith to the test but also refines it and proves its wisdom. Aware of today's ecological crisis, and aware as well that women do not exist apart from men, Johnson makes explicit the need for a contemporary theology to include non-human creation, and the need for it to benefit both sexes.

The new language of feminist theology is nothing so standard as a glossary of politically correct terms, but a mainstream of "feminist" Christian theologians agrees on such significant matters as the sexism of the patriarchal traditions, the inclination of women to think relationally, the appropriateness of feminine images for God, and the deficiencies of a hierarchical outlook that leads to domination – a will to subjugate either nature or other human beings. The traditional language of scripture and classical theology contains a wisdom and saving power that no serious Christian wants to neglect or devalue. The story of Jesus, and the creative interpretation of that story by geniuses such as Augustine and Origen, Aquinas and Luther, Calvin and Rahner, must remain a great legacy, a much admired thesaurus, of which all serious Christian reflection takes advantage. Combined, the feminist and traditional theologies amount to a "code" of religious insights, not in the sense that they are a secret language, but in the sense that they put into words, forms that we can work with developmentally, the root metaphors, the basic feelings and convictions, through which Christians have long found "salvation" and "divine life."

Johnson's definition of feminist Christian theology stresses the primacy of God, but also the solidarity of women that emerges, when one becomes conscious of how the equality of women with men in the possession of humanity has been violated. This violation, for which "sexism" can stand as shorthand, is a model, a paradigm, of injustice generally. For Johnson, much if not most of what is wrong in human history, what manifests human sinfulness, shows its basic, recurrent character and ways in the abuse of women by patriarchal cultures.

Johnson needs 300 pages to develop the implications of this beginning, but from this outset the dialectic, the play back-and-forth,

of her feminism and her Christian faith is clear. She does not accept
an either/or relationship between the two. Feminism has become a
lens through which to look upon Christian revelation, scripture, and
tradition afresh. Alternately, Christian faith provides the outlook on
ultimate reality, the divine mystery, that feminism and all other
considerations require if they are to reflect "under the aspect of
eternity" – from the most adequate perspective.

A second example: after explaining that the main "sources and
resources" for her constructive theology will feature scripture, tradition, and experience, Sallie McFague describes scripture and tradition as a flexible, varied, patchwork. Of scripture, for instance, she
says, "It is precisely the patchwork, potpourri character of the Hebraic
and Christian Scriptures with their rich flood of images, stories, and
themes – some interweaving and mutually supportive, others disparate, presenting alternative possibilities – that gives Christian theologians 'authority' to experiment, to find grids or screens with which
to interpret God's transforming love within the givens of their own
time."[10]

McFague is not explicit in this text about the consonance of her
characterization of scripture and the relational character of reality
that feminists tend to favor. Nonetheless, her underscoring of the
patchwork character of scripture brings it close to the experiential
basis of credible wisdom that feminists have stressed – the need for
revelation, special wisdom, to manifest strong roots in what actually
happens to people, women as much as men, and to square with the
worldviews, the life-ways, that such experience, reflected upon
faithfully, tends to develop. In contrast to views of scripture that
make it inert or monolithic, McFague primes us to think of the
scriptural books as coming from people like ourselves who had to
struggle to find their way through life's darkness, to hold their own
against the divine mystery, ultimately realizing that so immense a
love deserves our *carte blanche*.

When she becomes explicit about the "formal criterion" for her
theology, McFague again stresses "experience," which is virtually a
shibboleth in feminist circles:

> The formal criterion for theology, then, is that it reflect in tough-
> minded, concrete ways and in the language and thought forms of
> one's own time, about what salvation could mean now, to us. . . .

> What the formal criterion does not allow, however, is resting in an interpretation of God's salvific love from some bygone time, for this will invariably be escapist and, finally, destructive: that gospel will be good news not for our time but for another.[11]

Johnson and McFague are working, in these texts, as constructive theologians. If we go to feminist theologians whose expertise, specialization, is scriptural exegesis, we find similar convictions. For example, the work of Elisabeth Schüssler Fiorenza on the place of women in early Christianity and the elements of a feminist hermeneutics (interpretational theory) for scripture both respects the core of traditional Christian faith and offers, as tools for mediating that core to today's cultures, feminist sensitivities.[12] So does the exegetical work of Phyllis Trible.[13] As our own project here unfolds, we shall draw on parallel feminist work in other areas of Christian theology: sin, grace, ethics, prayer. Regularly the point will be to look afresh at wonderful old convictions and images, using the cutting blade of women's pains to get to the flesh of the matter in question.

The feminist revisions of traditional Christian reflection on faith that I treasure are not captious or casual. The credentials that convince me are manifest love of "the faith long handed down" and manifest awareness of the inhibition of such handing down that women have suffered – the damage wrought by sexism. If one loves Christian faith, for its revelation of the God to whom Eastern Orthodoxy prays confidently in the words "for you are a good God, and you love humankind," then one takes one's stand with the church, in all its historical folly and current weakness, not being ashamed of Christ or the gospel. If one stands in solidarity with the women of the world, the women of history, sensitive to the justice of their requests for the redress of sexist damage, then one asks that the gospel be freed of patriarchal fetters, allowed to apply its wonderful powers of liberation wholly, at full bore, for females as much as males. Together, these two allegiances amount to more than a double cord, a reinforced binding to what is right and holy. Such a binding is a religion (*re-ligio*) well worth entertaining, embracing, and serving.

Study Questions

1 What is the significance of revelation for Christian theology?
2 What is the significance for feminist theology of the fact that the Christian scriptures came from largely patriarchal cultures?
3 Explain the main dynamics of "traditioning."
4 How would you determine whether the history of the Christian church has kept faith with the view of women that Jesus had?
5 What sort of revelation ought constructive Christian theologians to find in the non-Christian religions?
6 When feminist Christians set out to revise traditional theology, what criteria should they consider binding?

Notes

1 See, for representative brief studies of "revelation," Avery Dulles, "Faith and revelation," in Francis Schüssler Fiorenza and John P. Galvin (eds), *Systematic Theology*, vol. 1 (Fortress, Minneapolis, 1991), pp. 89–128; Mary Catherine Hilkert, "Experience and tradition – can the center hold? Revelation," in Catherine Mowry LaCugna (ed.), *Freeing Theology* (Harper San Francisco, San Francisco, 1993), pp. 59–82; David A. Pailin, "Revelation," in Alan Richardson and John Bowden (eds), *The Westminster Dictionary of Christian Theology* (Westminster, Philadelphia, 1983), pp. 503–6.
2 See Giulia Piccaluga, "Knots," in Mircea Eliade (ed.), *The Encyclopedia of Religion, vol. 8* (Macmillan, New York, 1987), pp. 340–2.
3 See, for example, Catherine Mowry LaCugna, *God for Us* (Harper San Francisco, San Francisco, 1991), which redoes the central Christian doctrine of the Trinity.
4 See Jaroslav Pelikan, *Jesus Through the Centuries* (Yale University Press, New Haven, CT, 1985). On the general history of women in Europe, see Bonnie S. Anderson and Judith P. Zuisser (eds), *A History of Their Own*, two volumes (Harper and Row, New York, 1988).
5 See, for example, John Hick and Paul Knitter (eds), *The Myth of Christian Uniqueness* (Orbis Books, Maryknoll, NY, 1987).
6 See Mircea Eliade, *Shamanism* (Princeton University Press, Princeton, NJ, 1964).
7 See, for example, Marija Gimbutas, *The Language of the Goddess* (Harper San Francisco, San Francisco, 1989).

8   Huub Oosterhuis, *Your Word Is Near* (Newman Press, New York, 1968), p. 147.

9   Elizabeth Johnson, *She Who Is* (Crossroad, New York, 1992), p. 8.

10   Sallie McFague, *Models of God* (Fortress, Philadelphia, 1987), p. 44.

11   Ibid., p. 45.

12   See Elisabeth Schüssler Fiorenza, *In Memory of Her* (Crossroad, New York, 1983) and *Bread, Not Stone* (Beacon, Boston, 1984).

13   See Phyllis Trible, *Texts of Terror* (Fortress, Philadelphia, 1984).

Chapter 4

CREATION
NATURE AND ECOLOGY

How the World Was Born

Having sketched the nature of our project, looked at its foundations in the dynamics of our human searches for meaning, and considered the basic fonts of Christian faith, revelation and tradition, we turn to constructive work proper. The next four chapters – creation, ecclesiology, anthropology, and theology – probe the irreducible constants of reality. For Christians, the natural world, human beings in their togetherness, individual selfhood, and God are distinct yet coordinated. One cannot collapse any one of these four into another legitimately. Despite the full dependence of nature, society, and the self on God, one also cannot confuse any one of these three with God, legitimately, any more than with one another. When we have constructed our Christian feminist understanding of these four irreducible constants of reality, we shall have presented a comprehensive worldview. However germinal or incomplete, it will in principle stretch as far as Christian intelligence can take us. So we should be aware of the boldness, perhaps even the hubris, in our venture. What we enter upon now, in the viscera of the book, is a new effort to think after God the thoughts structuring all that is.

For Christian faith, the natural world, the entire span of creation, comes from God, as a free work. There is no necessity in nature, the universe. God would be God without nature, as God would be God without human beings or angels or anything else less than God. Now more clearly, now less, Christians have developed the instincts of the

Bible in this regard, moving from key passages in Genesis and Isaiah to equally key passages in John and Paul. The upshot has been, in technical terms, a conviction that creation comes from nothingness. There is a condition (an accurate assessment of reality) in which creation is not, and probably there was a time when creation, everything less than God, was not. The likelihood, as Christian faith sees things, is that the world, the universe, is not eternal. It probably came into being in time, perhaps through a "big bang," and probably it will pass out of being in time, through entropy. These are not theses of astrophysics or the physics of nuclear particles. They are intuitions of faith, developed with some awareness of current theories of how the universe was born and operates but guided more directly by traditional Christian understandings of divinity – what God is like, and how the world is unlike God.

Let us consider two of the key texts that have long shaped Christian instincts about the nature of the physical world:

> In the beginning when God created the heavens and the earth, the earth was a formless void and darkness covered the face of the deep, while a wind from God swept over the face of the waters. Then God said, "Let there be light;" and there was light. And God saw that the light was good; and God separated the light from the darkness. God called the light Day and the darkness he called Night. And there was evening and there was morning, the first day. (Genesis 1:1–5, NRSV)

These are the first lines in the Bible. They alert us to how the compilers of the canonical text oriented themselves in the world, in reality. Instinctively, they arranged the sacred writings so that, from the outset, readers might have a realistic estimate of their situation. The world in which such readers live began, gained its present shape, when God made the heavens and the earth. Prior to that making, that creative process, there was something – a formless void, a darkness over the face of the deep, but how this vague something stood to God is not clear. For the authors of Genesis 1:1, though, the point alpha probably was not "nothingness" in the metaphysician's sense of "non-being." On the other hand, "void" is a negative image, giving all the positivity, all the desirable reality in creation, to God. The process of creation began from humble raw materials.

The wind from God sweeping over the face of the waters can be the spirit of God, the vital breath. It stirs things to life, including the spirits of human beings. The formation of creation, through the "days" of God's work, comes from the action of God's spirit and word. The making of the natural world is a process of intelligent craftsmanship. God's choice to begin with light, make light the first "let there be," goes along with this stress on spirit, mind, intelligent craftsmanship. The world is not being born, coming into being, as a gestation. The divinity is not bringing forth its new life as process of birth. The motif is of a building, a designing, a clearing and assembling.

God sees that the light is good. God likes what God is making, how the work is going. It is hard to overemphasize how important the theme of God's pleasure in creation, God's satisfaction with the work of fashioning the natural world, ought to be in Christian theology. In contrast to many religious worldviews that view nature, space, and time suspiciously, Genesis is clear that the biblical God takes pleasure in creation, loves the world.

The first phase of creation leaves light and darkness, night and day, as the primordial basis of order. Not only is this the primitive rhythm by which human beings have always lived, waking and sleeping, it is the primitive binary structure of consciousness: knowledge and ignorance, awareness and shadow.

The model of craftsmanship dominating the account of creation at the beginning of Genesis suggests the patriarchal controls at work culturally. In using this model, and giving only bare hints of an alternate or complementary feminist one (the wind moving over the waters), the canonical writers make the relationship between the natural world and its source less intimate than they might have.

Biblical scholars tend to find in the creation account of Genesis notes of dependence on older or then-contemporary myths of the ancient Near East.[1] By the time the text came into its current literary form and position in the Bible, fear of their Canaanite neighbors' fertility religion may have inclined the authors to steer clear of imagery in which God would give birth to the world (from what sort of fertilization is not clear). Whatever the historical, psychological, and religious forces at work, we may note that there is no necessity in the use of masculine language for God, no reason not to picture the divine workman as a workwoman.

The question of how best to imagine the relation between the

source and the product, the divine maker and the world that has
been made, is more complicated. For the moment, let us simply note
that none of the advantages stemming from picturing this relation as
ideal (creation by spirit and word) requires a male divinity. A female
could breathe and speak as effectively as a male. In creating, as well
as all other aspects of the sole God's divine activity, holy ultimacy
transcends sexual limitation – is no more captured by "male" than
by "female."

The creative sovereignty of God, beside whom there is no other
maker of the world, leads a prophet such as Second Isaiah to believe
that history moves as God chooses to have it. The following verses
from Isaiah 45 dovetail with the assurances of Genesis that the
natural world is a work of God, fully under divine control from the
first, foundational word by which God gave the primitive rhythm of
light and darkness:

> I made the earth, and created humankind upon it; it was my hands
> that stretched out the heavens, and commanded all their host. . . . For
> thus says the Lord, who created the heavens (he is God!), who formed
> the earth and made it (he established it; he did not create it a chaos,
> he formed it to be inhabited): I am the Lord, and there is no other. I
> did not speak in secret, in a land of darkness. I did not say to the
> offspring of Jacob, "seek me in chaos." I the Lord speak the truth. I
> declare what is right. (Isaiah 45:12, 18–19)

The context is Israel's suffering in captivity in Babylon. The essential
message is that deliverance is nigh. The one who gives this message,
offers this comfort, is the sole God, the creator of the world, the Lord
with whom Israel stands in covenant. Isaiah stresses that the One
who gives the wonderful, redemptive word has complete authority,
because all of creation stands by his word. He made everything, in
order not chaos. There is nothing under heaven, nothing running in
the processes of nature, that does not derive from his work or admit
of his control.

Creation is not something that God, the Lord of Israel, did once
and for all, as though it carried no further, ongoing, indeed constant,
consequences. Creation is the continual context, situation, reality in
which all creatures find themselves. Creation is the comprehensive
plan, work, construction of our universal, ecological reality. What

happens among the nations, through their power plays, only occurs in and as part of the single plan of God, as does what happens through the action of the sun, the rain, the earth, the hunters, gatherers, and farmers.

Once again, there is no sexual inevitability in this sketch of the control, the providence, of the Creator. The One who stretched out the heavens and commanded their host probably comes to mind as a colossal workman and military general, stereotypically masculine, but only a little imagination could replace him with a female architect, designer, or queen. The core of the message does not depend on the patriarchal cultural trappings that the text may assume. The core of the message is that the biblical God can run the world, move history this way or that, because he or she or it made everything in the beginning, gave all basic ingredients their being and form.

How we ought to correlate this fundamental biblical instinct with modern scientific views of the universe, biological evolution, historical causality, and the like raises a host of complicated questions. For the moment, it is enough to note the enormous impact of the biblical texts that assure readers of the Creator's power and control. In the final analysis, Christians still affirm that their God, the Father-Son-Spirit, is the Creator of the world, and that the world stands under God's judgment (control), headed for the final disposition, the ultimate consummation, that God intends. They still think of providence, a divine plan, not a hair of their heads going unnumbered.

As with the matter of the basic goodness of the world, this conviction about divine providence has been enormously influential. If God has not made the world a chaos but an inhabited order, then believers can be confident that, whether they see it or not, feel it or not, their lives must make great sense.

How the World Is Maintained

Let us turn now to two explicitly Christian texts, drawn from the New Testament, that bring the matter of creation, and providence as well, into direct relation with the divinity of Christ:

> In the beginning was the Word, and the Word was with God, and the Word was God. He was in the beginning with God. All things came into being through him, and without him not one thing came into being. What has come into being in him was life, and the life was the light of all people. The light shines in the darkness, and the darkness did not overcome it. (John 1: 1–5)

The parallel with Genesis 1: 1–5 is conscious, deliberate. The author of John is harking back to the first pages of the Bible, resetting the account of creation given there. The Prologue to the Johannine version of the good news available in Jesus makes the Word of God the agent of God in the very fashioning of the universe. Inasmuch as this Word took flesh in Jesus, the deepest identity of Jesus the Messiah is the eternal speech, self-expression, through which God (the Father) uttered the various "let there bes" of creation.

The Word was with God – alongside, ever-present, identified with what God is in himself, herself, itself. Divinity, creative love without limit, is intelligent, full of rational life, directive and planning. The author of John thinks of everything in the natural world as occurring in the mind of God, the reality of God, through God's intellectual light. This thought need not conflict with a parallel, rounder thought: everything in the natural world may also occur in the spirit of God, the encircling love we might associate more with God's "heart" than God's mind, Word, or reason. Seldom with God are we forced to dichotomies, choices between either this or that. Indeed, though the orthodox interpretation of the Christian God as a Trinity is at best inchoate in the New Testament, including the Gospel of John, the seeds of it are germinating. So the stress here on the verbal, intellectualist side of the divine creativity need not rule out a complementary stress on the love of God for all the things God brings into being. The Word carrying all things in it can be cordial, a gracious blend of light and warmth, of strong making and gentle caring.

Because the extent of creation occurring in the Word is complete, to the point where the author feels obliged to say that without the Word not one thing came into being, the divinity of the Word seems beyond dispute. The Word is not a limited agent, a demi-urge, a lower, deputed creator. Whatever occurs, from mite to stellar giant, is "spoken" into existence. It takes its place, plays its role, as part of a narrative, a story, told by God from the divine bosom.

The implication is as providential as what we saw in the text from Isaiah. If all things come to be in the Word, and nothing comes to be apart from the Word, then all things move in the single, comprehensive pattern or blueprint or speech that God has used in bringing the world into being and keeping it going – developing, evolving. For the moment it is not necessary to distinguish the natural and human parts of creation. In the beginning, *everything* is implied. The Word is as extensive as divinity itself. Creation is much less extensive than divinity, and all of creation therefore can occur in the Word, be seen as a function of the outward activity of divinity that the Word effects, without there being any problem of "space."

The author of John shades the effect of creation toward life and light. The life that he, or she, implies is physical, yes, but perhaps spiritual even more. What has occurred in Jesus, historically, is an offer of divine life. By faith in Jesus, disciples can become deathless – partakers in the relationship with God, the Father, that Jesus enjoyed. What Jesus is physically, naturally, through the incarnation of the Word in the flesh that Mary gave him, followers of Jesus, believers, branches of his vine can become in him, through the identification with him that their faith and love create. So he is a Word, a good news, of eternal life – spiritual, moral power stronger than death, sin, ignorance. He is light, moving beyond the implications of God's work on the first day of creation according to Genesis, to the point where he becomes the privileged revelation of God. What Jesus makes clear, through the entirety of his being and work, is what God chooses to be for us, how God appears in our human parameters of space and time, grace and sin, spirit and flesh.

This light refers to our basic humanity. We are the creatures who can know that the natural world makes sense, carries in its being, its occurring, an intelligibility, a correlation with the Mind that ordered it. But the reference is moral as well as physical or ontological. There is a rightness, a lightsomeness, of the heart, the good will, as well as of the clear mind. The image of the Creator in us is fuller than our simple ability to grasp the order of our situation, appreciate that God has not made the world a chaos. We ought to express in the world of space and time the goodness of God, the moral clarity, the love.

Love makes light, even more than light makes love. When John is pushed to give his best word about God, it is that God is love. Love is the human force, the experiential reality, closest to the divine mystery from which all things come into being with God's blessing. Love is the "reason" offering us what explanation God can for the goodness of Jesus that makes him the savior. In Johannine theology, one cannot get behind love to something more basic. At the divine love one must stop, bow low, simply adore.

The light of the creative divine love shines in all the darkness of what is not God, what is ontologically or morally lesser. This darkness has never grasped the light of the creative divine love – never controlled it, been coextensive with it or equal to it, understood it or defeated it. The light shines in the darkness. The light happens, operates, whenever and wherever God is and divine activity occurs. For John the center of the drama of salvation through which God brings people to the light and so the possibility of divine life, a share in the divine deathlessness, is the revelation of Jesus – the revelation that Jesus was, through the incarnation in him of the eternal divine Word. When the Word took flesh and dwelt in the world, pitching its tent in the midst of human beings, becoming a participant in history, matter gained its fullest potency.

The deeds of Jesus that John records in the first half of the gospel (chapters 1–12) are signs of the eternal life that God has made available to those who open themselves to Jesus in faith. These signs – turning the water into wine, multiplying the loaves of bread, healing the man born blind – show the power of God at work in Jesus, the credentials he carries. They are eternal life operating in sinful time, to transform it. If received with faith, given an honest hearing, they can draw people into the orbit of God, the love of the Father, so fully that the existence of such people becomes eccentric – they live more and more as Jesus did, defining themselves by their relationship with God, making their foremost identity their abiding with God heart to heart, love to love.

We could play nearly endless variations on this theme of the Johannine reconception of the sense of creation at work in Genesis, because John's sense of Jesus is so rich that all the major motifs admit of a new, sacramental understanding radiating from the Word made flesh. Inasmuch as that flesh comes from Mary and situates creation, revelation, salvation, and all the other modalities of the divine action upon us in the intimate world of our bodies, food, sex, birth and death, it includes women as much as men, feminine motifs as much as masculine. The Johannine Jesus teaches female disciples as well as male (apparently unusual for a rabbi in his time). Martha and Mary are as good friends as their brother Lazarus. As a result, much of the vicious potential in the patriarchy of Jesus' day goes by the board, because of the freedom with which Jesus lives. He moves lightly, directed by his intimacy with the Father, the intercourse he has with the divine spirit. So in this gospel he seems singularly uncoopted, open to whatever images, illustrations, and interactions facilitate the disclosure of God's light, life, and love for all people, adults as much as children, women as much as men.[2]

A second classical New Testament text bearing directly on the Christian reconception of creation in the light of faith in Jesus as the incarnate Word of God occurs in the first chapter of the Pauline epistle to the Colossians. This text is probably an early Christian hymn, taken up by a disciple of Paul for a meditation on the status of Christ:

> He is the image of the invisible God, the firstborn of all creation; for in him all things in heaven and on earth were created, things visible and invisible, whether thrones or dominations or rulers or powers – all things have been created through him and for him. He himself is before all things, and in him all things hold together. He is the head of the body, the church; he is the beginning, the firstborn from the dead, so that he might come to have first place in everything. For in him all the fullness of God was pleased to dwell, and through him God was pleased to reconcile to himself all things, whether on earth or in heaven, by making peace through the blood of his cross. (Colossians 1: 15–20)

Just as Genesis and Second Isaiah work with different images, organized according to different senses of creation, so do John and Colossians. Only the slightest study of biblical documents shows the sensitive reader that scripture includes enormous variety. Here the central Pauline interest, the death and resurrection of Christ, gives the reflection on creation a different cast from that given by the central Johannine interest, the Word's taking flesh. John does not deny, indeed in the full sweep of the Gospel he stresses greatly, the death and resurrection of Jesus, while the author of Colossians makes the risen Lord the site where the fullness of God was pleased to dwell. But the angle, the feel, is different in each case, resulting in their creating together a richer presentation of both creation and Christ than either text could provide alone.

The very first sentence in this text joins both resurrection and the original creation. We ought to remember always that the New Testament comes from the faith of the first Christians that God had raised Jesus from the dead, making him Lord of all and "firstborn" of a new creation. Easter Sunday is the great imperative behind the gospel, both the reason the disciples rushed out to preach a good news and the substance of what they preached. The "image" associated with the risen Lord here is cognate to what the Word connotes in John. In each case, an expression of God, a self-manifestation, becomes available, and this expression illumines both the processes of history and the processes of the natural world.

Inasmuch as all things hold together in Christ, he is the linch pin of creation. Spiritual beings as much as physical take their ordering, gain their parts in the universal story, through the logic of God that Christ represents. The church relies on him in the same way, and the entire process of reconciliation through which God works human healing depends on him, passes through him, centrally. What happened in the death and resurrection of Jesus the Christ is the middle panel, the constitutive format, of any triptych structuring creation or history into what was, is, and will be.

Jesus the Christ is the fullness of the Godhead in corporeal, delimited, sacramental, enfleshed terms – choose what words and images you will. The cross of Christ, so shameful to his contemporaries, has become the still point of the turning world. The blood of the cross, reminiscent of the paschal lamb, to say nothing of all the other sacrifices important in the intercourse between divinity and humanity down the ages, has brought a definitive reconciliation. What had been at odds, estranged, is now evened, restored to peace and intimacy. The evils and pains of history, the cracks and sufferings of evolutionary creation, have found their medicine, their healing, their solution. Less serene than John, more conflicted and convoluted, the Pauline author nonetheless finally achieves a similar serenity. In the power of the resurrected Christ he or she finds creation restored to all the goodness that God saw in the beginning, when first God gave it light.

Once again, though the stated imagery of the text is male, because the focal object is Jesus the Christ, there is little sexist or sexually delimiting about the main ideas. It is the humanity of Jesus, as well as his particular masculinity, that serves as the instrument of reconciliation. It is the fact that he has a body, and so can be a sacramental center, as much as the fact that this body is male or female.

Certainly, the priestly overtones in the sacrificial symbols call to mind a patriarchal institution, but these overtones do not determine the message. When the discussion focuses on the divine image, the one in whom all things hold together, it is fully historical or personal but also transcendent, more than what finite creation can contain. So although the inevitable association of the Word and Lord with the man Jesus of Nazareth tends to make explicitly Christian views of creation and reconciliation more masculine than feminine, this association does not mean that the Creator is only male, only a patriarch, and must inevitably appear anthropomorphic, less than transcendent of the limitations, cultural even more than physical, that "Fatherhood" or "craftsmanship" might suggest.

Feminist theologians can accept the cultural limitations of the Johannine, Pauline, or other New Testament texts that they receive without feeling fettered to the patriarchal imagination that may seem to predominate. By reflecting on the core meaning that the images construct or suggest, feminist theologians can even begin a process through which, for example, "reconciliation" might stir pictures of restoration to the bosom of a family, return to a motherly love.

The Signs of God in Nature

A constructive Christian feminist theology is bound to think well of creation. It is bound, as well, to contemplate the intimate ties between God and the world, for "creation" means that the world comes from God directly, as a free grant of existence, a gracious work of art that need not have been. If there is a world, it is because God liked the prospect of sharing what God alone is necessarily or unfailingly with lesser beings, compounds of necessity and contingency. The most basic question in philosophy is why there is something rather than nothing. The Christian answer to this question lives in recesses of the divine mystery. The only reason there is something besides God is an act of interest, love, generosity on God's part.

Consequently, the things that exist "outside" of God, the creatures that constitute the world, bear witness to the divine generosity. How they receive and express divinity-up-to-a-point, how, for example, they stop the divine fullness of being at borders of matter, remains inexplicable, but even as limited they suggest wonderful things about their unlimited source. Thus, alongside scripture and tradition, many Christian theologians have studied nature as a source of revelation about God. The heavens and the earth, the seas and the mountains, the plants and the trees, the creeping things and the birds of the air – all have offered the reverent beholder clues to what God is like, how ultimacy may be in itself. All the more have human beings offered such clues, opening halls of reflection upon the ways of mind, spirit, will, and love.

A simple series of verses from one of the Psalms can suggest how many biblical believers have thought about the signs of God filling creation:

> Praise him, sun and moon; praise him, all you shining stars. Praise him, you highest heavens, and you waters above the heavens. Let them praise the name of the Lord, for he commanded and they were created. He established them forever and ever; he fixed their bounds, which cannot be passed. Praise the Lord from the earth, you sea monsters and all deeps, fire and hail, snow and frost, stormy wind fulfilling his command! Mountains and all hills, fruit trees and all cedars! Wild animals and all cattle, creeping things and flying birds! Kings of the earth and all peoples, princes and all rulers of the earth! Young men and women alike, old and young together! (Psalm 148: 3–12)[3]

The mood is not scientific analysis, not even sober appreciation. The mood is praise, worship, thrilled admiration. Much of what we think about the world in relation to God depends on how we think about God. If we are convinced that God is wholly good, then we are inclined to think that the world must be good, the myriad creatures in their variety and beauty must reflect an infinite divine splendor. On the other hand, if things are going badly in the world, and we doubt that God is caring for us well, we can find the natural world to be opaque, oppressive, even cruel. Rather than rising from an admiration of the frost or the snow to a song of praise for God, our spirits may resist, even revolt, because for the moment the frost or the snow gives us no lift, shows us no help or beauty or wonder. The fault may indeed lie with us, but often we cannot remove it. The fact seems to be that sometimes we experience the natural world as helping us to believe in God's care, convincing us that we can relax and feel at home, while at other times we experience isolation, alienation, even dread. God is in the world, making the divine fullness of being known, but the world never captures God, and always God insinuates how the world is less than ultimate, no fully lasting home.

Christians can believe that the limits of the natural world, like the limits of human goodness, serve their growth in wisdom. The core symbols of Christian faith are fully positive – good news, salvation, divine life, the love of God – but these symbols do not remove the harsh realities of finitude, sin, suffering, and death. The imperfection with which all human beings must contend is daunting. Until people realize that everything less than God can trouble them, they have not taken the first steps outside the nursery. (We ought to note, also, the more advanced matter of how divinity itself is the most daunting reality, but we need not deal with that now.)

"Finitude," being limited, is so basic a feature of both our own human reality and the processes of the natural world that we can forget the more basic reality, the unlimited, infinite character of God. The sweeps of cosmic space and time can lull us into thinking that the universe is endless, but harder analysis suggests that the galaxies do not measure the width of God's thumb. We cannot imagine in-finity, end-less-ness, existence outside of time and change, eternity. We can only affirm that everything we meet has borders and then push those borders away, to make a God completely uncontained. There are no conditions to God, no lets or stops or hindrances. God flows or is or occurs *tota simul*: completely and all at once. Now and then our souls can thrill to this, but our minds can never grasp it. Though the infinity of God gives us the very horizon we require to think, we cannot see or estimate this horizon directly. It can never become objective for us, a clear other standing "over there" where we might get it in our sights. God is prior to, the source of, the light by which we think of God, and we only think of God, as we only exist from God, because of God's own action.

So the term of reverent contemplations of the signs of God in nature tends to be silence. We do best when we hold ourselves rapt in attention, abiding in a basal sense of wonder. This attitude need not disable us, keep us from acting. But it ought to stabilize us. Nothing in creation competes well with God. "Monotheism," best correlated with a doctrine of creation from nothingness, is a dark writ of freedom. "Idolatry" is the deep spiritual mistake of making something seem to compete well with God. It is the error, crude or subtle, of losing the infinite qualitative difference between the Source and the effect, Being and a being, Power and a given kratophany.

Lest this all become impossibly abstract, let us enter the reverent world of the evangelical Christ, to remind ourselves of how Jesus seems to have moved through the fields and valleys of Galilee and experienced the signs of God in nature. The sixth chapter of Matthew is famous, justly, for Jesus' use of natural imagery to inculcate great trust in the providence of his God:

> Therefore I tell you, do not worry about your life, what you will eat, or what you will drink, or about your body, what you will wear. Is not life more than food and the body more than clothing? Look at the birds of the air; they neither sow nor reap nor gather into barns, and yet your heavenly Father feeds them. Are you not of more value than they? And can any of you by worrying add a single hour to your span of life? And why do you worry about clothing? Consider the lilies of the field, how they grow. They neither toil nor spin. Yet I tell you, even Solomon in all his glory was not clothed like one of these. But if God so clothes the grass of the field, which is alive today and tomorrow is thrown into the oven, will he not much more clothe you – you of little faith? (Matthew 6:25–31)

The creatures of the field thrive through God's care. The processes of nature express a husbanding, a provision, of the Creator. God knows what he is doing running the world. The unselfconsciousness of the animals and plants is wise. The followers of Jesus do well to imitate this unselfconsciousness, this lack of concern. God wants their trust, their confidence. Perhaps the distinctive hallmark of the teaching of Jesus was this trust: we cannot exaggerate the goodness of God.

For Jesus, God was always reliable, loving and good. Mysterious as evil might be, difficult as its reconciliation with God, the slippery point was the evil, not the goodness of God. God was a rock, a certitude. The stability of nature, the constancy of the heavens and seasons, ought to move the believer to repose in God peacefully. Worry, anxiety, upset – none does any good, and each shows that we have much to learn about God. Certainly, each is all too human, all too reasonable. But the perspective that Jesus seems to have reached relativizes them greatly. If the goodness of God becomes the guarantor of the goodness of both creation and our own lives, then the world is a secure, beautiful place. We all have to answer for ourselves whether experience has made such an inference credible. The Jesus of Matthew is either the most naive of men or the most lucid reader of creation.

The Place of Human Beings in the World

Our species, *Homo sapiens*, is one of the animal factors in evolution. Nowadays, it seems clear that much of the future of the planet earth will depend on how our species acts. Having gained the scientific knowledge and technological power to control natural processes much more than our forebears could, we face the problem of using this knowledge and power wisely. The delicacy of the interactions among the different creatures in a given ecosphere, and the immensely complicated question of how to think of the entire earth as a living, integral system, make any prudent person pause. The gift of human intelligence is also a great burden. The ability to choose, do this or that, brings the responsibility to choose well. We cannot move through nature on mere instinct, as the fishes and big cats can. We have to keep struggling to understand the implications of how we are mining the land, using the air, trying to harvest the seas.

Eventually, we may discover that the most frightening implication of our situation is that we cannot understand creation adequately, as we must if we are not to ruin it. We may realize that we can never get ahead of our interactions with nature, see down the road far or clearly enough not to do immense harm. At that point, the need to receive salvation from God could become cosmic. We might see that what we are immersed in, how the universal act of creation unfolds, is bound to be tragic, unless the Creator chooses to rescue it, by powers always beyond us.

In biblical terms, this is the wonder of human beings at the wisdom of God. For the Bible, the great signs of divine wisdom are the processes of nature. When Job tries to bring a lawsuit against God, for injustice, the instinctive response of the defenders of God is that Job has no status. He does not understand how the world works, because he is not the Creator. Only the Creator understands how the world works, so only the Creator can judge whether a given fate is just. This means finally that Job must trust God to give him justice – let God hold God to fair dealing. The charming, encouraging aspect of the text is that God praises Job for seeking justice. God wants Job to hold divinity to fair dealing. The smarmy assurances of Job's false friends that God must be right, Job must be wrong, and God is not likely to heed Job's cry for explanation fall away. God does not want facile agreement to the injustices of history, the wastes of natural evolution. God does not want "the wisdom of God" to countenance cruelty, absurdity, any enormity that may occur. When human beings think about their place in the world that God has made, they ought to bring to bear all their pathos and hurt, as well as all their brains. They ought not to still the cries of their hearts that many things are wrong, the goodness of God is not clear.

A capital text for this entire issue occurs in Proverbs. Just as the first verses of the Gospel of John carry echoes of the first verses of Genesis, so the Johannine theme of the Word of God, the incarnate Wisdom of God, carries echoes of the conception of Wisdom in Proverbs: Wisdom was with God in the beginning, when God fashioned the world. The feminine overtones to this conception make it pregnant: divine wisdom moves like a lovely woman, with grace and delicacy; the Word of God, the Light that the Light of God generates constantly, is no more male than female. Let us first take up the key images of Proverbs on their own terms, and then reflect on their Christian and feminist implications. Here is the crucial text:

> The Lord created me at the beginning of his work, the first of his acts of long ago. Ages ago I was set up, at the first, before the beginning of the earth. When there were no depths I was brought forth; when there were no springs abounding with water. Before the mountains

had been shaped, before the hills, I was brought forth – when he had not yet made earth and fields, or the world's first bits of soil. When he established the heavens I was there, when he drew a circle on the face of the deep, when he made firm the skies above, when he established the fountains of the deep, when he assigned to the sea its limit, so that the waters might not transgress his command, when he marked out the foundations of the earth, then I was beside him, like a master worker; and I was daily his delight, rejoicing before him always, rejoicing in his inhabited world, and delighting in the human race. (Proverbs 8:22–31)

Wisdom is a lady, the daughter or lover of the Creator Lord. She appears as the first of God's creative acts. The conceit is that God begins making the world by bringing forth the first necessity, the skill and plan on which the comprehensive work will depend. Wisdom, the wherewithal to effect creation, appears when God swings into action. Before deciding to create, launch the venture of Genesis, God did not need any wisdom other than the bare divine being. God was as God was, with nothing else required or entailed or brought on the scene. Why did God choose to make things different? What moved God to fashion a world? We cannot know, but the suggestion in this text is that the prospect brought God delight. Just as the drumbeat, the tattoo, in Genesis is that God saw that the works and days of creation were good, so the leitmotif in Proverbs is that creation was delightful – sprightly, a joy, a dance.

Most of the text stresses the priority of Wisdom. It came first and before. The earth, the depths, the springs, the mountains, the hills, the proportions of the current world – all were subsequent. Why? Because all gained their design from wisdom. In wisdom God made them all. Draftsman, engineer, masterworker – Wisdom took charge, oversaw everything. As the text from Isaiah stressed, God did not make the world a chaos but an order. Wisdom provided the order, the reason, the logic. And wisdom made this provision gladly, in delight. She worked before God, pleasing him. He loved the work she was accomplishing, and she took special pleasure in making creation habitable. Human beings, standing out for their extension of creation through reason and culture, drew a singular affection. Genesis stresses that human beings carry the image of God, have been made to a closer likeness than other creatures. The theme of workmanship here can square with that stress. Wisdom finds the human species most congenial because that species has the fullest measure of what she is herself.

So the place of human beings in the natural world depends on their participation in divine wisdom. Because human beings can know their way around the world, they can appreciate God's doings better than animals or inert beings. The biblical authors assume that God gives reason to human beings directly. No scientific theory of evolution prompts the biblical authors to sketch an ascent of human consciousness from merely animal beginnings to reason proper. Consequently, there is no biologically evolutionary dimension to the participation of human beings in what Proverbs considers divine wisdom. When Wisdom looks down on human beings from her designer's circle, they are already in place as rational.[4]

Though this text from Proverbs is intriguing, and though it exerted considerable influence on patristic speculation about creation, a more important text for the matter of the place of human beings in nature is Genesis 1:26–8:

> Then God said, "Let us make humankind in our image, according to our likeness, and let them have dominion over the fish of the sea, and over the birds of the air, and over the cattle, and over all the wild animals of the earth, and over every creeping thing that creeps upon the earth." So God created humankind in his image, in the image of God he created them, male and female he created them. God blessed them, and God said to them, "Be fruitful and multiply and fill the earth and subdue it; and have dominion over the fish of the sea and over the birds of the air, and over every living thing that moves upon the earth."

The likeness of God that characterizes human beings emerges as dominion. Human beings have a capacity for rule, just as God does. Implicitly, they possess the basis for rule (reason), but in this text the rule itself, the power, is to the fore. Human beings stand out from the rest of creation, because they are commanders and the rest are commanded.

Women share in this power of dominion as much as men. The image of divinity that God has created, the reflection or miniature of the divine rule, occurs in the shared being, the mutually specific reality, that men and women create together. Whether sexual sharing and creativity of this sort constitute the core of the divine image, and so symbolize something (fertility?) central in the dominion of God, is not clear. On the one hand, the Bible is slow to depict divinity as a force-field of fertility. On the other hand, the biblical God is vital, and the fruitfulness of creation gives God delight. The God of Genesis is not inert, static, remote, and dispassionate. Rather, he seems to move, interact with his raw materials, crackle with energy.

Human beings ought to do the same. The world is a garden for them to till, an operation for them to command, a wonderful series of projects to which they can set their hands, their hearts, their minds and so test themselves, bring about new arrangements, imitate God in fashioning new wonders.

Last, we should underscore that God blesses the species made in the divine image. It is good, in the sight of God, that women and men should hold the dominion God gives them. It pleases God to establish men and women at the head of the animal world, as the overseers, the commanders, of the biological venture. Certainly, the biblical authors are more interested in food management than deep ecological engineering. Much in this sketch of human dominion reflects the key, then-still-recent, move of human capacity from hunting and gathering into agriculture and animal husbandry. But such modesty is no reason to veto the extension of God's blessing to later, more ambitious conceptions of the place of human beings in nature. Such a veto ought to depend on damning data, not a premature failure of nerve.

If nature turns out to be immensely more complicated than what human beings can manage, then human beings will have to be more modest. Since we have suggestive evidence nowadays that this is the case, Genesis 1:28 can sound naive or anachronistic. But the blessing of God on the venture of human beings in managing the natural world can extend to such revisions and maturations as the venture itself requires. God can hallow the moment when we realize that we have been bungling things, because of our irreverence or selfcenteredness. The dominion that we human beings have, based on our both possessing reason and being required to use it, challenges us to measure up to the rule that divinity itself carries out. If this rule be suave, conservative, a guidance bringing out the best in those it guides, so should the rule to which we aspire be. If the creative plan of God makes most creatures thrive, so should our cooperation with God's plan.

Eco-feminists, thinking well of mother earth and lady wisdom, have much to offer the project of creating such a rule and cooperation. The *delight* of God in wisdom and creation ought to be a giveaway. The play of those drawing the plans, whirling the compasses, ought to be telltale. Light is the touch that the best ecological reporters stress. If we heed the messages of the otters and the aspen, we shall not be ham-handed, slew-footed. We shall be patient, obliging, interactive, relational. We shall think of our being images of God as a commission to a ministerial (serving) rule. Our task is to help all of creation to flourish. Our joy ought to be to serve the welfare of all the other species with whom we share the planet. These can remain vague, pious feelings, or they can tie religious energies to practical tasks of reclamation. We can think of Lady Wisdom, as of our share in the creative dominion of God, with a purely contemplative mind, or we can use such biblical imagery to hone our ecological managements, anoint them with more finesse. What is our choice to be, and what the criterion for it?[5]

Ecology as a Religious Issue

Stimulating as the imagery of craftsmanship can be, nowadays our theologies of nature require more. The "environmental" character of creation, the constant mutual influence from niche to niche, makes a simple model of construction inadequate. For example, if we investigate the human immune system, we find that staggering complexity is involved. We also find that this system is not a island, existing apart from the body's other systems. The chemistry of the body is an operation that would put Dow or Merck or Sandoz to shame. And the chemistry of the body obviously does not operate apart from the physics of radiation or the genetics of RNA. So when we start to evaluate ecology as a religious issue, we can hear a humbling song. Living, actual creation is more than wheels and epicycles, more even than boxes within boxes. Living, actual creation is systems, families, environments on the move, ebbing and flowing, overlapping, going awry and coming back. The strongest constant is the processiveness, the stable change. The most central religious implication is an old wonder: who has been God's counselor, that thus she made the world?

The upshot of a leisurely Christian reflection on ecology is a prosaic but crucial balance. Without wonder at the unlikely character of the natural world, as those investigating it most sensitively describe it, we do not sense the mysteriousness of creation, the ancient elementary boggle laid out in the new images, sounds, and smells that cosmologists are negotiating nowadays. Yet without a discipline to contain our wonder, a reason to move into mysterious nature that can free us from terror at the possible consequences of our movement, we cannot bear the responsibilities that being human seems to impose. Let us ruminate on both sides of this equation, both pans of this balance, searching for a Christian feminist sense of the natural world, appreciation of ecological processes and human responsibilities, that may turn out to be distinctive.[6]

Grossly, the failure of the majority regarding ecology appears to be a lack of wonder. Despite several centuries of modern science, few human beings seem to think of themselves as confreres of the other animals. Go to San Diego, stroll through the magnificent zoo, and you will find most visitors leaving as provincial as they came. The animals are the others that our kind has captured and organized, for our interest, education, self-satisfaction. Yes, the artifice may be only another bit of mental plastic, another index of how superficial we human beings tend to be in civilization, but the result is still damaging. We need a very different view of natural creation, evolutionary animality, if we are to manage the earth adequately in the next century. As long as we human beings remain spectators at the zoo, think ourselves exceptions to evolutionary systems theory, we won't have a snowman's chance.

However, isn't it precisely the biblical heritage of dominion, special imagery, the peculiar delight of wisdom in the doings of humankind, that has kept Western cultures from a properly egalitarian, confraternal sense of the natural world? Isn't it the hubristic claim that our kind has been commissioned to till the garden? As soon as one opens the Bible to human literary processes, a full range of critical questions opens up. What were the authors of Genesis doing, other than padding their anthropocentric claims? Are not all positions ideological – views of the world laid out to defend particular privileges? Such questions or charges are hard but inevitable. Historically, some of the most exploitative cultures have developed on supposedly Christian soil. Both the modern technological subjugation of nature and the modern venture in colonialism owe much to a biblical sense of dominion. With God transcending the world, the world became less than God – relative, even profane. One can exploit a profane world at will. With God surely offering divine life only to disciples of Christ, other people became less holy than Christians, less sure to be saved. Exploiting a *massa damnata* can seem to be a sacred work. Whether these inferences were necessary is a nice question. More pressing at our present juncture is how we ought to think about ecology in the wake of the damage done.

I believe that we ought to emphasize religious wonder but tie it specifically to the materialization of grace. We ought to emphasize religious wonder at the occurrence of physical creation, the natural world, because until we re-establish it as a holy presence of divinity we shall have no radical measure to counter ecological exploitation.

In human affairs, an at least residual sense that the individual is sacred, an image of God, continues to maintain the barriers against complete exploitation or abuse. Most human beings still cannot murder or maim without qualms. The situation is murkier when it comes to the land, the sky, the waters. The ways we act suggest we no longer feel resonances of mother earth, father sky, sister stream or ocean. What is inanimate seems taken as merely given, available for whatever use we human beings imagine. What is animate but not human seems assumed to be lesser, subordinate, an item falling in the order of means not ends. Therefore, most human beings apparently think that they can burn trash, dump manure, blast shotguns at rabbits just as they please, autonomously. Most human beings apparently find no divinity in nature, get from rock and moss neither veto nor prayer.

We have to change this spiritual state if we are to save the earth from devastation. No longer can we treat nature as our skivvy. In India and China, as well as the United States and the United Kingdom, we have sinned our way into a cul-de-sac. The only adequate exit is a saltus of conversion. Until we repent and return to the good news that nature is a gift of God, a presence of what is most holy, we shall lack the wisdom to see nature aright and interact with it healthily. Does Christian theology, either traditional or present-day, offer effective prods toward such a conversion? Where would you send a person of good will looking for a radical reappreciation of nature?

Appreciate intermediate places like new wicca rites,[7] but go beyond them for the ontological jugular. The crux of the new naturalistic spirituality that we require is the insight that bare being creates a claim to respect. Any creature owes its being ultimately to God, and so ultimately any creature is more like all others than different. No creature, consequently, has a right to exploit others. *Pace* Genesis, human beings ought not to use animals or plants without respect. The Inuit who begged forgiveness of the seals they killed for food felt this prohibition in their bones. At the base of cultures of hunting and gathering lies a dread at the necessity for life to take life. We modern human beings have become accustomed to exploiting animal and plant life. We cannot return to the primal naiveté of hunters and gatherers. But we can move toward a second naiveté, on the far side of our present insensitivity. We can look soberly, rationally, at the state of the earth, the decimation of the animals, and discern the new spiritual state that living well with present-day ecological nature requires.

I have said that we should tie our religious wonder to materializations of grace. Here the theological note could be distinctively Christian. Let the conversion to the sacredness of bare being interact with a Christian appreciation of divinity's having taken flesh, and a sharply sacramental spirituality might result. Francis of Assisi exemplified what I have in mind spiritually when he spoke to brother sun and sister moon. Hildegaarde of Bingen nodded to it when she spoke of the original blessing in creation. Neither thought of being human as an exception to nature. For both all creatures constituted a family, a single household of the Creator.

Brother fire and sister water could intrigue us similarly. We could retrieve some of the wonder long invested in standing stones. This can sound quixotic, until one considers the alternatives. Without wonder, religious poetry, we have laid waste to nature catastrophically. Consider the northern vastnesses of the former Soviet Union. Miners have exploited them so brutally that their return to health is a very long shot. Consider Lake Baikal, one of the world's largest, now practically dead. Yevtushenko has immortalized Baba Yar. Who will immortalize Lake Baikal? Whence is the redemption of nature to come?

Suppose that divinity itself has consecrated matter. Suppose that matter, compact energy and antagonism, is not the opposite of divine spirituality but an illogical synonym. We have no reason for this supposition more compelling than the Incarnation. If the Word of God became material flesh, grace can take rock-simple forms. Zen Buddhists find such a proposition obvious. Most Christians still find it novel.

Time is running out on such Christians. The twenty-first century will not deal with their retardation kindly. They, we, must begin to *see* the grace of the inchworm, the fuzzy caterpillar. Seeing, they, we, must begin not to stomp on it reflexively. Rather, we must begin to let it be, until we know what to do with it, how to interact with it well. Indeed, we must begin to bow before it, sensing in it a funny presence of God.

God is everywhere, so a mature religious sensibility is always finding new presences. Any mark or moment of beauty can alert us, but so can any episode of pain. The coincidence between God and meaning makes human awareness religious inalienably. The central place of ecological awareness nowadays means that God is apt to shine in a cobweb, ripple in a wombat's fur. These are not thoughts of a spirit pagan or anti-Christian. They are what John of the Cross might call darts of an incarnational faith. The reason of God has come into material forms. Grace, the divine life proper, moves in endocrine systems, erodes grand canyons on the wind. The nub of ecology as a religious issue is getting beings with minds to move along with grace.

Diminishing Dominion

If people reverence nature as a prime place to wonder at the materializations of divine holiness, they tend to move along with grace. Nowadays, tutored by a growing appreciation of ecological interactions, they can see that most systems are dynamic. That means that grace is lively, does move, is nearly restless in its work to bless material creativity. It also means that we who would be religious about material creativity, properly incarnational about grace, have to be similarly restless, willing to be lured forward and grow. Certainly, we continue to need moments of stability, sabbatical times. But we can make our own, in a new key, the old biblical theme that we have on earth no lasting city. We can rework Paul's images of a creation that is in labor, groaning for redemption. The traditional accent of pilgrimage can return, perhaps applied less to jaunts to Santiago de Compostela or Jerusalem than it used to be, more to liminal times at new views of deserts, mountains, sites of natural beauty by the sea.

Liminal times are thresholds, when we stand between something old and something new. Watching the sea otters sporting off Point Lobos in California, we can gasp to realize that nature can be playful. Trolling along Loch Ness, we can understand that we seldom need to see a monster to return home recharged. The spring flowers of Estes Park in Colorado can strike our heart like a fist. The waves rolling in on Maui can regularize our heartbeats, give us a *pranayama*, a yoga for breath control. Each such experience is ecstatic, taking us out of ourselves. If we have been doing our naturalistic homework, any can take us into the materialization of grace. The otters, the lake, the flowers, the waves are all solid stuff. They beguile the eye, seduce the mind with pleasure. And they all say that here, in the midst of creation, God is lovely in limbs and works other than those of human beings. Here, in very material ways, ultimate reality is consoling its creatures, repairing its works, and launching new starts. Can we not enter in and do the same?

If we enter in gently, as the experiences tend to whisper that we should, any crude sense of dominion will lessen. The invitation tells us that we are guests. Yes, we have rights, because we too are simply creatures whose lives are short, who have never seen God. Yes, because we have bodies, matter down to the nub of our definition, we move in the chemical systems, suffer the effects of the tides and stars. But historically we human beings have thought of ourselves as more than natural, exceptions to natural laws. Because of our reason, we have developed cultural systems to rival those of nature, often to take nature to war.

Liminal times make it easy to rethink all traditional relationships. A new view of nature, the angles of a gnarled cypress in Monterey or the wave of green grass in the Kansan Flint Hills, can take us back toward the beginner's mind with which the first human beings grappled with our continents. We can find conception stopping, categorization slowing down. Abiding more simply, connecting from the belly and bowels, we can feel more solid, less heady, encouragingly rooted in the earth.

Think of the meso-American god Quetzalcoatl, the feathered serpent. It crawled on the ground, in contact with the earth constantly. It flew to the heavens, in high flights of spirit. Or think of the werejaguar, half spotted cat, lightning quick through the forest, yet carrying a human face, because it was like us in being and guile. The iconography of the world's religions is full of complex symbols of our immersion in nature, yet freedom from nature. The sphinx of Egypt is no anomaly. When Isaiah saw the creatures powering the divine chariot, his imagination overflowed. The creatures came from deep in him, and perhaps he sensed that that would have been a better place to apply the burning coal.

Dominion in any crude sense is a mark of immaturity, unsophistication, lewdness or vulgarity in their old meanings. As we come of age, religiously as well as scientifically, we see the need to become more suave. The grace of God in dealing with us has made us humbler. As Loyola says in his rules for the discernment of spirits, it is the way of the good spirit to deal with the generous gently, come like drops of water onto a sponge. It is the way of the wicked spirit to enter and leave our spirit loudly, violently, leaving us upset. Think of the patience of God, waiting not only for nature to expand billions of light years but also for us to come to ourselves, repent, and return home to her prodigal love. Think of the constancy of ultimate reality, never not providing us light. God has not been ashamed to be our God. The dominion of God has not cuffed us about. Is the lesson not obvious? Should we not blush to cuff others about?

At this point the work we have done on the analogous character of all images and concepts for God may prove helpful. If it profits our construction of a new theology of nature to think of creation as an offspring of God, a child dear to a nursing mother, we should recall that we have the freedom to think this way boldly. The biblical prophets did not hesitate to depict Israel as the child of God, minded on leading strings. We may depict nature as the child of God, led most subtly, through a quasi-infinite series of delicate interventions. To move the nuclear particles, the genetic proteins, the electrical impulses of the brain, the drift of the cosmic antimatter, God has to be with "us" always, beyond and below the promise of Exodus 3. The covenant of God with Israel can be a paradigm of the covenant God has struck with creation. We can know the creative being of God, how God makes and brings forth, by what we experience day by day. Through our telescopes, our microscopes, our runs with butterfly nets, we can take in something of the divine name. God is as God is with us. God is what nature requires, to keep going as nature does.

Now and then the dominion of God seems violent, when stars erupt or earthquakes rip the land. Now and then a tornado or a flood or a fire frightens us terribly. If we are liturgically minded, we may recall that the beginning of wisdom is fear of the Lord, the very first psalm. If we are radically honest, we may read natural disaster as a reminder that no technological achievements have insulated us against primordial power. The grass withers. The flowers fade. The oceans can howl and rage. We feel our dominion shrinking, and this feeling can be good. Self-importance is a heavy burden. Not lasting long, in the final analysis not being able to change much, can be good for our religious spirits. A narcissistic time wears calluses on its palms from clapping itself on the back. Let go, step back, strip away. Then it may become clearer that any good rule of nature depends on rule of, deep knowledge of, ourselves. Twisted by disorder, we cannot fail to wreak havoc in nature. Humble before God, we have a chance to manage nature well, become stewards the Master will reward.

Here we can revisit Lady Wisdom, who not only played before God at creation but manages his household well. She is irked with the simple, who do not appreciate the graciousness of her provisions, but she continues to deal with them as a generous hostess:

> Wisdom has built her house, she has hewn her seven pillars. She has slaughtered her animals, she has mixed her wine, and has also set her table. She has sent her servant girls, she calls from the highest places in the town, "You that are simple, turn in here!" To those without sense she says, "Come, eat of my bread and drink of the wine I have mixed. Lay aside immaturity, and live, and walk in the way of insight. (Proverbs 9:1–6)

The provisions of Wisdom are homey, but they admit of symbolic interpretation as the highest spiritual gifts. The nourishment that we need, if we are to be faithful stewards of creation, is one that takes us from simplicity, in the sense of a narrow, immature estimate of our situation, to proper sophistication, breadth, maturity. The bread and wine of Wisdom, fulfilled for Christians in the eucharistic body and blood of Christ, are solid fare: unblinking encounter with daily reality, spiced by mystical contact with the ground of that reality, the unlimited being and beauty of God. The way of insight is a reverence for the material forms of the holy grace of God that energizes us to handle such forms well. This is a path of life. We grow to the measure of ecological responsibility that God asks of us nowadays by shouldering the task of interacting with nature humbly, delicately, yet with all the intelligence that we can muster.

The advantage of taking Lady Wisdom as our model is that she can keep joy, subtlety, and grace to the fore. In contrast to older models, which could risk brutal power-plays against nature, Lady Wisdom suggests a guidance, a dominion, with a much lighter touch. She wants to nourish the simple. Her delightful play before God at creation has given her a love for the human race. If we will come to her table, accept her nourishment, she will initiate us into the circle God drew on the face of the deep. She knows the ways of creation, the inmost designs. And she reminds us that God has made the world in good pleasure, as an act of generosity, sharing, desire to make available the divine bounty.

We need so positive, wise, hopeful a view of natural creation and evolution if we are to develop an ecological spirituality with confidence. We need strong counters to the reams of depressing data about pollution, uncontrolled population growth, the awesome complexity of the ecological systems we must struggle to understand. A hard look at the operations of the AIDS virus can make us wonder whether nature doesn't harbor a diabolical strain. A sober confrontation with the many painful ways we die can stir all the old problems of theodicy.[8] So we do well to take ourselves outside ecology proper on a regular basis. We do well to meditate on the free, revealed character of a help, a wisdom from on high, that God has promised. In Christian terms, Lady Wisdom is the love of God poured forth in our hearts by the Holy Spirit. Equally, she is the gentle operation of the Risen Christ, the incarnate Word freed of all debts to sin and corruption, able to move lithely at the head of a new creation, because she is the first born from the dead and Lord of all.

The figures overlap, supporting one another mutually. The point remains simple, in the good sense of this term. When we follow the allure of material grace to its transcendent sources, we find regularly that life in the natural world seems to become more possible. The challenge becomes more attractive, more stimulating, than the burden. The passion to understand becomes stronger than the passion that is mainly suffering, pain and discouragement. It is the way, the property, of Lady Wisdom to encourage and nurture us. It is the characteristic of the disciples of Lady Wisdom, the friends who gather at her table regularly, to find the world at whose beginning she danced delightful and so to rejoice that God should have given them bodily being in its midst.

Study Questions

1　What is the significance of believing that God created the world from nothingness?
2　Does the Christian location of creation in the divine Word offer Christian feminists insuperable problems (for example, does it make the world androcentric)?
3　Why is there something rather than nothing?
4　Should women think differently about the place of human beings in the world than men?
5　In what ways is ecology not a religious issue?
6　What are the assets and liabilities in the biblical image of "dominion"?

Notes

1　For representative, mainstream scholarly commentary on biblical texts, see James L. May (ed.), *Harper's Bible Commentary* (Harper and Row, San Francisco, 1988), and Raymond E. Brown, Joseph A. Fitzmyer, and Roland E. Murphy (eds), *The New Jerome Biblical Commentary* (Prentice-Hall, Englewood Cliffs, NJ, 1990). For the Torah, the first five books of the Hebrew Bible, see Gunter W. Plaut (ed.), *The Torah: a Modern Commentary* (Union of American Hebrew Congregations, New York, 1981).
2　Two recent thorough studies of John are John Ashton's *Understanding the Fourth Gospel* (Clarendon Press, Oxford, 1991) and Thomas L. Brodie's *The Gospel According to John* (Oxford University Press, New York, 1993).

3 For succinct commentaries on individual psalms, see Roland E. Murphy's *The Psalms Are Yours* (Paulist Press, New York, 1993).

4 On wisdom in the feminist reconstruction of the Christian sense of God (theology proper), see Elizabeth A. Johnson, *She Who Is* (Crossroad, New York, 1992), pp. 124–87.

5 See Charles Birch and Jay B. McDaniel (eds), *Liberating Life* (Orbis, Maryknoll, NY, 1990). The debts of this book to the process philosophy of Alfred North Whitehead bring, positively, categories compatible with a dynamic, evolutionary natural world. Negatively, they can seem to envision a limited God and dilution of the radical mystery of creation. For a European feminist perspective, see Catharina J. M. Halkes, *New Creation* (Westminster/John Knox, Louisville, KY, 1991).

6 Sallie McFague has become a leading voice on this issue. See her *Models of God* (Fortress, Philadelphia, 1987) and *The Body of God* (Augsburg Fortress, Minneapolis, 1993). See also Rosemary Radford Ruether, *Gaia and God* (Harper San Francisco, San Francisco, 1992).

7 An interesting avenue into this topic is to begin with an influential wicca's first writings and follow her development. For Starhawk (Miriam Simos), the place to start is *The Spiral Dance* (Harper and Row, San Francisco, 1979). For Mary Daly, the point of departure is *Beyond God the Father* (Beacon, Boston, 1973) and *The Church and the Second Sex* (Harper and Row, New York, 1975). Christians have to read Starhawk's poetry with a critical metaphysical eye, since it verges on the pantheistic. Daly's historical interpretations can be ideological. Perhaps the most stimulating historian of the rise of feminist (not necessarily witchy) consciousness is Gerda Lerner. See her *The Creation of Patriarchy* (Oxford University Press, New York, 1985) and *The Creation of Feminist Consciousness* (Oxford University Press, New York, 1992). Lerner's horizon is secular, so more flattened, less mysterious, than what Christian feminists usually desire, but her awareness of cultural dynamics is wonderfully sharp.

8 See Sherwin B. Nuland, *How We Die* (Alfred A. Knopf, New York, 1994). The medical horizon is both instructive and compassionate, but the restraints laid upon hope seem pessimistic, ultimately (for the Christian) because there is no opening to the passover of Christ from death to resurrection.

Chapter 5

ECCLESIOLOGY

SOCIETY AND POLITICS

A Vision of Community

At the end of the second chapter of Acts, after the Ascension of Jesus, the coming of the Holy Spirit in power, and the confident, successful preaching by Peter of the good news of the resurrection of Jesus, we find a moving description of how the first little community of Christian disciples lived together. Scholars of Lukan literature tend to consider this description more ideal (what the author thought life in the Christian community ought to be) than what actually obtained historically, but the famous word *koinonia* (common life) mentioned in it has remained a powerful symbol of the social unity that Christian faith ought to create.[1] Let us first consider the relevant verses from Acts themselves, and then start to construct from them our Christian feminist sense of community:

> Awe came upon everyone, because many wonders and signs were being done by the apostles. All who believed were together and had all things in common; they would sell their possessions and goods and distribute the proceeds to all, as any had need. Day by day, as they spent much time together in the temple, they broke bread at home and ate their food with glad and generous hearts, praising God and having the good will of all the people. And day by day the Lord added to their number those who were being saved. (Acts 2:43–7)

The mood is religious: awe, wonder, encouragement – because of the power the apostles (the original disciples of Jesus, such as Peter) were showing. The members gathering in the earliest days felt filled with a spirit they attributed to the resurrection of Jesus, and it moved them to preach effectively that Jesus had been the Messiah. This same power soon enabled Peter and others to effect dramatic acts of healing, reminiscent of the marvelous cures that Jesus himself had worked. All in all, the time right after Pentecost, when Acts has the followers of Jesus begin to make their common response to the new, resurrected life into which their faith has brought them, is a uniquely vivid moment in Christian history. The church is coming forth, being born, and the Holy Spirit is the midwife. From the midst, the womb, of quite ordinary men and women, is emerging an ideal brother-and-sisterhood.

Often the later history of the church mocked this pristine beginning, but the images from Acts 2 never faded completely: At the outset, when the victory of Christ was newest, the followers of Christ found it easy to live together in nearly pure love. That was the message many readers of the New Testament took away. That was the golden moment of Christian community, setting the standard ever after.

Throughout even the darkest ages of later Christian history, the implication remained that, were faith again to become pristine, fully connected to the power of Christ's resurrection as it had been originally, the disciples of Christ would again find it easy to live together in nearly pure love. This implication was the hope of many a Christian reformer, many a Christian initiator of a new religious group. Though virtually all Christian (as other) ventures in both reform and innovation have soon run into stubborn resistance, impressive human limitation and sin, the idyll sketched by Luke has stimulated some great tries. Much in social theory finally boils down to one's estimate of what is possible among human beings. These verses from Acts 2 tended to keep estimates hopeful, the heavens open wide, encouraging people to think that common experience of divine power could make them into profound friends.

The bonds of the ideal community that Luke sketches for us in this text are both practical and spiritual. The members share their resources, their material goods, and they also share their spiritual lives, by praying together. At this stage of Christian history, they are still pious Jews, assembling in the temple. But the note that they broke bread at home suggests that such distinctively Christian rituals as the eucharist were developing rapidly. (In fact, the description is surely anachronistic, reading back into the first days in Jerusalem a maturation of doctrine and ritual that took a full generation. See also Luke 24.)

The breaking of the bread was itself a primary sign of the sharing that the early Christians prized. In memory of Jesus, as the images associated with both his final passover meal with his disciples and his death on the cross specified what God had made him, the earliest Christians gathered at table for communion. Their communion was with one another as well as with Jesus, their Lord and Christ. In believing that they encountered the full reality of Jesus in the bread and wine of their ritual, the early Christians of Acts drew together among themselves. Indeed, characteristically they felt that their glad ("eucharistic") celebration of the memory and sacramental presence of Jesus the Christ, their risen Lord, was the prime mover of their common life.

The eucharist, the Lord's Supper, the breaking of the bread – this ritual created the church, the Christian *koinonia*, as much as it derived from the church. Just as the relationship between the Christian scripture and the Christian community has been dialectical, each forming the other, both developing together, so has the relationship between the Christian sacraments and the Christian community, the church.

The breaking of the bread has been the most central sacrament, the most important ritual remembrance of all that Jesus was and did. That Luke underscores the central place of this memorial ritual of communion at the very beginnings of church history is enormously significant. The followers of Christ ought not only to live simply and generously, sharing their goods; they ought not only to pray regularly, alone and together, in the house of God; they ought also to celebrate together commemoratively at the center of their faith, recalling and re-enacting the prime historical moments in the career of Jesus, and understanding their eucharistic celebration to be the very food, the very lifeblood, of their common life.

The last note to stress from the text is the movement toward salvation. The idyllic early community is growing in number, because many people of good will are finding in its message and common life the salvation of God. "The salvation of God" is my elaboration of the text's "being saved." In the original Jewish context, being saved probably meant gaining righteousness before God, coming to stand as acceptable morally. The members of the early Christian community in Jerusalem probably had sought such righteousness as Jews and felt they were now finding it through faith that Jesus was the Christ.

By believing that Jesus had been, indeed still was alive as, the Messiah, the early Christians brought their sense of religious anticipation to term. The great treasure they had been seeking, the consummation for which they had so long longed, seemed to them to have arrived, become present, now stand accomplished. Certainly, they looked forward eagerly to the full return of Jesus, at the definitive (eschatological) consummation of history. But from the time of the first Pentecost, at the completion of the foundational Christian cycle of days from the resurrection to the coming of the Spirit, the followers of Jesus could also relax. The victory of salvation, the profound healing of humanity's relationship with God, had occurred. At the root, in the principle, of the redesign of creation itself (the risen Christ as the firstborn of a new, deathless order), God had restored the (fallen) world to uprightness, given back to what had been wobbling badly its pivot for sanity and health.

The tensions tacit here between "now" and "not yet" have pushed the Christian understanding of history, the flux of both cosmic and human time, into creative patterns indeed. On the one hand, the full elaboration of sacramentality implicit in the sense that salvation has essentially been won could develop from Johannine sources a profoundly incarnational humanism: the flesh of Christ saves the world. On the other hand, a Pauline impatience with history, to say nothing of the brutal sufferings that history itself could impose, has always kept Christians pressing forward to improve the world, even to escape from the world. Because there are experiential data, as well as data of faith, to support both sides of this psychological balancing act, wisdom has tended to repose in the middle. Overall, both "now" and "not yet" have received their due. In the main, the Christian community has felt called to live well in the world, responsibly, without getting so bogged down that it forgot the priority of heaven.

The eucharist proved to be a highly creative response to this tense, potentially dualistic situation. In the measure that members wished, they could open their community to all social ranks, ethnic groups, ages and sexes, by making faith alone the requirement for communion. Generally, the local communities did open their fellowship to all comers who professed faith in the Lordship of Christ. Though few churches lived so poorly or purely as the one depicted in Acts 2, no church could get away from the memory of Jesus' familiarity with "sinners" and his willingness to eat with them. Equally, no church could get away from the backbone of the early proclamation of the gospel: Christ died for all people, sinners of every stripe. The thrust of the death and resurrection of Christ could not have been more radical.

As a result, the eucharist had always to remain open to anyone professing faith in the saving power of the death and resurrection of Christ. And, as a further result, the church could not become a merely ethnic or social or even religious group. It had to keep defining itself as the community formed by a eucharistic memory of Jesus, and so it had to remain an open community, called by God to welcome any whom God inspired to believe in Jesus as their Lord.

For Christian feminists, the openness of the ideal community, the biblical paradigm, has to be heartening, just as the historical failures of Christians to keep faith with this paradigm have to be discouraging. In principle, as Paul says in Galatians 3:28, there is no male or female, Jew or Greek, slave or free. Such social distinctions are relatively trivial, compared to the equality, the commonality, created by faith in Christ. The people who celebrate the eucharist of Christ together are friends, brothers and sisters, members of a common body and life more than they are strangers, aliens, nonmembers. Women have all the basic rights to membership and services that men do, just as women have the same obligations to make the church flourish. Any rules for the administration of the community's affairs, the ordering of the community's rituals or teaching or good works, ought to be contingent arrangements, thought to be as good or bad as the practical results they bring about. Few rules ought to depend on a member's sex.

Though men led the original Christian community in Jerusalem, because that was the prevailing social pattern among Jews of their time, the crucial source of the early *koinonia* was not any human contrivance, traditional or new. The crucial source was the power of the Spirit of God, in witness to the nearly violent new creation that had swept Jesus out of the grave. Christian feminists are therefore bound to feel that restrictions put on the full equality of women in the church are a sign of impotence and decline. In the measure that the Spirit of Christ is powerful, the eucharist of Christ is glad and shining bright, women are the equals of men in gratitude and joy. In the measure that the idyll of Acts 2 remains a parable for all ages of church history, feminists are likely to think that social justice, healthy community life, is still both present in germ and capable of rich realization. That is why the Lukan vision of the community that Christian faith ought to create is always relevant.[2]

Social, Structural Sin

The bane of human existence is that so much seems to be or go wrong. Many children are born into bad circumstances, appear from the start to have little chance for a happy life. Many adults sicken before their natural time, and all human beings die. Ignorance and cruelty twist lives out of shape in home after home, country after country. Justice is on vacation as much as on the job. Certainly, there are many boons in human existence – healthy children, fair days. But only a fool, a culpable innocent, thinks that human existence is what it ought to be. Only a person of midget soul does not groan deep in the night.

"Sin" is the theological word for why we ought to groan deep in the night. Finitude (simple limitation in knowledge and power) plays a key role, but the nefarious villain is sin. Sin is wrong, evil, that we choose – to do or accept or abet. Sin is irresponsibility, or irrationality, or malice that might not have been, ought not to have come into being. It came into being because we made it or let it happen, and its coming into being resulted in disorder, injustice, pain. People did not have enough to eat because their tribal warlords hijacked the grain. Women suffered pain and disease because the manufacturers were not honest about the silicone implants. Entrepreneurs in Nigeria, Colombia, and other sick lands created cartels for the growth, manufacture, and distribution of cocaine, assuring the world more years during which millions would suffer addiction. Looking at any epoch past, any period completed, one's nostrils flare, because the cynicism is so reeking. Disrobe sin and your head will fly back from the stench.

"Sin" is an analogous (variable) concept, not a univocal one. Though the primary analogue, the key instance, is the individual human being choosing freely to do what is wrong, a great deal of sin is inertial, systematic, structural. Patterns have developed, momenta gotten under way, that virtually guarantee injustice, distortion, and suffering, regardless of the acts of any given individual. For example, some American urban ghettos are now older than three generations. Life in them has been wrong for so long that crime and hopelessness appear inevitable, normal. New children enter old arrangements, ways of doing things, bound to continue the blight. The more things change, drugs and guns carry new names, the more they stay the same.

Structural sin is the sand in the machine that no one is running. Structural or systematic or (with historical brackets) "original" sin is the slant that makes all human beings seem to walk oddly, move with less than grace. Unfortunately, it can seem to be the bias on which our whole cloth has been cut. As Paul experienced (Romans 7), with some anguish, the good that we would do we do not, but the evil that we would not do we do. The result is that we are unhappy. Pain clouds our conscience, remorse saps our will. We have all sinned and fallen short of the glory of God, the image we ought to have burnished. We have all experienced that more than external nature is flawed. Human nature too is flawed, carries its own toxins and lesions. The self in our own belly is sick.

The most influential biblical story of sin occurs in Genesis 3, where the cause of the wrongdoing is disobedience:

> Now the serpent was more crafty than any other wild animal that the Lord God had made. He said to the woman, "Did God say, 'You shall not eat from any tree in the garden?'" The woman said to the serpent, "We may eat of the fruit of the trees in the garden; but God said, 'You shall not eat of the fruit of the tree that is in the middle of the garden, nor shall you touch it, or you shall die.'" But the serpent said to the woman, "You will not die; for God knows that when you eat of it your eyes will be opened, and you will be like God, knowing good and evil." So when the woman saw that the tree was good for food, and that it was a delight to the eyes, and that the tree was to be desired to make one wise, she took of the fruit and ate; and she also gave some to her husband, who was with her, and he ate. Then the eyes of both were opened, and they knew that they were naked; and

they sewed fig leaves together and made loincloths for themselves. (Genesis 3:1–7)

The symbolism in this little story has entered the wellsprings of the Western imagination. Think, for example, of how "figleaf" functions nowadays to suggest a pathetic, feckless defense or covering. Moreover, on analysis the story proves to be quite sophisticated. The serpent (often a highly ambiguous figure in tribal mythology) is both crafty and inclined to challenge God. We do not learn why the serpent wants to incite the woman to disobey God, but we suspect that he himself has already become God's enemy and so wants an ally in rebellion.

How can the serpent assure the woman that she will not die? Why does she take his word? In fact, the woman does not die physically, though perhaps something more precious dies, her life of intimacy with God in unquestioned grace. But at the outset the woman cannot know any of this, either that she will not die physically or that she will die spiritually. She must make her move, listen to the serpent, take his word rather than God's because that is the bent of her heart. She must already be, as the crafty serpent intuits, half in rebellion, as her husband who agrees to her disobedience must be.

The benefit that the serpent holds out, the reason for disobeying God and eating the fruit of the forbidden tree, is that the woman's eyes will open and she will know good and evil. Moreover, this new knowledge will make her like God. The promise is breathtaking, though once again there is no good reason why the woman should accredit it. Who is the serpent to guarantee that eating the forbidden fruit will bring a leap forward in knowledge? Why should the woman believe that she will become like God?

In this story, as in the tawdry chronicles of everyday sin, huge parts of the action make no sense, are irrational. Had the woman questioned the serpent, and herself, rigorously, she would have been hard put to sin. Had she not given in to her rebellion or ambition or desire to please the serpent, she would have smelled the taint on the air. But she did not, because, with her husband, she was an archetypal, paradigmatic, exemplary sinner. And she still does not, because in all us sinners Eve and Adam continue to be slovens, too lazy to pay attention, think straight, tamp down their self-centered excitement.

In making the great, original sin of human beings a fall through disobedience into the knowledge of good and evil, Genesis 3 bristles with ambivalence. The author sympathizes with both the serpent and the primal couple, supporting their independence from God, not wanting any of them to chafe from submission. As well, the author suggests that any primal intimacy with God, uncomplicated amiability, would have been naive and bound soon to shatter. Human beings have to know good and evil, right and wrong, if they are to be mature. They have to be like God, capable of discernment and choice, if they are to be significant images of divinity. By such a logic, the fall was necessary, a happy fault. However painful the consequences of opposing God, siding with the serpent, entering the thickets of evil and good, the "first" woman and man had to do what they did in order to become the progenitors of real human beings. Real human beings live with moral ambiguity. It is remarkable that the author of so old a text as Genesis 3 is emphatic on this point. To be human is to struggle for one's clarities, sometimes apparently with God.

In this part of the story, the man is barely an adjunct to the woman, the president as vegetable. But eating the forbidden fruit, disobeying God, alters the relationship between them. They become aware together of their nakedness – a wonderfully succinct image. From sex to brains, they see one another in a new light, and what they see is shameful. Here the loyalty of the author returns to God, the Creator. Though the author was cheering the serpent and the primal couple forward, in the aftermath he, or she, turns grim. The first human beings seem shriveled, diminished, by their episode. Indeed, they seem foolish, clutching themselves like "September Morn." All the artifice of clothing and sexual manners lands upon them, all the distortion of culture.

We are dealing with a powerful myth, so there is no way to extract a tidy logic. We should note, though, that the result of disobeying God is chaos. True, God takes compassion on the couple and clothes them. But they have to leave the garden, and from the time of their first children, Cain and Abel, human history becomes a story of murder. Abstractly, we can say that when people lose their proper connection to God, their souls go out of order and their human affairs run downhill. The proper connection of a creature to its Creator is submission, obedience, doing what the One who made it has made it for.

Concretely, however, this is not a simple task or relationship. If the Creator made the creature to find its way strugglingly, developing its reason through experience, then the obedience of the creature cannot be unimaginative or accomplished once and for all. It cannot be the mental submission of the fundamentalist, who takes biblical texts and texts of life literally, as though human beings were inert clay or God were not a poet. Because God the poet breathed into clay a living spirit, nothing about human obedience is easy, little is obvious. The story in Genesis 3 is realistic about sin because it suggests the complexity.

In the final analysis, though, the message is terribly clear: We human beings do commit sin, both personal and social. We do stand before God as guilty. We do not know precisely how or why this happens. We cannot get the distance, the clear rationality, necessary to see exactly by what mechanisms. Sin is like an experiment in physics analyzed by Heisenberg. The standpoint of the observer enters into the equations so significantly that all the observations are smudged. There is no pure, undistorted observation. The saints (lesser sinners) do better than the rest of us, and their conclusions run to the complete praise of God. But even the saints suffer from moral failures. Even the best of our kind must plait figleaves and beg God for forgiveness.

As the rest of the "primeval history" encapsuled in Genesis 1–11 unfolds, the consequences of life outside the garden, human inter-course in knowledge of good and evil, nakedness, and shame, lead to such disasters as the Tower of Babel and the great flood of Noah. For our purposes, the point is the confluence of personal and social sin. Eve and Adam have unleashed mechanisms that shape the family lives of all their descendants. Individuals ratify the disordered relations with God, one another, and the natural world that their progenitors got going. So both milieux and personal consciences develop in distorted fashion. Both the structural aspects of good and evil, responsible living and sin, and the private, intimate aspects tend to go awry. Our final inquiry takes aim at their relationship: how does my sin relate to the sin of the world?

The sin of the world, the welter of distorted relationships swirling around me, pushes my personal actions out of true, off base. Equally, often I ratify the distorted relationships swirling around me, evaluating and choosing as though I agreed. So, I take a demeaning view of an immigrant, or chisel on my income tax, or slip away for a guilty afternoon, because, in part, "everyone does it," it's in the air, calls the tunes. Yes, we may hope, I also stand against this tendency, at least now and then. I also defend the rights of the innocent, and do business honestly, and keep faith with those I love. But I can never escape completely from the pools in which I swim, the currents in which I move. I have to struggle hard to gain significant independence. And at night, when I examine my conscience, I tend to find that I have agreed to the wayward flux as much as I have opposed it. I have tired of fighting for the right against so many drones. I have lost hope of making a difference.

These are the murky, troubling, all-too-human voices of an ordinarily sensitive conscience. The inner atmosphere is gray. I am not a saint, splendid in moral clarity. I am not utterly depraved, a soul lost in a moral Calcutta. If I am willing, I can draw from this humble mixedness considerable religious consolation. The good news flowing from Jesus the Christ is that God's predilection is for sinners. The ground for hope that good will prove stronger than evil is that God wants the life of the sinner, not her death. The way to life, the entrance upon the riches of the good news, is repentance. For John the Baptist and Jesus, the first step is to turn around. Thus the examinations of conscience that make most headway against sin are those that feature creative pauses. Letting myself get close to a raw area, letting myself touch my responsibility with tender hands, I can stop in realization that, yes, I have been missing a mark, indulging a bitterness or blindness, doing wrong. Yes, I have no excuse, the proper response is to ask forgiveness.

In the next section we shall ponder the stereotypically different psychologies of repentance and reform that some commentators pass out to men and women. Here the basic psychology seems quite common. Come to ourselves, by some ultimately unknowable mixture of grace and inner effort, we see that we have gotten off course. Were we blown there by prevailing cultural winds, or did we take the rudder in hand boldly? Usually we cannot say precisely, and it doesn't finally matter. We have gone with a bad drift, making it our own. But now we have the chance to get back on course, patch things up, make a new beginning. With the God of Jesus, always we can make a new beginning. In the measure that we feel the oppressions of sin, hurt from its work on our bones, this assurance will seem wonderful – almost too good to be true. In the measure that we enter into the redemptive work of Jesus, the sufferings of God in the world, we shall realize that the love with which God has addressed the problem of evil comes from an absolute goodness. That is a rock upon which one might build a solid life. That is a container able to hold the worst of our sins.

Christian Feminism and Power

The stereotype is that men sin through pride, women through weakness. Men get angry, throb with ambition, ride waves of testosterone, are schooled to competition and violence. Women get confused, lack a sharp sense of self, find it hard to stand against men directly or be considered tough. Let us first consider a provocative selection from John Keegan's fine work, *A History of Warfare*, and then muse about the constructive implications of women's relations with power. Here is the selection:

> Half of human nature – the female half – is in any case highly ambivalent about warmaking. Women may be both the cause of warmaking – wife-stealing is a principal source of conflict in primitive societies – and can be the instigators of violence in an extreme form: Lady Macbeth is a type who strikes a universal chord of recognition; they can also be remarkably hard-hearted mothers of warriors, some apparently preferring the pain of bereavement to the shame of accepting the homeward return of a coward. Women can, moreover, make positively messianic war leaders, evoking through the interaction of the complex chemistry of femininity with masculine responses a degree of loyalty and self-sacrifice from their male followers which a man might well fail to call forth. Warfare is, nevertheless, the one human activity from which women, with the most insignificant exceptions, have always and everywhere stood apart. Women look to men to protect them from danger, and bitterly reproach them when they fail as defenders. Women have followed the drum, nursed the wounded, tended the fields and herded the flocks when the man of the family has followed his leader, have even dug the trenches for men to defend and laboured in the workshops to send them their weapons. Women, however, do not fight. They rarely fight among

themselves and they never, in any military sense, fight men. If warfare is as old as history and as universal as mankind, we must now enter the supremely important limitation that it is an entirely masculine activity.[3]

This is a reading of history past. Presently, women in various branches of the US military, to take only one example, are moving closer and closer to combat. The end-results of this movement are not yet certain. Whether they will require a complete revision of Keegan's thesis no one can say. If they do require any significant revision, the debates about stereotypes of the sexes' relations to making war should gain a sharp critique. For our purposes, however, the establishment of women as, for instance, combat pilots has yet to become a pressing datum, demanding that we rethink an entire preconception. For our purposes, the historical location of women outside the operations of war remains the more significant focus for meditation.

Keegan does not ask why women historically have not fought and have been at best ambivalent about war. His discussion of the female half of the race comes after a discussion of other factors that limit people's capacities for making war: weather, terrain, population, wealth. Clearly, the female half of the race has not restrained the male half from making war. Indeed, recorded history can seem nothing more than a record of armies moving back and forth across darkling plains. The ambivalence of women has been impotent, if one requires that power issue in effective change. Does this mean that women have supported warriors more than opposed them? Does the impotence of the female half of the race imply that women have seen in men's constant going to war something inevitable, even something good?

These are not questions that one can answer surely, with either empirical data or unassailable logic. They serve better as probes, stimuli, moving us to investigate the psychological relations among such contrasting phenomena as fighting and getting along, direct confrontation and oblique manipulation. I think that the remarkable difference in the basic attitudes of women and men in the matter of making war is no mystery, and it surprises me that Keegan should not at least nod at the cause of it. Women bring forth life. Biologically, emotionally, culturally, and in a dozen other ways, women grow up with a vocation to conceive, bear, and nurture new life. Warfare aims, more or less directly, at killing – cutting down life, both new and old. The sexual dualism and difference is almost crude.

In many primitive tribes, women and men live apart, segregated, so that the generative power of women will not conflict with the killing (warrior) power of men. Just as women require purification after menstruation (the demonstration of their fertility), so men require purification after warfare (the demonstration of their power to kill). This primal antagonism-and-balance appears in most Native American cultures, most native African cultures, and aboriginal Australia. The frescos on the walls of caves used by prehistoric Europeans suggest (they do not prove) a similar dualism. Though the ancient Great Goddess of Europe had charge of death as well as life, her first form was that of a Magna Mater, a great mother.[4] From the beginning, the obvious mystery about women was that new life came from their midst. The nearly equally obvious observation was that women tended to hate the butchery that destroyed their children.

Now, when Christian feminists analyze social realities, guided by such interests as an ideal community (on the model of Acts 2) and the operation of structural sin, how does the good news of Christ color or reshape what history and secular psychology say about women's relationship to warmaking? More broadly, how ought constructive thinkers to reason about a feminist use of power – one that would make women the equals of men in the possession, wielding, and, no doubt, abuse of power? These are questions that become only too pertinent at this point.

Suppose that feminists, female and male alike, accepted Keegan's thesis about the historic exclusion of women from war, and accepted as well his remarkable opinion that war has become outmoded – no longer serving to humanity benefits outweighing its costs. What consequences might follow for a new conception of how to use power more humanely? What blend of force and persuasion, confrontation and cooperation, might emerge as the most cogent strategy for dealing with human evil, structural and personal sin?

I believe that negotiation, in the broad sense of dialogue, entering into another person's or party's world through patient imagination and emerging with an agreed plan for fruitful change, might develop fairly easily as a methodical way to such a strategy. I think that were partners to relevant dialogues to move beyond conceptual games to responsible outlines of collaborative works aimed practically at peace and justice they might embarrass our politicians into becoming adults. The fact is that we continue to have endemic, useless warmaking in such notorious places as South Africa, Israel, Armenia, Azerbaijan, Somalia, Sri Lanka, Bosnia-Herzegovina, etc., because no one wields a knife capable of cutting the Gordian knot.

The Gordian knot is past history, seething with resentments and injuries too numerous to count. The knife required gains its edge from several whetstones. First, it derives from a sickness at death, maiming, destruction. People will entertain new options if their pain has become intolerable. A realistic negotiation, dialogue, tells, ideally convinces, the participants that they are fools if they let their soldiers or politicians or terrorist neighbors keep ruining their lives.

Second, it taxes all parties to the negotiation, all parties to the conflict, with responsibility, and it requires all to contribute resources, both material and spiritual, to the solutions. If one side has three times the number of starving people that the other side has, while the material resources of the two sides are equivalent, then the other side must come forward with help. Until such a notion becomes credible, realistic, the two sides have yet to develop a cause, a negotiation, a vision of the actual people involved, the actual suffering, common enough to be worth a farthing.

Negotiators have to make clear to the parties involved these home truths. They have to brave the scorn of warriors and supposed patriots obsessed with vengeance long enough to penetrate their blood-soaked souls. The historical patience of women in mediating conflicts within their families, among the murderous macho men of their tribes, suggests that often women will be good at this supremely important work. Be that as it may, I believe that the development from feminist reflection of conversational models for negotiation, circles rather than opposing four-square conference tables, could be one of the most creative ways to move in the future from antagonism to common cause, Newtonian stasis to Darwinian development, ecology, interaction, mutual responsibility. Less and less does nature, or for that matter sophisticated history, let us think in terms of simple dualisms of mine and thine. More and more do the actual facts of time, both natural and human, suggest that all significant causalities have been complicated, dialectical, intriguing blends of stereotypically male and female ways of proceeding, patterns of both violence and peace contingent yet recurrent so varyingly as to make studying them both a terror and a delight.

Third, I must note some specifically Christian angles to the whetstone that I think is required, though I do not have the space at this juncture to describe them adequately. (They will return later, when we deal with the suffering of Jesus.) For instance, a Christian view of creation, sin, and human nature stresses the gratuity of the world, the radical dependence of human beings on God for their being, the mystery of sin that Genesis 3 primes us to find terribly powerful in human history, and the *hope*, indeed the bold confidence, that the central symbol of the eucharist (the memorial of the death and resurrection of Christ) engenders that human beings really can do better, need not always be stupid screw-ups.

For further instance, as several of the early Christian fathers taught, what the many require as necessities for survival are more important than what the few desire as luxuries. In other words, in negotiations about just redistributions of resources, Christians ought to differ from secularists dominated by supposedly neutral views of common human rights, let alone by *laissez-faire* economic philosophies that plump for a completely free market (in fact, a completely free market is virtually impossible to find). For Christians, the goods of the earth come ultimately (and in terms of their being quite directly) from God, and God remains their first owner. The intention of God, as Christian tradition tends to render it exegetically, is that these goods serve the well-being of all the earth's people. Logically, this intention opposes the view that private property is a right so basic as to be untouchable, cordoned off rather than set in the midst of numerous ecological relationships.

So, as the fathers argued, the right of the poor to survive is stronger than the right of the wealthy to survive well, luxuriously. The poor may have no political or military power to enforce their right (and I believe they are ill-advised to become Marxist guerrillas attempting enforcement by terror), but for Christians the moral right of the poor is obvious. Jesus blessed the poor, served the poor, and told the rich that their entry into heaven would be more difficult than the passage of a camel through the eye of a needle. Any lively remembrance of Jesus, any alert reading of the New Testament or celebration of the eucharist, brings a withering antagonism to the view that might makes right, the rich can ride over the poor roughshod, push the poor about as they please.

I believe that this means, at the end of the day, that Christians ought to avoid analyses of power, the redistribution of resources, the resolution of military conflicts, and cognate matters that take a secular horizon of human rights and legal entitlements. All that is a house of cards. Christians ought rather to insist that the justice at issue, the progress and healing, any peace compatible with the biblical *shalom*, requires a horizon of grace: the free creation of the world by God, and the consequent establishment of all human beings as stewards rather than owners.

To make this insistence audible, and then (one hopes) credible, outside their own ranks, Christians need not, probably should not, insist on biblical imagery. They can, for example, stress rather the priority of the single, integral ecosystem of our current planet earth – how nature as a whole is more basic and crucial than any particular, national or regional, systems, whether biological or economic or technological or historical. Nature ought to compel all negotiators to push themselves out of the center of concern. The global planet ought to shrink, relativize, all chauvinisms.

If tough arguments on behalf of nature, the most common weal, have created any space for calm, supra-tribal analysis, negotiators may be able to move on to a properly religious (ultimate, reverent) horizon. War seems especially stupid, sacrilegious, when people possess a wonder at the gratuity of being. That is why Buddhists are pacificists almost constitutionally, called to make *ahimsa* (non-injury) a stable cast of soul. Christians are divided, both historically and theologically. The Christian community has arguments, loyalties, in favor of warriors – self-defense, punishing criminals, waging just wars in protection of aggrieved innocents. It also has arguments, paradigms, in favor of pacifism: turning the other cheek, loving one's enemies, doing good to those who persecute us. At its best, this variety and tension has been creative, pushing Christians toward a political science both much fuller than what Buddhism has developed and arguably more realistic. At the worst moments in the history of Christian social reflection, there has been no tension, rather near absolutism or fanaticism, on one side or the other.

A constructive Christian feminist theology dedicated to promoting social justice on grounds both traditional and present-day could opt deliberately to incorporate both realism about how to resist evil-doers and idealism about compassion for the widow and orphan, help for people down and out. Presently, such ventures need not carry loads of baggage from past commitments. Presently, they can assume that much is healthy in their intellectual environments, as yet unpolluted by mentors with teeth set on edge. The fathers have eaten sour grapes, but now the daughters are sniffing better wine. I hope, I believe, that this can be more than California dreaming.

Sacraments as Acts of Christ's Body

Where are Christians able to find nourishment for their hopes that a gracious view of the world, inspiring a generous attitude toward the resolution of conflicts, could enable antagonistic, warring peoples to break out of their cycles of violence and make new starts? Exactly where they are able to find all the other images, memories, recalls to the heart of their matter: Scripture and sacrament. We have noted the function of Scripture as the constitution of the Church, what one might call its paradigmatic history. Let us now reflect on the function of the sacraments as acts of the Risen Christ to forgive, reform, and nourish his people. To the degree that Christian feminists can find through these acts the power to rethink how social relations ought to flourish, in the church as well as secular society, they can ground their constructive work in the center of the gospel.

Any group needs myths and rituals to keep alive its sense of itself, where it came from and what it exists to do. In the Christian case, the crucial collection of myths, sacred stories, is the Bible. The crucial collection of rituals is the sacraments, the official ceremonies through which people enter the church, come of age, marry, are com-missioned for service, receive formal forgiveness for their sins, are strengthened in time of mortal illness, and, above all, remember actively, performatively, for communion their constitutive story: the work of Jesus, from birth to establishment in heaven as resurrected Lord.

Historically, these seven rituals that Roman Catholicism has can-onized were only some of the ceremonies through which believers gathered for a formal re-expression, reaffirmation, of their faith.[5]

Baptism, the rite of entry, and the eucharist, the active weekly remembrance of the story of Jesus and believers' communion with the Risen Lord, always stood out as the most important sacramental rituals. The laving of the new member of the church, whether child or adult, signified a washing clean of sin, the creation of a brand new being, consecrated and made full of spiritual power by God's own life. The eating of Christ's body and blood signified the crucial nourishment on which Christian life depended: the grace of God given through Jesus the Messiah and Lord, come in the power of his Spirit.

The other sacramental actions had more or less similar status among Protestants (less) and Eastern Orthodox (a greater variety, less concern about a tidy seven) than in Roman Catholicism. Protestants have feared that focusing on material actions, honoring the saints, venerating icons, and the like would take people into idolatry. The abuses in the Western church at the time of Luther, the prods to his revolt in 1517, made this fear all too well grounded. Eastern Orthodox have insisted that the entire church is sacramental, filled with the Holy Spirit, pneumatic, so as to make both nature and human activity extensions of the Incarnation. Christ the Pantocrator, the Lord of All, presses to fill every nook and cranny. The symbolism of the Orthodox Divine Liturgy, replete with solemn chants, incense, gorgeous vestments, icons, and more makes this conviction plain. If anything, the intense sacramentality of the Orthodox tradition runs the danger of suggesting that ordinary earthly life merits little consideration. The implications for political theory, sexuality, family life, and the administration of church affairs are complicated, but history indicates that often they have been unhappy, in some ways especially so for women.

In itself, though, the key notion of Christian sacramental theology, that the acts through which the church regenerates its sense of what it is and thereby strives to sanctify its people are acts of the Risen Christ, is startling enough to catalyze interesting reflection. For Pauline literature, the distinction between the spirit of the Risen Christ and the Holy Spirit, the third person of the Trinity, who also acts in the Christian community, is far from clear. Certainly, the distinctions among the three divine persons are relational, and their threefoldness never takes away their unity. Whoever sees the Johannine Jesus, the Word incarnate, sees the Father, the source of Jesus, where Jesus gets his mission and definition. Equally, the Holy Spirit is "merely" the love between the Father and the Son, considered hypostatically, as so full as to be consubstantial with them, as infinite and powerful as they are. Paul was more interested in the power, the manifest spiritual force, that the early Christians found through their worship of the Risen Lord than in nice distinctions between what came from the Christ and what from the Holy Spirit. John, probably writing some forty years later, places more stress on believers' *abiding* with all three persons – remaining in *koinonia* with the community that Jesus' own prayer (John 14–17) reveals him to have enjoyed.

The divine life so important to John is the life of the godhead itself: Father-Son-Spirit. Certainly, John does not make the sharp distinctions that the medieval scholastics will make, after Aristotelian logic has become a standard theological tool. But in the second half of John, the "Book of Glory," where Jesus is living in heaven as much as on earth, it is clear that all three of the persons confessed at Nicaea, Chalcedon, Constantinople, and the other most important early church councils are present, somewhat distinct, and working in the soul of both Jesus and all others who enter his reality, become part of his fullest being, through faith. Faith in Jesus brings believers into the divine life that Jesus had from the beginning, that his earthly sacramental actions (the seven signs that structure the first half of John) demonstrate to be powerful for healing, nourishment, and convincing people of good will that his presence is the definitive *kairos*, the crucial moment of both judgment and opportunity when God is offering to cure sick human history and nature, when human beings can find an utterly radical redemption and new creation.

How can all this work out in ordinary sacramental practice? Consider the following account of an anointing ("last rites"), and note the maternal motifs (important to the identification of women with the church, under a broad rubric that embraced them both – the "bride" of Christ):

> Lying in my narrow hospital bed, feeling the oil of gladness and healing, I knew I had little time. More importantly, though, I felt, by your wondrous grace, that this was the first time in my effective memory that the Church, in the representative figure of one of its

priests (who, at a still deeper level, stood for Christ), was praying for me individually, by name, to deal with painful circumstances, suffering, and needs uniquely my own. . . . Something maternal really did appear. I felt taken to the bosom of a holy mother, a loving family, that cared for me. It knew about my muscle spasms and dismal prognosis. It loved me despite my manifest failings and my worst sins. And it dismissed the past history, the tubby clerics, the mutual estrangement and disappointment of mother and child as irrelevant . . . the church at prayer in my anointing said, "We ask God, who is wholly good, to strengthen your body and spirit, for we love you and care about you, as God does infinitely more. We are not clerics, bureaucrats, bloodless functionaries. We are your family, your brothers and sisters, mortal and sinful like you, sure one day to need anointing ourselves. Come close, into our embrace. Become part of the communion of saints as we intercede for you with God. Be at peace."[6]

No doubt, this is an exceptional moment, not an ordinary experience. But it reveals the awesome power of human rituals, when they match exactly with human need or desire. Through the blessed oil, the man feels on his forehead, and other parts of his body, a cool, smooth touch of God. His body is broken, his sentence is terminal cancer. But the response of both his body and his spirit draws him into peace, even joy. His community has found a way to touch him, through and through. At a stroke, his ambivalence about life in the church, which can be smarmy or tawdry, stands resolved. Because the church, the body of Christ, really has been a community of holy power, a source of healing acts, he has verified all the laud given it in the creeds, all the faith reposed in it.

The church is not this of itself. As the man intuits, the deepest agent of his anointing is Christ, the head of the church, the high priest to whom all its lower priests are assimilated. In an organic model of the church, whether the Pauline one of the body or the Johannine one of the vine and branches, a single life circulates. The members vary, each having an honorable place and role, but the life is common. And the life, the reason to be, the transforming power that the sacraments convey now and then, is that of Christ, Christians' God. (The Eastern Orthodox liturgical phrase, "Christ our God," is a wonderful mantra.) The body, the branches, have their importance, because God loves them and went out of her way to join them to herself. But the treasure, the salvation, the coruscant wonder is only Christ.

The promise of the sacraments is that they convey Christ without fail. After all the huffing and puffing about whether the sacraments operate *ex opere operato* (by their simple occurrence), the ecclesiological point stands clear. If the church cannot guarantee that its formal acts, its official liturgy, is efficacious, sure to make present holy things, then it is no eschatological, definitive community of salvation. If the sacraments are not unfailing, they are not acts of Christ. This does not mean that they are not also fully human, may not be performed badly or well. It does not mean that their actual impact does not depend on the faith, attention, purity, and other qualities that those receiving them can muster. It simply means that the sacraments must be as objective, as independently real, as the existence of the risen Christ and the existence of the community he keeps going.

A mythological time grows uneasy with such objectivity, thinking it naive. I am puzzled that many women rush into mythological thinking, into Jung and such disciples as the bestselling American Thomas Moore, like drunken lemmings. Here is the sex that bloats and bleeds, bears children in pain and wipes most of their little asses. Here is the sex that does most of the nursing. How can it disregard so piously its anchors to Christian incarnationalism, realism, clear-eyed encounters with what is, what fortunately transcends its own psyche? The narcissism in a significant amount of contemporary feminist spirituality would be amusing, did it not retard so many. It is a small comfort that what we now call the men's movement, with its analogously burgeoning spirituality, seems equally narcissistic, waxing on about "scrotal power" and other images not quite to be believed.

Christians should not deprecate psychology, but they should make sure that it does not substitute for theology. The four cardinal realities that we mentioned at the outset of chapter 4 (nature, society, the self, and God) are irreducible: we cannot collapse any one into any other legitimately. Too many Christian scriptural scholars deprecate the thrust of the gospels toward an objective representation of what Jesus did, said, was. However different the conception of history with which the evangelists worked, when we compare it with our own contemporary conceptions, it is a slander to say that they were not trying to tell the truth. They wanted to render the full reality of Jesus, as their experience of him, their living with him, their commitments to him in faith brought that reality out. They were saying, always failingly but with considerable confidence that their work was not vain, "This is who he was, what he remains."

All readers of the gospels have to decide for themselves what they can, ought to, accept. Any educated readers can accept the fact that the gospels are human literary products, arrangements of imagination, and even polemics, as well as confessions of faith inspired by God. Is the story of the transfiguration of Jesus (Mark 9, Matthew 17) transplanted from the time after his resurrection? Doesn't the presence of Moses and Elijah stand for Jesus' illumination of the Law and the Prophets, rather than for any literal presence of these dead heroes with Jesus on the mountain? Different readers, like different scholars, have the right to answer questions such as these differently, as their information and instincts prompt. But, in my opinion, no fair reader concludes from the symbolic density of the gospels either that they are completely subjective, never getting outside the writers' psyches, or that they are mere propaganda, tales told with no reference to actual history, for the sake of proselytizing.

The same holds for what I take to be a fair analysis of the thrust of the sacraments. Certainly, they create their meaning in human minds, because that is where meaning occurs for us rational animals. By operating on our senses, they raise up images in which we may see again the meanings of our faith, perhaps with new angles or depths of appreciation. But this does not mean that they do not claim to express a faith handed down from the beginning, the first Christian generation, when the primary sacrament was the historical flesh of Jesus himself. It also does not mean that they cannot be the common possession, the objective ritual matrix, of hundreds of millions of believers, receiving anointing or the eucharist or penitential forgiveness in dozens of different lands.

I would have feminists champion this objectivity, this wonderfully common, material obviousness and simplicity, and reject the implicitly gnostic, anti-incarnational thrust of archetypal psychology. Women no more profit from being locked in their psyches, made obsessive about their souls, than men do. Women may be more vulnerable than men to promises of fine feeling, experiences of tender swooning, but they ought also to be more aware of the pathology behind the vapors. The Teutonic fog emanating from Jung, Rilke, Heidegger, even Tillich, is not the clean breeze of Christ's Spirit. What Ralph Waldo Emerson stressed as an infinity of soul is not the infinity of God.

Idealistic spirituality, from the Platonists to the modern Germans to some important Buddhist schools (for example, Yogacara), does us the favor of showing how God must be the light of our light, but it is not specifically Christian. What is specifically Christian, the *sine qua non* of an orthodox confession, is that the Word of God took flesh and dwelt among us, the man Jesus became for us human beings and our salvation the abode of God, as much as any creature can be. The early Christian conviction that Mary is the *theotokos*, the bearer of God, buttressed this distinctively Christian conviction. Mary gave God the wherewithal to enter space and time, become like us human beings in all things save sin, make the flesh we know intimately the primary presence of absolute holiness, deathless sanctity.

The sacraments organize the words, the material stuff, the smells, the tastes, the touches fitting for an incarnational faith. They call us to raise our voices in song, praise, choruses of agreement. The stained glass and incense and vestments, the bread and wine and water and wax, the light and shadow and color and quiet all become more and more iconic, images for life, as we mature in our faith, become habituated to the liturgy, take on sacramentality as our natural mental horizon, think analogously, metaphorically, as a primary instinct.

Of course, each of these aspects of traditional, catholic faith has its dangers, and the reforming vigilance of the protestant assemblies is a crucial counterbalance. In the stripped bareness of Zwingli's Fraumunsterkirche in Zurich, and the parallel plainness of Bullfinch's Congregational churches in New England, one sees a helpful, chastening counterbalance. Only God is God. Even the incarnate Word cannot capture God fully (because Christ is finite, limited in space and time), and the Incarnation does not make Christ an answer man.

To say the least, it is a great irony that women have seldom been ordained as priests, asked to officiate ministerially at the altar to confect the sacraments, administer the liturgical rites that materialize grace. To say what is necessary, it is a scandal, a great revelation of sin. Without becoming anachronistic, and so asking earlier times to display later sensitivities, we still have to say that so to exclude from priestly ministry women, the sex who carry physical life, incarnate spirituality, directly within them, the sex whose hands have most often patted and poked new life into its first squalling overture, betrays a stunning ignorance of the Incarnation.

We women are no more material than men, but no less either. We women are no less rational than men, but no more either. In fact and performance, if not clear judgment, the men ruling the Christian church have through most of history denied both of these propositions. The propositions seem to me patent, so I shall not waste time defending them. The denial seems to me to reveal a terrible self-service: the clear desire of many men to remain in power, regardless of how they have to bend the facts, avoid the truth.

To close here, let me merely urge feminists to exert themselves regarding sacramentality. Until we have figured out how the sacraments are acts of Christ fully appropriate to our cause of realizing in all ways the equality of women with men in the possession of humanity, we feminists will have missed a great opportunity, overlooked a key citadel or territory we must gain. The materialization of divine grace in the Christian sacraments ought to be neither Jewish nor Greek, slavish nor free, male nor female. It ought to be (in fact, to a remarkable degree it already is) simply human: the exfoliation of the lovely planting of grace, both healing and elevating, in Jesus, the root of Jesse, the child of Mary, the cedar of Lebanon, the star of the sea, the gate of heaven, the type of the church.

The Social Location of Redemption

We are trying to build, or at least sketch, a Christian sense of human sociability. The *ekklesia* that we place at the center of this effort, the Christian community, is composed of those called by God to become together the social location of the good news, the familial and institutional site of redemption. But what is "redemption," and does it go on only in the church? How does God seem to be at work in our world for the repair of all broken communities, the making of justice and peace anywhere? These are the questions begging treatment at this juncture.

"Redemption" stems from an image of "buying back." People sold into slavery are bought back into freedom. People indentured to death, sin, injustice are released, manumitted, to divine life, grace, social relations running as they ought to run, fairly and kindly. Those are the overtones, the implications, of the basic image of redemption, as Christian theologians have developed them.

"Salvation," where the core image is of healing, making what was sick well, what was broken whole again, differs little from "redemption." "Redemption" can appear more forensic, legal, and "salvation" appear more medicinal, curative, but both designate the effects of God's gracious action to bring humanity out of its alienations, return our kind to harmony with divinity, one another, physical nature, our own selves.

Redemption occurs wherever people are in fact liberated from slavery, manumitted into freedom. It does not occur only in the Christian church, any more than grace occurs only in the Christian church. Grace and redemption, deriving directly from the action of God, occur wherever God chooses to be present, loving, liberating. That can be in palaces or slums, schools or hospitals, churches or soccer fields. That is wherever people come to themselves, seize their human potential, strike out again after the light that has never failed to shine in the darkness. The function of the church is to illumine these processes, both by explaining who God is, how God stands revealed in Christ, how God works in the world, and by exemplifying, in its own common life, the new range and intensity of social relationships that grace makes possible.

The church ought to be a sacrament, an ongoing demonstration, of the new, liberated humanity, the freed, gracious social intercourse, that the reign of God, the advent of the *kairos*, the time of opportunity, come in Jesus the Messiah, has made possible. It ought to be the eschatological community of salvation, the definitive social body showing the world human potential coming to beautiful actualization. This is the ideal being and function that the church would keep burning brightly before the secular world, drawing all who observed its beauty forward toward their own analogous fulfillments.

Suffice it to say that the failures of the church, all the ways in which it has not been in history such an eschatological community of salvation, have greatly marred its sacramental mission. When the church was gouging medieval Europeans, or torturing people through the Inquisition, or fighting modern scientists such as Galileo, it was proving to be the enemy of redemption, one of the worst foes of humanity's liberation into freedom. It was failing so egregiously that it was bespoiling the name of its master, sometimes even making Jesus odious among the best and the brightest (for example, Nietzsche).

This is perhaps the saddest story-line in Christian history: how the church often became a stumbling block to faith. Let us tuck it away, with the suggestion that by besmirching its own reputation for honesty and goodness, the church has greatly reduced its capacity for influencing troubled peoples such as those we now describe. In other words, the Christian community has greatly reduced its value to its master and God, who has always to mourn all the places in the world where hatred and violence twist his children out of joint, keeping them captive to sin and destruction.

During the first week of January 1994, I was in Jerusalem, participating in a Jewish–Christian–Muslim "trialogue." The previous year I had met with the same people in Graz, Austria. Graz is only an hour from the border with the former Yugoslavia, while Jerusalem was enjoying a moment for making peace between Arab Palestinians and Israeli Jews. Soon the massacre at Hebron would take this moment away, but at the New Year hopes were running high that a peace accord would begin the process of establishing some sort of quasi-autonomy for Palestinians, lessening greatly the conflicts endemic since 1948.

In early 1993 the terrible war in the former Yugoslavia was featuring the systematic raping of Bosnian Muslim women by Orthodox Serbs (to pollute the blood line), as part of a calculated, genocidal effort to destroy Bosnian Muslim culture completely (mosques and archives were the other principal targets). The infamous "ethnic cleansing" was in full force, and the lessons in human depravity, crying out for redress through redemption, could not have been grosser. Our group studied the evils occurring nearby, but even our relatively objective, detached scholars could not agree on even the simplest outline of the past 500 years of "Yugoslavian" history. Representatives of the Bosnian Muslim, Catholic Croat, and Orthodox Serb groups all blamed others for their violence. Each claimed that its people were only reacting, protecting their rights, seeking justice. The disagreement among the representatives was less sickening than the military operations featured in the papers, but not a great deal more consoling. All parties seemed wedded to their hatreds. The emotional level, overall, was primitive, tribal.

Things were not manifestly better in Jerusalem a year later. Jews told us that "justice" was not an appropriate word to use in our communiqué supporting the peace process. "Forgiveness" was beyond the pale. The past could not come up for review, if that meant Palestinians' expecting any financial reparations for damages done, or any significant return of property. For their part, the local Muslims with whom we met near the Dome of the Rock insisted that we get clear three things. First, they were not terrorists. Second, their "occupation" by Israeli Jews was intolerable. Third, Islam itself is perfect, the consummation of Judaism and Christianity, so any interreligious dialogue or cooperation would have to be more a matter of courtesy or cosmetics than of substance. Islam could never change, because its foundation, its basis, is the eternal Word of God given in the Koran.

The relatively small Palestinian Christian community lived in a third zone, dealing with Palestinian Muslims more intimately than with Israeli Jews, but inevitably coming into conflicts with the government similar to those visited on Muslims. For example, the Palestinian Christians living in Bethlehem were subject to the same harassment at checkpoints that infuriated their Muslim neighbors. They needed the same special passes to be in Jerusalem after dark. From petty harassment to brutal suppression, the government used a variety of ways to remind Palestinians each day that they were second-class citizens. The result, so predictable as to make the government seem moronic, was to keep resentment seething, assure that the *intifada* and the terrorism of groups like Hamas would keep burning on.

The most hopeful visit I had with a local group was accidental. A member of our group wandered into a center for nonviolence in Jerusalem, near an Arab studies center flying the flag of the PLO, and came back to bring me along. On the walls of the director's office were pictures of the Mahatma Gandhi and Martin Luther King Jr. The Muslim director described the main programs: publishing colorful reading primers for Palestinian kids, running a weaving cooperative through which Palestinian women could sell cloth goods, teaching people in the Palestinian villages how to deal with the hated army less confrontationally, more along the lines of Gandhi's *satya-graha* (relying on the force of the justice, the truth, of their cause), planting trees, and cleaning up their villages. The director was cheerful, one of the few Palestinians I heard laugh. Though he had lost some of the sight in one eye to a soldier's club, he spoke without rancor, seeming to find his work itself, the whole idealistic venture in nonviolence, sustaining spiritually. This visit was a high point for me, one of the few moments or meetings I love to remember. The reason, I now realize, is that it was one of the few times I could believe that redemption was possible. Orthodox Jews seemed hell-bent on ruining the peace process. In the Hasidic communities opinion ran solidly against the government's efforts to hand over control of Jericho to the Palestinians through the PLO.

Radical Muslim Palestinians did not scruple at terrorism. I found no justification for their position, but I did note one truly horrible symbol of what their people were suffering. In the refugee camps of Gaza, where some of the people have never known another home, there is an altogether disproportionately high incidence of blindness in children. It stems from a parasite infecting the local drinking water. A doctor friend back in America assured me, with manifest disgust, that this condition can be avoided for peanuts – the easy administration of a simple prophylactic drug. He said that there is no way that the government could not know about this, and that mounting a program to safeguard the children from blindness, or cure those infected by treating them early, would not be difficult at all. Letting this condition, this epidemic, develop in the camps of Gaza was therefore deliberate. It struck me as one of the purest evils I've ever encountered, right up there alongside the systematic rape of the Bosnian Muslim women. It will be a long while before I forget it.

There is no sense in pussyfooting about what a constructive Christian feminist response to such evils has to be. There is no avoiding the words "forgiveness" and "reconciliation." If these words, and even more the processes, both external (political, economic, cultural) and internal (changes of heart), that they denote cannot rise to the top of all parties' agendas, there will be no peace in Israel or the former Yugoslavia. Israelis and Yugoslavs will only come into peace, experience the return of their lives and countries in healing, by coming to love their enemies and doing good to those who have persecuted them. This is the golden rule, extrapolated in the light of biblical experiences of redemption.

At present virtually all the parties to the peace processes sputtering in the former Yugoslavia and Israel consider forgiveness and reconciliation hopelessly idealistic. *Realpolitik* continues to be their horizon, pragmatic considerations their coin. Certainly, many of the problems they are trying to resolve, many of the moods they are trying to change, rise from enormously basic material needs and roiling emotions. But the slowness of their progress, and the vulnerability of their work to the depredations of fanatics, who in an hour can destroy months of inching ahead, ought to make the leaders more open to radical propositions. It ought to make a venture like the center for nonviolence a central symbol, rather than a marginal little operation housed on a side street.

The Jewish leaders we met, including the Israeli President Ezer Weizman, were smart, tough people, almost wholly men. They were soldier-politicians, in the case of the foremost Israelis people formed by the wars of 1967 and 1973. They were secular rather than religious, and generally the better for that, since the "religious" parties were the most immovably conservative, showing little opening to the peace process.

The few idiosyncratic, deeply dovish Jews we encountered – for example, the theologian David Hartman and the philosopher Paul Mendes-Flohr (member of both our trialogue group and the Rainbow Coalition, a longstanding, truly ecumenical, Jerusalem group) – shed some light on where the creative energy necessary for any lasting peace might come from, but the very irony in their voices, sadness in their smiles, showed how marginal they felt. Their business was witness, not direct construction of peace. Their witness was crucial, but most of their neighbors considered them fools.

Is Christ's call to forgiveness, to reconciliation, to a new start under God, always bound to sound foolish? Will Christian redemption always appear, at least initially, as a stumbling block to the Jew and as foolishness to the Gentile (1 Corinthians 1:23) – that is, a problem for all sorts of people? It would seem so, in which case what ought Christian feminists to think, how ought they to counsel their souls?

Christian feminists ought to remember that no overhaul of patriarchal sexism is likely to eradicate the mysterious passion apparently necessary for the otherness of God, the holiness that places a great divide between the Creator and us creatures, to break through and refashion us from mortality to deathlessness. Why this is necessary never becomes clear, though as we respond to the sufferings that life imposes and do in fact through generous responses lose some of our egocentricity, we may glimpse a strange rightness, even a savage beauty.

If we human beings are deeply flawed, marred, set off kilter in our original casting (the better being we continue to know ought to be), then the scandalous necessity for suffering, crucifixion mild or deep, may carry a charge of mercy. It would be precipitous to assert this boldly, especially if we ourselves have not suffered lacerating pain and the person to whom we are asserting it has. Yet, as well, not to mention this possibility, which imposes itself again and again in the writings of the deepest Christian mystics (for example, John of the Cross), would be to default on an absorbing, ultimately profoundly hopeful, possibility.

Suppose that the passion of Christ is, displays, a form, a pattern, through which the Creator regularly, and usually undramatically, brings her rational creatures beyond where they would go on their own. Suppose that pain, and unavoidable death, amount to a growth and education, so thorough as to penetrate every bit of our marrow and blood, that carry us away from the self-centeredness of spontaneous biological units,[7] carry us toward the absolute mystery of divinity itself. If that were so, then our sufferings, our inescapable immersions in the widespread dynamics of redemption, could be part of what we might call an evolutionary soteriology – a process of salvation as constitutive of *Homo sapiens* as our being primates.

The agreement of feminists to the evidence for this possibility need be no more credulous than that of any other group. The proposition is bound to strike the secular, faithless reader as wild and unlikely, regardless of that reader's sex or sexual politics. Even believers who live at the merely doctrinal level of faith are apt, in their hearts, to make little of it. But people who have actually suffered, whether physically or emotionally or spiritually, may find it possible, even desirable, to pause for a more serious consideration.

In moments of respite, when the pain is not taking away their capacity to absorb what it may be teaching them, people who have actually suffered can note a nearly inevitable detachment. Much that they considered important they now see clearly never really was.

Life becomes much simpler, the accidental separates itself from the essential. If women have any advantage in this matter (and it is not patent that they do), it may come from their living on the margins of social power more frequently than men. On the margins, trappings and perquisites tend to be fewer. Spareness and neglect can prompt a sustained meditation on what is essential. Combine this marginal status with primary responsibility for children, which implies inevitably direct involvement with such basic matters as food, clothing, health, and education, and you suggest a cadre of human beings, half the race, who have to look at the essentials, and the difficulty of providing them well day after day, with little blinking.

In her 1985 Madeleva Lecture, the American theologian Monika Hellwig reflected along these lines as follows:

> To be deprived of the power of domination, to have little or no access to bullying power, to be unable to compel or persuade by threat of use of institutional sanctions, is necessarily to be thrown back upon other resources. And that may well be to discover that divine power, the power of grace, is of a very different kind, effective inasmuch as it empowers and liberates human freedom – freedom for self-transcendence, freedom for true community with others, freedom for God and God's purposes in creation and history.[8]

If suffering, of any sort, brings about this sort of freedom, the final import of which is unending union with God, the absolute bliss, we have to entertain the possibility that even crucifixion may be a mercy of God, and that the "fault," the so painful crack running into the soul of human nature, which the myths of Eve and Adam spotlight, may, very paradoxically and mysteriously, finally turn out to be "happy:" a *felix culpa* that merited so great and such a Redeemer and redemption that death became no more.

Women in the Church

We have seen the image of Eve, the first female, in the story of Genesis 3 about the primal disobedience that sits at the heart of human alienation. Let us now consider the image of Mary, the second Eve, who has symbolized for Christians the possibilities available through the redemption that her son accomplished. As a passing, almost accidental, illustration of how millennial traditional Christian devotion tended to regard Mary, observe the following prayer from a thirteenth-century English manual composed for anchoritic women (those secluded, walled into the side of a village church, to do penance and pursue intimate union with God): "Rejoice, mother of God, immaculate virgin; rejoice, you who have received joy from the angel; rejoice, you who have borne the eternal splendor of light; rejoice, o mother; rejoice, holy virgin mother of God. You alone are pure virgin and mother. All things created by your Son praise you, mother of light; be for us a faithful intercessor."[9]

The prayer stresses the conjoined motherhood and virginity of Mary, locating it from the Annunciation. The images are wholly positive: immaculateness, joy, light. The twofoldness of Mary reflects the humanity and divinity of Jesus, the basic mystery of the Incarnation. It is no more amazing that Mary should be both virgin and mother than it is that Jesus should be both divine and human – indeed, it is considerably less. Mary derives all her privileges from her status as the *theotokos*, the one chosen to bear eternity into time, to give the Word of God his flesh. If we accept the Incarnation, we should not boggle at Mary's virginity, at least not on the grounds that it contradicts maternity, is not possible biologically. (However, we may argue on theological grounds that *virginitas in partu*, Mary's remaining a virgin even in giving birth, as well as in not conceiving through ordinary sexual intercourse, does not fit the materialization of grace at the heart of the Incarnation as well as would her being like other women in all things save sin, which giving birth certainly ought not to imply.)

The end of the prayer suggests Mary's present heavenly status. She is the Queen of Heaven, and the faithful look to her for intercessory help. She is the premier saint, to whom traditional Catholic and Orthodox Christians have gone when they wanted a mediator before God or Christ. She has been "Our Lady," *Notre Dame*, with all the grace notes that romantic, chivalric medieval Christianity created. She has been the sad, often stunningly beautiful ikon prominent in many Byzantine churches, the sorrowful mother, the Eastern *pietà*. It is hard to exaggerate the wealth of images or the visual impact that Mary, the virgin mother of God, has focused for traditional Christianity. In all of them, powerful messages about female human nature have instructed the entire Christian community that the redemptive grace of God can rework the liabilities of Eve, just as thoroughly as it can rework the liabilities of Adam.

It would be easy enough to document the major limitations that the patriarchal character of Christian authority imposed on women's free, joyous exercise of faith down the centuries. The fact that no women could officiate at the eucharist during most historical periods epitomizes the whole. The fears of matter, the body, the flesh that Christianity nurtured from Platonic and Gnostic sources tended to work to the special disadvantage of women. Bleeding and giving birth tended to mark women as unclean, polluted, in need of purification on a regular basis. In many places and times, women were not supposed to receive eucharistic communion if they were menstruating. Taboos going back to Leviticus tended to place ritualistic, priestly activities as far away from supposedly carnal female nature as possible. A celibate clergy and corps of monks, religious professionals, usually regarded women as dangerous temptations.

In a dozen ways, therefore, women had at best an ambiguous, marginal status in the traditional Christian church. They possessed little institutional power, though regularly they constituted the majority of active church members, and the images they bore tended to be extreme. Whereas men were ordinary, normal, median humanity, women were either Eve or Mary, whores or mothers who lived like virgins. The wisest women simply laughed and did their religious business directly with God, who they knew had to see things more clearly than most of the men running the church. But a great many women suffered cartloads of frustration, sometimes feeling as brutalized by the church as by their saturnine peasant husbands.

If all this is close to a commonplace reading in Christian feminist circles nowadays, what can we say that might go beyond the commonplace, to provide a better stone for the theological building we are constructing, one dressed better, perhaps even marbled pink?

The work of redemption goes on like the growth of the Kingdom, the Reign, of God: organically, subtly, largely hidden. Two of the famous parables of Jesus about the Kingdom that we find in Matthew 13 make this clear:

> He put before them another parable: "The kingdom of heaven is like a mustard seed that someone took and sowed in his field; it is the smallest of all the seeds, but when it has grown it is the greatest of shrubs and becomes a tree, so that the birds of the air come and make nests in its branches." He told them another parable: "The kingdom of heaven is like yeast that a woman took and mixed in with three measures of flour until all of it was leavened." (Matthew 13:31–3)

This organic imagery of Jesus implies the constant presence of grace in history, and the constant priority of God. More than we know, God is at work in all people's hearts, all people's circumstances, inviting them into the light, insinuating a largely blind, mute longing for an absolute future, a being beyond the imperfections and vicissitudes that make so much of human experience, time present, painful. The reign of God is the rule, the predominance, of a better experience. The potential that early Christians such as Matthew found in the teaching and work of Jesus was nothing less than the establishment of God, the Lord of Israel, as the closer ruler of people's lives, the steady invader, encroacher, who would free them from the oppressions of Gentile (Roman) rule, free them, more profoundly, from suffering and sin themselves.

Women felt these forces and hopes as fully and frequently as men, and women mediated these forces, served as channels of the graces of the reign of God, as successfully as men. We may lay down this proposition, assume this thesis, with little argument, for two reasons. One, there is no empirical way to disprove it (as there is no empirical way to prove it), since grace, a sense of being moved into the reign of God, is not susceptible of what we might now call sociological establishment. Two, if women carry the image of God as intimately as men do, and so are the complete equals of men in the possession of humanity, then we may assume that the lives of women, the interactions of women with nature, other human beings, themselves, and the divine mystery, are as full of divine life as are the lives of men.

The marginal status of most women, in terms of the power they could gain and the roles they could play in patriarchal societies, did not prevent women from putting leaven into the rise of the Kingdom. It did not keep them from showing other people, especially children, the kindness necessary for faith in a good God (as well, sometimes, as the cruelty that makes faith in a good God hard to accredit). So the most significant function of women in the church has been identical to the most significant function of men. Women have been members of Christ, branches of his vine, half the singers in the great chorus of the 144,000 who have praised the Lamb that was slain and raised as worthy of all honor and glory and power and might. In that way the lives of Christian women have been as revelatory, as apocalyptic, as caught up in the glory of the resurrection of Christ as the first-born from the dead and Lord of all, as have the lives of their fathers, husbands, sons, male friends, and priests.

Many Christian women have gone through dark nights searching for God, just as many Christian men have. And now and then Christian women, like Christian men, have felt their souls take fire from a living flame of love, as the dark God has consumed their dross and made them burn with light. At such times, above all, they have known, immediately and indubitably, that we are all made for a consuming love, an absolute intimacy with holy ultimacy, and inasmuch as Christian women have realized that this incomparable knowledge has come to them through the community of Christ, their grievances have seemed minor. The love of Christ has redeemed the church of Christ from its patriarchal cruelty, not in such a way as to lead any wise person to alter the historical record, but in such a way as to relativize even gross evils. Where sin has abounded (flourished, raced like a raging cancer), grace has abounded the more. The abounding of grace over sin is the major stupor in Pauline theology, stopping our mouths, arresting our hearts. It is enough to make the life of any person, female or male, eucharistic: compelled above all to give thanks. It is even enough to make God seem good for having done the divine work through a church of highly imperfect male leaders – for having done it as God has, and in no other way.

Study Questions

1   What would be the best use of the idyllic view of the Christian community presented in Acts 2?
2   What are the main dynamics of social, structural sin?
3   Are there any solid feminist reasons for objecting to Christian sacramentality in principle?

4 What examples of the social structure of redemption can you find in your own experience?
5 How can feminists remain in the Christian church in good conscience?

Notes

1 See Richard J. Dillon, "Acts of the Apostles," in Raymond E. Brown, Joseph A. Fitzmyer, and Roland E. Murphy (eds), *The New Jerome Biblical Commentary* (Prentice Hall, Englewood Cliffs, NJ, 1990), p. 734.
2 See two works by Wayne A. Meeks: *The First Urban Christians* (Yale University Press, New Haven, CT, 1983), and *The Moral World of the First Christians* (Westminster, Philadelphia, 1986).
3 John Keegan, *A History of Warfare* (Alfred A. Knopf, New York, 1993), pp. 75–6.
4 See Marija Gimbutas, *The Language of the Goddess* (Harper and Row, San Francisco, 1989).
5 See Bernard Cooke, *Ministry to Word and Sacraments* (Fortress Press, Philadelphia, 1976); also Edward Schillebeeckx, *Ministry* (Crossroad, New York, 1981) and *Church: the Human Story of God* (Crossroad, New York, 1990).
6 John Carmody, *Cancer and Faith* (Twenty-Third Publications, Mystic, CT, 1994), pp. 55–6.
7 See Richard Dawkins, *The Selfish Gene* (Oxford University Press, New York, 1989).
8 Monika Hellwig, *Christian Women in a Troubled World* (Paulist Press, New York, 1985), p. 24.
9 Anne Savage and Nicholas Watson (trans.), *Anchoritic Spirituality: Ancrene Wisse and Associated Works* (Paulist Press/Classics of Western Spirituality, New York, 1991), p. 62.

Chapter 6

ANTHROPOLOGY
THE SELF SICK AND HEALTHY

Finding Oneself in God

The anthropology that I envision begins where the ecclesiology ended. The self of the Christian feminist that I want to describe belongs to Christ as branch to vine. Moreover, the center of that self is joyous, because the life of the vine flows in it, the grace of God holds it well. I believe, as I believe that all Christians must believe, that God is any person's deepest need, best fulfillment. I also believe that God is available to all people, hearing them before they speak, wanting their flourishing and hating their laceration of themselves through sin. How can we move from poetic language such as this to the hurly-burly of actual history, daily struggle on the cobblestones, where most of the personal maturation of most people goes forward and backwards and to the side with more mess than theological clarity?

Perhaps we can accomplish some of such a move, traverse one day's portion of such a journey, by looking at Catherine Fisk, a character in Frank Conroy's dazzling novel, *Body and Soul*. The hero, a boy-wonder pianist, had been devastated by Catherine when they were both adolescents. In her cruelty and selfishness, she had displayed all the arrogance of the wealthy and powerful for the poor. Now, more than a decade later, when they are both in their mid-twenties, the hero meets her unexpectedly in London, on the eve of the premier of his first important orchestral work.

The force of the encounter derives less from its unlikeliness, its chance, than from the great change that has come over Catherine. Having eloped at seventeen to Australia, become the mother of a young girl, and then been divorced, she is now living the bare life of a graduate student of history. Gone are both her wealth and her arrogance. Come is a spiritual vitality, an intellectual joy, that makes her seem a wholly new being. Here is how she describes her work:

> "I really know more about 1000–1500 – just up to the start of the Renaissance. It's a tremendously exciting period to study because so little work has been done. Practically fresh territory, you could say. Good for somebody young." She leaned forward in her enthusiasm. "I can actually make *finds*."
>
> "You mean, what, manuscripts?"
>
> "Well, that's always a remote possibility, but I mean more tracing influences across languages, across cultures, seeing things appear to sink forever and then show up unexpectedly someplace else, sometimes the last place you'd expect. Lots of hunts. I'm a huntress."
>
> "Aha," he said, recognizing a flash of the old Catherine.
>
> "I've published two papers. I'm good at it, and I love it."
>
> He nodded. "You've found your work." After a moment he said, "I know it sounds old-fashioned, but I think it's terribly important to have real work. You know? It doesn't matter what it is, just so it's something that tests you, so when you go forward you grow. A lot of people seem to go around in circles." He felt a twinge of guilt as he realized he was talking about Lady [his former wife, Catherine's cousin].
>
> "Well," she said, looking down, "without work I don't know what would have become of me." She stated it as a simple fact, somehow conveying that further thought on the matter was irrelevant.[1]

What would have become of Catherine without work is what becomes of any of us when we fail to engage with the primary challenges of life. For Freud, the primary challenges, meeting which developed the capacities crucial for mental health, were to love and to work. Until people could love – themselves, the natural world, other people, the basic condition in which they found themselves – they were at best immature, were more likely at least half sick. Similarly, until people could work well – make something, do something, explain something, serve something worthwhile, something that forced them forward in growth and gave them the wherewithal to help others – they were likely to wallow in frustration, seem to themselves and other people only halflings, women or men *manqué*. Without good work, Catherine would not be leaning forward in enthusiasm, would not be confident that she is a good huntress engaged in a worthy hunt.

Freud says little positive about what I consider a third crucial capacity, the ability to pray. In this neglect he is a typically secular analyst, and all the flatter for that. If we look at Catherine with a prayerful openness, a contemplative predisposition to find the touch of God in her life, in her change, deeper possibilities start to assemble. Catherine's sense that she has clarified her calling gives her more than psychological security. It does more than take her from the confusion concerning personal identity that we associate with adolescence. It gives her a blessed challenge, a wave against which to set her board and so channel her rush. It takes away her distraction, her lack of discipline, brings her spirit to a focus acute enough to make her wonder, blink at mystery.

How has it happened that Catherine has stumbled into medieval history and found there a great love? Why was she so fortunate as to discover a work, an absorption with a mysterious making of meaning, that could redeem her life from the pit? These are questions that move us outside a Freudian horizon, into religious contemplation. These are questions that send rockets into providence, predestination, the guidance or oversight or design of universal history by the Creator. As we let them instruct us,[2] Catherine becomes an ordinary miracle. Her experience is nothing that would commend itself to prime-time television, prurient for vulgar miracles, but for those with eyes to see, it offers a shy sacramental lesson. She has felt the lure of a spiritual life, a dedication of her talent and passion to discovering meaning. In responding, she has left the fleshpots of Egypt, started out for the desert and covenantal life. Her cloud by day and pillar of fire by night may be scholarship, the holiness of the British Museum, but inasmuch as it keeps her going, we can consider it manna.

Manna always comes from heaven, according to heaven's own inscrutable schedules. The Confucian sage Mencius discovered this, when he ruminated on the mandate of heaven (*ming*), by which traditional Chinese dynastic power came and went. All profound theologies of history discover it, and any good *Bildungsroman* like

Body and Soul is bound to suggest it. Just as the genius to make music that lodges in the soul of the precious composer is finally a humble miracle, a prodigy no one can fully explain, so is the rescue of a life like that of Catherine Fisk, her once being lost and now feeling found in a worthy work.

A worthy work, like a worthy love or a worthy regime of contemplative prayer, moves with the undertow, the deep breathing, of the divine mystery, our ontological and soteriological source. It knows what Paul means when he speaks of the sighs of the Spirit (Romans 8:26), or at least it pricks up its ears. The work or love or regular contemplative prayer has set the person into a labor of growth, a struggle to clarify and deepen her understanding, simplify and purify her volition, motivation, ambition. She may not realize that she has signed on for all this, but the process she has entered, the dynamics giving her joy, are ruthless in entailing it.

There are no shortcuts in the spiritual life. There are no lazy man's, lazy woman's, ways to wisdom. Many current bestselling gurus, such as the American Thomas Moore, disgrace themselves by ignoring this.[3] They make a lot of money but, in my experience, draw a judgment from serious seekers that they are lightweights, embarrassingly ignorant of traditional Christian wisdom, or calculating whores.

Presently, Catherine Fisk knows little of implications such as this, and she need not. It is more than enough, grace amazing enough, that she has found her work. If she perseveres, keeping faith with the light of discovery that draws her forward, letting her spirit deepen as the work presses her down into matters of evaluation, the siftings of data and argument and horizon required for good judgment, she will find in ten years or so that her work is substantially more intrinsic to her self than it was when first it hooked her. Another ten years of fidelity should put her in sight of Confucius, who came to love the Way (*Tao*) almost without thinking, to obey the Way almost without effort.

At fifty, Catherine may know why Aristotle wanted no one younger than fifty to discourse on ethics, tell us how we ought to live. Beyond fifty, most bets are off, most tracts of wilderness unmarked. Many people burn out, in ways more or less embarrassing. Some, with or without burnout and renewal, shift "work" to the back burner, realizing that they must now be about unmediated sharing with God. It is not thoughts or theories or even symbols that absorb them. It is silence and suffering, the purer the better.

Those who know do not speak, and I have revealed enough of my ignorance. Let me conclude this section by noting one more dimension of the typical line forward, through which the self tends to find itself in God. We might call this dimension moral, the matter of vices and virtues. It is not accidental that the authors or assemblers of the Christian classics that come out of the desert show themselves fascinated by the seven capital sins (pride, covetousness, lust, anger, gluttony, envy, sloth) and the four cardinal virtues (prudence, justice, fortitude, temperance). The great heroes of the desert, beginning with Antony, sought nothing less than the remaking of human nature. Unremade, it was badly crippled, mottled like blue cheese by sin. Through a combination of hard ascetical work and the unmerited grace of God, a monk or nun could heal much of human nature, fill in many of the mottles or at least compensate for them.

Certainly, reading the desert classics, we may find ourselves having to enter serious cautions about the views of human nature and the body that some of the harsher heroes pass on. At points they can seem far more Stoic than Christian, if "Christian" means being shaped through and through, in mind as well as imagination, heart, and emotion, by the Incarnation. Nonetheless, we should mark well the moral concerns of the desert teachers, who in many ways function as the founders of serious Christian spirituality, because questions of morality, basic character, remain central to all psychological development that Christian feminists can call healthy.

For example, a person such as Catherine Fisk – bright, passionate, focused – may find it hard to put up with lesser colleagues, be impatient with dullards, let alone fools and knaves. If her spiritual horizon remains limited to the virtues of academic scholarship, which take little explicit notion of personal character, she may take unduly long to develop kindness, become as gentle as her own failings, as well as the intrinsic sociability of human existence, make fitting. She may need a few midnight examinations of conscience before she feels ashamed of having laid a rough tongue on others, having baited gladly the cross-eyed bear. But Catherine seems well on the way to becoming a good woman, as well as a good scholar. She is a responsible mother, and she will not let the musician-hero make more of their affair than it merits. She insists that he see it for the exhilarating yet transient meeting it must be. They are not suited for a life-long marriage. They are not mates from deep in their souls. Whatever the similarities in the first stages of their spiritual trajectories, Catherine senses that the later stages will diverge unbridgeably. This honesty, this moral awareness, marks Catherine as considerably more mature than the musician, and it gives the reader considerable confidence that she will age well. Indeed, it gives me, and I assume other Christian feminists, confidence that she is finding herself deeply enough to locate her maturation in the mystery of God.

A Christian Feminist View of Love

Having worked on work, the first of Freud's two crucial capacities, let us now work on love, the second. To do this somewhat graphically, let us begin with Anna, a woman of notable passion. She has just left the hospital bedside of her best friend, witnessing her death by cancer. Wracked in soul, Anna contacts her lover, a married doctor from whom she has been trying to stay away. He comes to her immediately, and her wan beauty moves him deeply. Feeling the need to reaffirm life, Anna responds to his movement:

> "I love you to the breadth, depth, height. I love you whether I see you or not. If I don't see you, I still love you. Remember that." She leaned over him and kissed his forehead, his eyelids and earlobes and the hollow places of his neck. Then she got out of bed and turned on all the lights and came back to him and made love to him like a cheerleader of love, like a panther of love, in view of being alive, of breathing without pain, in the light of being cognizant and alive she took the married man along and they made love.[4]

Anna is unlucky in love. Beautiful, a gifted novelist, a wealthy daughter of an old New Orleans family, she gets plenty of attention but little sustained connection, few relationships that so match mind and heart as to head for the long haul. For the Christian feminist theologian, this is a sad situation, because Christian theology makes love the best of our experiential analogies for God. Falling in love, being in love, serving others lovingly – these tell us more about God, the ultimate source of the world, and more about Christ, the redeemer of our lives from deadly lovelessness through passion into immortal union with God, than any other experiences. Despite all their liability to abuse, vulgarization, they remain the most powerful things that happen to us. Socrates spoke of love as a madness. *Eros* for beauty opens the soul as nothing else. The self-spending love that Christians locate in God, *agape*, is the pulse, the inner music, of Jesus' life. When we engage ourselves with love, even speculatively, we connect with what Dante saw moving the stars.

Anna is neurotic, divided, self-absorbed yet generous, able at times to move like a Princess, full of almost arrogant grace, reduced at other times to torpor and weeping, because her confidence has crashed through the floor. Her southern culture has formed her to act like a lady, but one allowed outrageous behavior now and then. She is expected to be quick, aware, complicated, changeable, manipulative, emotional, mysterious. It is an interesting, dramatic view of the self, allowing an intelligent woman of means considerable scope for exploring the world, but it also has its considerable limits, since few women gain access to independent economic or political power, run the businesses or control the Louisiana parishes.

Anna is a woman making do, coping well, in a particularly rich, sensuous form of patriarchal culture. She tosses down the liquor, laughs raucously over the crayfish, and keeps watch with an artist's eye. What she does not do is find more bliss in love than heartache. What does not come clear for her, despite her convent school training, is the divinity of love, the spark of holiness in even quite imperfect sex or artistic *eros*.

What is this divinity of love? I think it is the inclination of love toward creativity, making new being and life with body and mind, imagination and reason. I think it is the power of love to take the self out of itself, into broader horizons, larger states of soul, unwonted generosity. In love, we feel blessed, visited by a grace we did not make and do not deserve. For a little while, everything is right with the world, we know without doubt why we have been born. It seems that love pulses in every atom of the world, glances off every ripple on the water. We smile at our romanticism, perhaps even begin to dread our crash back into ordinary pain, which we still consider realism. But we cannot deny, if we have even minimal mental health, that these days of love have given our time new meaning. And we know, because the message greets us in the morning and closes our eyes at night, that we ought to remember these unique moments, making them key points around which we organize all the time that went before and all the time that will come after.

Mature love, we may think, becomes steady, even stodgy. Taking care of children, earning bread and tuition and fuel for the car, narrows our horizons and wears us out. We are almost too tired for long bouts of sexual passion. We begin to see that helping one another, putting the good of one another and the children or the good of the needy friend before our own is the practical demonstration of love that God asks of us.

If we are wise, and faithful to prayer, we shall let this vision ripen, wry and humbling as it may be. If we are wise, we shall not despise the more dramatic loves of our youth, but neither shall we canonize them as high points, for ever after beyond our reach. We shall rather start to let the Spirit of God make us content with trying to meet the obligations of the day directly, generously, be they attractive or dull. We shall enter upon a useful if unpretentious patch of Johannine abnegation, following the watchword of the Baptist that we must decrease, Christ must increase.

These are rather standard theses, sprung from rather standard experiences of ordinary Christian maturation. Christian women share most of both the experiences and the convictions in which they issue, though it is useful to hear women express their own versions, which can exhibit interesting variations. For example, romance seems to continue to mean more to women than it does to their spouses and male friends. Flowers, dress-up dinners, little signs of appreciation, little chances to feel attractive again, desired again, punctuate the dreams of maturing women, and sensitive men capitalize on them. Much of this occurs with considerable awareness, and so with significant humor. I see Anna making love as a cheerleader with a wide grin, sending up the prowling panther.

I also see her needing the embrace of her lover to erase death from her mind. At least for a few hours, she has to forget the corpse of her best friend, and what it says about her own future. Tangled as her adulterous affair has been, she carries a commitment to her lover that is in effect unconditional. Wisely or foolishly, she will never let him go, whether she sees him or not, can be with him or not. This is a depth of love, or an intensity of love, that translates nearly directly into what we find in the Christian mystics. God becomes virtually taken for granted, as the mystics write God a blank check. Beyond reason, prudence, criticism, they keep God always in the right. Though God slay them, yet will they trust him. Though God hide herself cruelly, yet will they keep roaming the hills, searching the valleys.

There are many good kinds of love: that between parent and child, teacher and student, friend and friend. Naomi and Ruth, David and Jonathan, Jesus and the Beloved Disciple, Jesus and Mary Magdalene – the Bible is especially rich in friendships. But the most passionate love, canonized in the Song of Songs, is a romantic heterosexual love that drew the great mystics like moths to the flame, bears to honey. Bernard of Clairvaux and John of the Cross are but two examples. Teresa of Avila and Teresa of Lisieux both drew on the nuptials depicted in the Song. If the Jewish rabbis tended to equate the female with Israel and the male with the Lord, the Christian mystics tended to equate the female with the individual soul and the male with Christ. They did not deny that the female might be the church, the comprehensive bride of Christ, but they were more inclined to dwell on the intimacy between the individual soul and the lover who had made it for himself.

The Song itself describes the lovers with a notable parallelism of imagery. Most of what one does the other does as well. The female takes considerable initiative, though she does more pining, because the male is absent more frequently. The seasons and moods of the spiritual life emerge as volatile and trying. The lesson is that the self must find itself through an ardent love of a mystery nearly bound to wound it regularly. Painful as its searches can be, they offer a nonpareil life. There is no life to compare with a life in love with God. Of that all the mystics are convinced, even those who kvetch at God constantly, complaining.

The first five verses of Chapter 3 of the Song are among the most famous, and they can give us the lines on which to end. For many of the Christian saints, of the greatest lovers of God, they have suggested the pinnacle of the spiritual fulfillment possible in this earthly life, while we still suffer the limits of time and the body. Note that the final stage in the progression of the search for love, and the finding of love, is simply a fierce clinging to the beloved, a passionate unwillingness to let the beloved go:

> Upon my bed at night I sought him whom my soul loves; I sought him, but found him not; I called him, but he gave no answer. I will rise up now and go about the city, in the streets and in the squares; I will seek him whom my soul loves. I sought him, but found him not. The sentinels found me, as they went about in the city. "Have you seen him whom my soul loves?" Scarcely had I passed them, when I found him whom my soul loves. I held him, and would not let him go until I brought him into my mother's house, and into the chamber of her that conceived me. I adjure you, O daughters of Jerusalem, by the gazelles or the wild does; do not stir up or awaken love until it is ready. (Song of Songs 3:1–5)

The Self as a Social Relation

Both love and work make plain the relatedness of the self, how it is social as well as individual, connected to the rest of creation, as well as its own keep or cell of isolation, unique and solitary. Even the monk or nun in the desert lives among other creatures, lizards and birds and rocks. The fully Christian monk or nun in the desert prays with vivid awareness of the communion of saints, the entire body of Christ. The official liturgy of the church requires such prayer, and the Bible common to all church prayer provides a link with all other believers. Many Christian theologians have realized that when we find ourselves in God, we discover that we are part of a family. God does not hold us or save us alone. Unique as our particular story may be, tailor-made as our vocation, we are wise to submit it to the common fund of Christian experience, to discern the spirits working in it according to the interpretational rules passed down through the centuries.

The relations that make the self social are four, precisely its connections to the cardinal dimensions of reality that have given us the four inner chapters of our Christian feminist constructive theology. The human self is immersed in nature, through its body and inalienable animality. We need food and shelter. We are vulnerable to disease and sure to die. We live on the earth, under heaven, depending every day on the sky or the stream for water. We measure time by the sun and the stars. We deal with the world, learn about reality, think of ourselves and our habitat dependent on our bodily senses. The first relation is with nature, our fundament. We need all the health we can find in this relation. We need the best possible connection to nature, physical and mental, that we can develop. That is why the environmental movement, the elaboration of ecological consciousness, is bound to bring fresh colors and emphases to our religious lives. That is why citizens of the twenty-first century are bound to think about God and themselves differently than their ancestors did a millennium ago, when there were no airplanes, no arctic ice-breakers, no combines harvesting broad sweeps of corn.

The second relation of the self is to other people, creating politics, culture, war, churches, family life, business. Most of us do not live in the desert or the forest. Most of us interact with other human beings each day, for both delight and discouragement. Our human kind remain the kind that most interest most of us. Whether with learning or mere common sense, we study human nature, shake our heads and laugh or weep. Among the wonders that the Bible mentions are the way of a man with a maid. More than two thousand years after that proverbial wondering, few members of either sex can claim confidence that they understand the other. Yet from our intimate dealings with the other sex, the very coordination of our bodies, we keep the race going. From our commonplace sharing of meals, we nourish our spirits as much as we fill our bellies. Both our materiality and our mentality conspire to make us social, and both gain their forms, their senses of where they ought to be going, how they ought to be developing, from the stories that we hear from other people, the liturgies, religious or secular, that we act out day after day.

The third relation of the self is to itself, with itself. This seems peculiar to our human species, though certainly we find intriguing analogues in the problem-solving of the higher apes, the play of the quick dolphins, perhaps even the ability of lower individuals to know themselves as distinct from all others through their pheromones.

Apparently uniquely, human selves can be both the subjects of actions and thoughts, and the objects. We can stand back, hold yesterday at arm's length, and pass judgment upon it. We can stop time in memory or send it racing ahead in imagination. The most interesting thing about us, most of our kind opine, is our minds, our spirits shaped by life and will. From our minds come our images of the world, including the world's Creator. From our minds, working in collaborations both formal and informal, we make ways of life, cultural paths through chaos into meaning. The languages that we fashion send meaning forth on puffs of air, fleeting sounds. The arts that we develop add depth of feeling, emotion. And all this comes from the self, even though Buddhist analysis says there is no such thing. There is only a temporary clump of "heaps," a fasicule sure soon to come unglued. So even the nature of the self, the being of our personal being, comes up for examination, study, argument. The self is a relation to itself, an inner conversation, a constant telling of stories, that makes it social even in solitude.

Fourth, those who have read Søren Kierkegaard, the marvelous nineteenth-century Danish existential theologian, know that he understands the core of human selfhood to be an absolute tie to God. His self is a relation relating itself absolutely to the Absolute. In my explication, this description is ontological. We are never independent of God. For us to exist, to be, God must give us our reality, share with us the *is* that only God possesses self-sufficiently. We must participate in the being of God if we are to stand out from nothingness. Creation is God's grant of existence to us, ultimately because of God's own goodness and love. We come into being, are made, because the being of God diffuses itself, mysteriously making finite beings, others who are divine to a tiny degree (and so thereby are also not divine).

Inasmuch as we respond to our condition of creaturehood, as it drives us forward like the inner spring of our selfhood, we relate ourselves to God actively. Not only does God grant us existence, like a stream flowing out of a font that nothing can contain, we drive ourselves toward God, struggle onward and upward with great desire. We have an *eros* for God, a great longing love. We may realize this clearly, or it may work in us largely unnamed, unrecognized. But every person ardent for beauty or justice or love is burning for God. All such people are also reflecting their origin in God, the fact that only their participation in the being of God makes them real. So God is not extrinsic to us, though certainly God transcends all our limitations. God is more our selves than we are, more the source of our identity than our parents or our genes or even our biographical stories.

Perhaps Jesus realized this to a unique degree, and his realization begot his intense relationship to God as his Father. Perhaps his favorite name for God, "Abba," bespeaks his sense that God had generated him, was always generating him, like a procreating parent. God was giving him his being, his life, his meaning and mission. Without his tie to God, the repose of his being in God, he would be nothing. The more fully he lived in and from this repose, the fuller and healthier his life seemed to be. When he looked at the lame, the halt, the blind, he sensed lesions in their connection, physical hurts and failings that seemed to call into question the goodness of the grant of existence from God that made them be.

Similarly, when Jesus considered the pathologies of sinners, the stubborn obtuseness of those who would not see the signs that the Father was working through him, did not want to repent and believe in the good news of the Kingdom, he was moved to pity. Their standing apart in sin, insisting on proud skepticism, was a refusal to relate themselves to God positively, lovingly. It was a rejection of the absolute, the ultimate, connection by which God constitutes all of us as ourselves. No sinners could actually accomplish such a rejection, because to accomplish it, sever the ties to God that made them both be and be themselves, they would have to send themselves into nonbeing, pop off the video screen like zapped fighter planes. But all sinners seem to try to do this, running from God as though God threatened their freedom. The truth is that closeness to God increases our freedom, while distance from God binds us to ourselves. The truth is that God is the best champion of our freedom, as the traditional liturgical prayer knew well: "O God, to serve whom is to reign, grant that . . . "

Overall, then, we do well to think and speak of the self as relational – not an island, rather a member of an ecological niche, a singer in a huge, grand chorus. As constructive Christian feminist theologians, we do even better to think that connection, relationship, is at the heart of both being human and being followers of Christ.

It is at the heart of being human, because the more human we are, the better we balance and coordinate individual difference (the *terminus a quo* of relationship, the point from which connection sets out) and common cause (the *terminus ad quem*, the goal of shared wellbeing). Individual difference, which the inclination of men toward independence and autonomy spotlights, is necessary if we are to have a strong, distinctive voice, be bold enough, confident enough, to go our own way, when our mission requires it. Common cause, working with others for the good of all – which the inclination of women toward cooperation, sharing, having a self more fluid than that of men, more permeable by children and friends at the borders, underscores – shows our solidarity with other creatures, the ecological character of our reality. Thereby, it shows that autonomy has severe natural limits (is more often a fiction than a fact). If the carbon, iron, and oxygen in our flesh and bones go back to explosions of stars, we cannot be alien to others in the universe, solitaries who become whole only in silent caves.

An incarnational faith such as Christianity tends to avoid severe dichotomies, forced options for either/or. Neither autonomy nor relationality, alone, is the whole story. Neither the stereotypical ways of women nor the stereotypical ways of men can claim validly to represent what "human" behavior denotes. All the qualities characterizing our kind deserve acknowledgment. Our debts to the earth and our aspirations toward heaven ought more to balance one another, keep one another from excess, than to fight to the death.

The wholeness of being human, the complete richness to which God invites the self, the "I" we know from both the mirror and the cries of our heart, is always a cloddish spark, a smoking flax, a feathered serpent. The Word of God, taking flesh, is the full type, asymptote, ideal according to which we are made. The relation of the eternal Son to the eternal Father, identity differentiated only through diction (the Father's being the Speaker, the Son's being the Spoken), only through generation (the Father's being the Begetter, the Son's being the Begotten), tells us that perfection is neither autonomy nor heteronomy, neither being complete-unto-oneself nor being the serf of an overlord. Perfection is the community of God that resonates most lyrically in human beings when we so love one another that our "our" encloses our "mine" and "thine."

The Sins that Shackle the Self

All its sins shackle the self. Every devolution from its high calling to love God with whole mind, heart, soul, and strength, and to love its neighbor as itself, diminishes the self, makes it blush whenever it comes to itself and sees what it ought to be. But in recent analyses of the peculiar, characteristic (or at least stereotypic) failings of men and women, two sins stand out.[5] For women the failing, the sin, the vice that gets most attention is weakness, cowardice, diffusion – having no self. For men the vice that gets most attention is the old, standard, most capital sin: pride. Discussing the supposed difference of the sexes with regard to their central failings may help our constructive work, inasmuch as any fully adequate theological vision has to provide for the full range of human failings, and has also to overcome, move beyond, the flabby versions of sexual stereotypes, to the deep stinking core that Christian tradition finds in all sin, all revolt against God, who is solely, always, wholly good.

Let us begin with pride, the standard worst sin, the "I will not serve" that we can find hinted in the account of the Fall in Genesis and that Dante depicts so graphically in *The Inferno* as the icy cold of the archfiend Lucifer. He who had been the brightest star in heaven, the luminary of the angelic host, now is a frozen lump of resistance living at the nadir of hell, at the farthest extremity, the exact antipode, of God's heaven. His is the sin not of bodily passion but of diamond hard will, spiritual resistance. Not to be God infuriates him. He cannot abide being a creature, a dependant, a nothing of himself. Why this is so is not clear, because his cold fury is the quintessence of irrationality. But there he is, nonpareil myth and symbol of the core sin, most egregious misser of the mark, leading example of the spiritual revolt that has made a shambles of human history, of human time an abattoir.

Augustine, who ranks behind no Christian theologian in rhetorical ability to turn a memorable phrase, has spoken of sin as love of self unto contempt of God – a description spotlighting pride. In contrast, proper religion, rooted in humility, begets love of God unto contempt of self. The "contempt" in question here is difficult for present-day Westerners to grasp. It is no unhealthy self-loathing. It is simply the stark realization that we creatures are thoroughly impure, compared to the blazing holiness of God. If we love ourselves inordinately, unduly, so as to assume or live as though we, rather than God, were the primary reality in our lives, the center on which to focus, we reject, as it were condemn, the objective order of creation, how things actually are in the universe. We have eyes for seeing but excessive self-love, narcissism, shuts them. We ought to hear the voices of all our fellow creatures, who chant day and night, "We are not God." Augustine heard them, because he had sought God for many years, and their chorus became for him a stabilizing mantra.

Pride is the overweening, overdriving, overly self-concerned, self-important self-regard that testosterone seems often to fuel. Pride is a will to power, a *libido dominandi*, a Nietzschean dreaming to become a superman, a blazing intensity of will that might blow away all obstacles to creativity or rule. Pride provides great energy for great projects. Without pride, there would have been no sweep of the Mongolian hordes across the steppes, no British Empire, no "westward ho" opening the American plains. People need to think well enough of themselves to be confident that they can bring their ambitions, their dreams, to fruition. They have to want to do good work, build deep foundations and lovely outgardens, if they are to persevere at improving the world. Virtually everything in both human culture and the human psyche is complicated, not handled well by a simplistic assignment of status as "good" or "bad." We have to judge case by case, and our main criterion has to be the fruits, the actual results in the given case, what is really happening. The pride that makes for craftsmanship, dignity, generosity is usually a blessing. The pride that makes for arrogance, willingness to crush other people, desire to exalt oneself and reap adulation is usually a curse, ruining the character of the individual inclined to it and spreading misery in the lives of those he bullies.

In the memorable imagery coined by the psychoanalytic writer Dorothy Dinnerstein,[6] the stereotypical male, source of so much suffering in history, is a minotaur, only half human, just as significantly bestial, a bull fixated on strength and lust. Parallel to the male minotaur, and in the final analysis just as destructive, is the female abortion, the mermaid. She is as watery, as labile, as the minotaur is earthy, stolid. She is as insubstantial as a siren's song, as unreliable. Half woman, half fish, she lives in the murkiness of the psychic deep, seldom enjoying clean clarity, usually swimming in circles, confused and unproductive.

Dinnerstein's images exaggerate both the roles that the sexes have exercised historically (at least in patriarchal times) and the contours of their representative personalities. But the images also strike home enough to rattle our confidence. We recognize them all too well. We know whenever we are honest that we have all colluded to polarize human nature sexually. Time after time we women and men have abetted one another to produce mythic malformations, gross distortions of both male force and female grace. Naturally, there are exceptions: effeminate, slippery men, and harsh, lumpish women. On the whole, though, our ideal images of ourselves as women or men run all too close to the mermaid and the minotaur. On the whole, a great many women would like to be subtle sirens, not mind greatly being mysterious, even slippery. On the whole, a great many men would like to be powerful enough to generate fear, paw the ground and make the earth shake.

In my view, the strength of Dinnerstein's theory of human sexual malaise and malformation lies in two convictions that she develops. The first is that men and women share responsibility for what our species has become. The second is that we have tended to perpetuate our aberrations, generation after generation, by relegating to women the majority of our care of children. Let us reflect on these two convictions with a Christian feminist theological sensibility.

First, it always gladdens my heart to find people taking responsibility, owning up to their own roles, their own contributions good or bad, in an enterprise. The now nearly standard feminist analytical assumption that patriarchal cultures have assigned history to men has many facts on its side, but it distorts reality badly to state it so baldly. Certainly, men have been the ones who have claimed the mandate to shape history, make things go, determine where the tribe would travel, what it would hunt, how it would divide the spoils. Men have been the more apparent actors, initiators, prime sources of the erotic energy required for chasing the large game, stripping the great forests, crossing the vast seas. Women have received the fertilizations of men, been more passive regarding culture, taken more instruction than they have given out.

However, under the surface of these apparent roles and relationships, actual influences may often have been more subtle, mutual, even egalitarian. Simply because men had to have cooperative women if the race were to survive and prosper, women exercised a strong attraction and held some high cards. Men had to please women, in the final analysis. They could push women around, beat women into submission, but until they persuaded women to be good wives and mothers the men's lives would never be peaceful. Women treated badly would burn the men's eggs, or would only *endure* being used sexually, suffering it with bad grace. Like rain falling on a tin roof was the nagging of a bitter woman, one who had little to lose.

By experiment, women learned that bursts of temper, calculated weeping, flattery and manipulation could be as effective as straightforward male force. They realized quickly that physical beauty could draw a man into thrall, sexual allure make him go weak at the knees, soft in the head. Good women hated learning all this, becoming adept at spiritual corruption. But so often was the fight at the level of bare survival, not fair, and for their children as much as themselves, that even good women could judge purity of conscience a luxury. The first charge was to secure food and shelter, survival today and hope for tomorrow. The second charge was to win enough victories, preserve enough confidence and dignity, to keep soldiering along, even walk with a skip or sashay now and then.

Second, because throughout recorded human history men have carried relatively little of the responsibility for raising small children, women have molded each generation to a pattern designed to continue to polarize the sexes as mermaids and minotaurs. Men have tended to think of themselves as the mavens of higher culture, the doctors and dukes commanding larger youth, but women have dominated the primary education, the crucial first years.

In psychoanalytical perspective, women have shown infants the countenance of the Madonna and the breast of bliss that have stood for paradise, primal innocence and happiness, the myth of an early, utter intimacy with the divine. Girls have responded to this countenance directly, intuiting that providing it was their own destiny. Girls might find their mothers all too like themselves, or all too domineering in matters feminine, but girls always knew that their bodily cycles would shape them just as their mothers' bodily cycles had shaped the prior generation of females. They always knew instinctively that the ways, moods, and tendencies characterizing the mother-dominated family atmosphere in which they spent their childhood were their legacy more than the legacy of their brothers.

Girls had to identify with their mothers as the sex that carried children and usually cared for the hearth, prepared the food, made most of the clothing, did most of the nursing, received more orders than it gave out, was smaller and weaker physically, softer and more liable to abuse, second fiddle more than first violin when it came to overt power, leadership, authority. Men proposed the courses of action and assumed that women would obey, run them, follow along. Women grouped together to care for the children, create circles of emotional support. The lives of women were ragged around the edges, the psyches of women were fluid, compared to the sharp edges, the right lines of rigor, that warrior-hunters venerated, the autonomy that military champions needed and arrogated.

Boys, sensing all this, had to distance themselves from their mothers. They had to break out of their primal enchantment by the Madonna, their blissful communion at the breast. They were not going to be mothers, nurses, keepers of the hearth flame. They were going to be hunters, warriors, chiefs. They had to be hard, for their lives focused outside themselves, where rocks and animals and harsh weather gave them no quarter. They did not have to be soft for children, round and patient and warm. They could love children and play with them well. They could long to teach their children everything that they themselves found valuable. But their first obligation, as human biology happened to evolve it, was to secure food and defend the tribe against its enemies. The first requirement in their psychic maturation was that they leave the undifferentiated track where infant boys differ little from infant girls in needing and loving their mother's lap, so as to find the patterns, the ways of carrying themselves, working, and thinking, that would make them what their fathers were, would allow them to be for their generation what their fathers had been for the fathers' prior one.

In a word, boys had to distance themselves from their mothers, and so from their sisters, even before they left the primary education dominated by female instincts and skills. Their revolt against the feminine milieu in which they came to responsible consciousness, conscience, tended to be clearer and cleaner than that required of girls, because more obviously necessary. If their revolt, their pursuit of their proper masculine difference from women, went well, they did not despise the feminine milieu they had to leave, but often it did not go well. Often the boys were ambivalent, or the mothers wanted to hold on to authority, or the fathers did too much or too little.

In those cases, irritations could start a rash that continued throughout the rest of the child's life. Sexual malaise, thinking ill of the female and having her think ill of the male in return, could become a stable cast of mind, only one step from misogyny or misanthropy. The sexes could shake their heads as a reflex, writing one another off. Men would always be difficult boys, revolting and pissing in the corners. Women would always be flighty girls, ever-changing bundles of emotion, constantly trying to wrap you around their favor, their sex, their applause. The atmosphere around women would always be dense, perfumed, dramatic. The atmosphere around men would usually be spare, harsh, laconic.

These differences held some attractions, but for the long haul each sex was bound to prefer its own bodily, emotional, mental, and social styles. Each was bound to suffer mixed feelings about the other, and the rule of women over children was bound to mark the sufferings of women into the psyches of all fresh human beings more sharply than the sufferings of men. Children were bound to grow up the allies of women more than the allies of men, and though some of this first alliance was sure to shift, when one combined it with the parallels between mother human and mother earth, the first divinities, the earliest personifications of the sources of life, were bound to be more female than male, more goddesses than gods.

The theological upshot of this psychoanalytical reading of the longstanding pathologies debilitating relations between the sexes is that both have sinned and fallen short of the divine glory, the healthy image of God that might have been. Both have colluded to keep women supposedly more emotional than men, men supposedly more rational than women. Both have even agreed to allow subplots to this main story in which women emerged as more sapiential than men, fuller figures of wisdom, while men emerged as more victimized than women, more crushed by war and heart attack.

What, in our sin, our coordinated brutishness and weakness, we men and women have not done is create the love, the fair-dealing, the cherishing of the earth and our own kind that a more gracious sexual mutuality might have created. Certainly, sometimes we have created love, good homes, happy children formed by two healthy parents. Happily, the record of sexual interactions has to note many successes, some of them heroic. Our coordination of supposed female weakness, diffusion, over-dependence, and supposed male strength, focus, autonomy, has been good enough, successful enough, to enable us to survive. If it is not always clear that, where sin abounded, grace abounded the more, at least it is undeniable that we have kept the species going for perhaps millions of years – no mean accomplishment.

In the present moment of historical awareness, however, where feminist sensitivities have become sharp, many analysts tend to stress the costs that the evolution of patriarchal history has exacted, and so to look on male independence, leading to pride, and female lack of selfhood, leading to cowardice, as states of soul we ought to leave behind. Together these vices, missings of the mark, have created sins that have shackled the majority of selves cruelly. Together they mount a strong case for taking new pathways, scrapping old arrangements and making new starts. So the Christian theologians among such analysts tend to draw from the sexual history of our kind familiar lessons in the need for us always to be converted, to repent again and believe in the good news that God has created us, male and female, for life and love and equality, not death and war and subjugation.

Faith and the Life-cycle of Women

All human beings pass through expectable stages, from birth to death, and a constant theme of poetry the world over is that we grow old too soon and smart too late, that youth is wasted on young people, that if we had known then what we know now our lives would have been much less painful. However, the more realistic fact is that we all move into a future we cannot know, and that probably we are all the better for that, pressured to obey the first precept of the spiritual life: pay attention.

The further fact is that efforts to lay out the characteristic trials and virtues that the main stages of the human life-cycle create can become fascinating reflections on the human self, human experiences of time, how individual personality and social setting interact mutually. So as we contemplate the relations between Christian faith and the ordinary periods of the life-cycle, we should let ourselves move into the depths of the intercourse with the divine mystery that such contemplations can suggest is the core of our temporal drama. We should remind ourselves, perhaps best by stirring up the force of the traditional Christian symbols for God's being with us as God chooses and Christ's passing over from death to life, that the most profound plot-line of our drama is divinization, *theosis*: God's taking us into God's own life, for our healing in time and our securement in bliss for eternity.

Most traditional cultures have offered their people at least rudimentary sketches of how the life-cycle is likely to go. For example, classical Hindu culture canonized an ideal scheme (based on 100 years) in which males of the upper three castes (those eligible for *moksha*, breaking out of the karmic system, the world of suffering known as *samsara*) would live in quadrants as students, householders, forest-dwellers, and wandering sages. In this ideal life, parents would apprentice their children to a guru, who would teach them the Vedic tradition, preserve them in chastity, and form them through obedience. Then, having gained sufficient book-learning, familiarity with the sacred texts, the children would take up the tasks of adulthood: marriage, procreation, earning a living, contributing to society through running a business, maintaining a social position, supporting a family.

This worldly activity would help keep society, general culture, going, but it would also give the individual rich experience, much of it painful. Through such experience, what had been only bookish learning might become real, existential, personal. People could start to understand why desire was like a flame sure to burn them, how detachment brought cool relief. They might start to hear the dicta, the symbols, the theses of the *Bhagavad-Gita*, or any other much-revered text, as dazzling revelation, words of the gods searing their own souls, luring and healing their own hearts.

The third stage (*ashrama*) of the classical Hindu life-cycle came when one saw one's children's children and the hair on one's head had turned gray. It was time for detachment, withdrawal from worldly affairs, assessment of what twenty-five years of experience in the world had taught one. The "forest" was the place of detachment, solitude, meditation in which to learn, assimilate, assess the meaning of one's experience of sex, parenting, work, business, politics. The assumption was that what one had experienced in the world would vindicate what the classics had taught, show that the wisdom handed down from the original *rishis*, the seers responsible for the Vedas, was stunningly accurate. If the assimilation succeeded fully, it would bring enlightenment. The person well-educated in the classics, and then richly experienced in worldly responsibilities, and then happy in meditational appropriation of such experience, would emerge fulfilled in a burst of light. The ignorance (*avidya*) that is the Hindu equivalent of original sin would disappear in a flash and the person would see.

Such seeing would bring a complete liberation, even a strong love of wandering naked to demonstrate the truth. Teaching by the example of such liberation, the enlightened person (*sannyasin*) would become one of the great benefactors of his time, demonstrating that the tradition was truthful, wisdom and liberation were not chimeras, all the sufferings involved in learning and living in the world and pressing hard for ultimate enlightenment were worth it.[7]

For many Western women, a wealth of Greek goddesses have helped to illustrate a sense of the life-cycle that paced it out in three different stages.[8] The time of classical females evolved through periods as Virgin, Mother, and Crone. The Virgin was sexually pure, not much involved with things libidinal or genital, but more importantly free, active, a huntress, an independent female as yet unattached to males, children, the earth, still at liberty to explore the world, wander bosky paths musing. She was Artemis rather than Aphrodite. She was strong, graceful, happiest when solitary in the woods. As yet reason predominated over bodily passion. Social relations were still simple, not warped by great need to please men, bow or scrape or flatter. The hallmark of the young woman of the classical myths, the prototypical goddess, is her independence, her autonomy. She is remarkably like an individualist male, though she may seem shyer, more modest, more self-contained.

However, the middle phase of the classical female life-cycle changes this imagery dramatically. When women become fertile physically, involved with children, echoing Mother Earth, they take on engagement, connection, relationality with a bang. Emotion races in them like a flood tide, pushing reason to the side. Menstrual cycles, tying them to the moon, give their lives a round, recurring regularity. Food and sex and shelter, weeping and bleeding and producing milk, make feminine life seem effluvial, amazingly liquid, so strongly sensual as to demote reason to something more instrumental, workaday, pragmatic than capable of detached speculation or mapping the stars. Cooking and nursing and making love predominate. Song and ritual and gossip weave through day after day.

If the immersion of classical Hindu men in the worlds of business and war and ritual (the worlds of traders, soldiers, and priests) provides them with wonderful laboratories in which to test the verities of the Vedas, the immersion of classical Greek (Indo-European, same-stock) women in the realities of marriage and parenthood provides analogous opportunities for verification and falsification. The mother, generatrix, representative of the Earth itself, who dominates the middle, mature phase of the classical female life-cycle, is as incarnate a figure as the world has ever known. Her fertile womb is both the most important source of life and the most powerful reminder that the same earth that brings us forth receives us back. The womb is also the grave. In this imagery, women are closer to both birth and death than men. Women are more natural, more instructive. The mother is the predominant form of femininity across the span of traditional (religious) cultures. The greatest wonder of women is that they are the source of new life, the opening through which sacred being emerges.

The third phase of the classical female life-cycle is that of the aging, post-menopausal woman. Here the hallmark is that she becomes a familiar of time ("crone") and so a figure of wisdom. Often she is a wicca, a good witch. She knows about herbs, spices, aphrodisiacs. She loves nature, the woods, the cycles of the seasons, all the turns and delicacies of mother earth, her divine patroness. With the end of menstruation, she breaks free of the sexual wars. The reason and freedom that she enjoyed as a virgin, prior to the onset, the onslaught, of the so-sensual, body-dominated middle phase of motherhood, return to gladden her heart. Much as she can be grateful for the passion, the pleasure, even the sufferings of sex, romance, and family life, ceding responsibility for her children, because they are now grown, and being relatively free of her husband, either because he has died (from earliest times, the crone was often a widow) or because aging has softened their sexual differences, showing them an androgyny in the human personality that is approaching wisdom, the crone can treat men less manipulatively, feel fewer slings and arrows from patriarchs.

She may in fact prefer to live in a coven, with other wiccas, but in many traditional societies (for example, the aboriginal Australian), elderly women and men stand free of the taboos and exclusions that marked their lives while they were still fertile. Just as the generative power of women fails with menopause, so does the killing power of men fail when they are too old to hunt or fight effectively. But, the body having declined, the spirit can wax fatter. In this new spiritual prosperity, the crone and the sage both tend to speak less and less, love silence more and more. The overwhelming reality absorbing them is not the sensual ego, the variable body, the riotous emotions. The overwhelming reality is nothing limited to the self, nothing self-centered. The whole, the creative divine mystery, the world of wonders that keeps putting on its kaleidoscopic show, oblivious of human attention or applause, becomes the great interest. The self heads out of itself, no longer obliged to think so much about the rent, what's for dinner, how to keep the kids from falling into the mammoth pit. A shamanic love of journeys, imaginative flights to all that might be, or a yogic love of interiority, pacific rest at the base of the meditative spirit, tends to become a predominant disposition. The elderly who are maturing best move through their last years, the end of their time, with an increasing interest in eternity. Some develop a great curiosity about what sort of moat death really is. A few even come to hope for an absolute future, a being taken into the bosom of their deathless Creator.

For a Christian feminist faith, the classical Western display of lifetime in three stages of virginity, motherhood, and sapiential maturity can be both stimulating and consoling. The schema suggests, for instance, that it is good for females to grow up independent, well-educated, formed to look to themselves, be confident in their selves, self-reliant. Such an education can do wonders to combat the stereotypical female failing, not having a self strong enough to resist overdirection by men and so over the long haul undercontributing to the common good from precisely feminine experiences, insights, graces. Whether this conception of the utilities of a virginal phase in the typical life-cycle of women creates a strong argument for an independent education of women that would afford them many chances at leadership is an interesting question. The pros and cons of coeducational institutions continue to cross and criss.

Clearly, though, whatever tells women from earliest consciousness that they are individuals, rational and free as much as emotional and related, is good in the sight of a mature Christian theology. How can women be healthy images of the divine if their lives are always cluttered, swamped by dependencies, indentured to others in excessive service? How can their spirits fatten, and then be stripped lean, if their bodies are all-important, constantly on display and duty for the pleasure of men? Virtually no men are anorexic. Virtually all women worry inordinately about how they look. It has been to the advantage of men to try to curtail the freedoms of the classical virginal goddess. The disparagement of Artemis, the castigating of her as cold and dikey, has usually been impure.

Girls need a latency period, a time of clarity and reason little bent by sex and emotion, just as much as boys do. It is unfortunate, sometimes even tragic, that girls tend to develop somatically and sexually more quickly than boys, shortening their years of latency, lessening their time of serene freedom from hormones and itchy desires. If we wished, however, we could accommodate our mores to provide adolescent girls a fuller moratorium for deep development. We could put aside excessive romance, as well as marrying and child-rearing, until sweet reason had established itself in well-trained brains.

Last, let me simply hint at the possible correlations between this classical mapping of the female life-cycle and the traditional Christian scheme of the three ways or times of the spiritual life. The traditional Christian scheme speaks of purgative, illuminative, and unitive stages. The novice setting out for virtue and intimacy with God has first to purge away sin, vice and distance from God. In the beginning comes repentance, *metanoia*, conversion. Discipline sets up as a liberation: silence, self-denial, prayer, and fasting. A new being struggles to be born. The old, sinful personality starts to sicken, pass away. With joy, the tyro works on her self, trying to overcome her vanities, distractions, sloths.

If she goes at this purgative work generously, she is likely to make great progress in a short time. Her prayer, which usually begins as meditation, starts to shift to something more contemplative: holistic, dominated by rest and love more than striving and reasoning. She is passing across the threshold into the second phase of the traditional

Christian spiritual cycle, the time of illumination. Here the point to the processes is to understand, make one's own, take to heart the precepts, truths, worked over in the purgative phase. Here one learns why the Sabbath was made for human beings, and not human beings for the Sabbath. The person becomes free to eat and drink, speak or hold silence, as the grace of the moment or the need of the neighbor counsels or requires. The letter of the law cedes to the spirit. The Spirit lists where it will, beckoning us gently to follow.

Moreover, no exemplar shines more usefully than Jesus, the very Word of God incarnate. The parables of Jesus, his miracles, everything suggesting how he put divine wisdom into sacramental action, poetic speech, redemptive suffering, become a great treasure. Christian faith develops as a profound humanism. Whatever is noble, true, good seems to stream down from the Father of lights. Equally, though, the Christian teachings about the depths of original sin, the extent of the cracks in human nature, come home with a new force. Regular revelations of the recalcitrance of human nature, including most pointedly one's own, first build and then sustain a strong pressure toward sobriety. The immense suffering of human beings, indeed all of creation, that sinful human resistance to grace creates takes an emotional toll.

In the final phase, a few fully successful Christians pass through a crucifixion like that of Jesus and become mystics proper, experiencing directly the love and carrying power of God. Usually this requires their enduring dark nights and thick clouds of unknowing. Normally God strips the mystic, the person chosen to commune with the divine being immediately, heart to heart, down to the bone. Normally the genuine mystic, the significant saint, has been broken and then remade. But each story tends to differ, because at the consummation of the traditional Christian life-cycle God deals with sharply defined individuals one by one, fitting the divine ministrations to their needs most sensitively.

If there is an agreement among Christian mystics about this process, it tends to be that God is much gentler, subtler, more gracious than any natural models, based on the physical power running the universe, would suggest God would be. God moves like a shy lover, careful at a work of persuasion. God wants full response, love, from the heart, with no compulsion.

This can be too wonderful to comprehend, too simple to seem

significant. We do well toward the end to recall the powerful images of the first chapters of Revelation, so as not to forget who is this Risen Lord working in our blood. Yet we must also let God carry the initiative, do with us what God will. The unitive way or period is one in which we write God *carte blanche*, find our soul tending more and more toward abandonment. We come to want only what God wants: Our Father, who art in Heaven, hallowed be *Thy* name, *Thy* kingdom come, *Thy* will be done. If women can head for this sort of climax, wanting God to be all in all, then their virginity and motherhood and wisdom from aging can assimilate them to Jesus and Mary. Beyond piety, in mystical substance, they can become children and friends of God. A constructive Christian feminist theology can think of no better achievement, no richer dividend for having been created either female or male.

Prayer as the Ultimate Freedom

We have looked at the psychology of Christian existence, considering the life-cycle of the self, the sins that tend to shackle it, its constitution as social (relational), its love, and how it finds itself in God (often through good work). To conclude, let us consider prayer, the ultimate act of freedom in which a Christian woman can find that no idol need enthrall her, nothing can separate her from the love of God revealed in Christ.

Prayer stems from two correlated realities. First is the quasi-unlimited outreach of the human spirit. From the time of Plato, analysts of human consciousness have realized that human awareness is both directional ("intentional," to enter the linguistic stream begun by Brentano and Husserl) and transcendent (always going beyond). Nothing finite, experienced in space or time, gives human awareness, our soul, need or ability to rest permanently, stop moving on. No work or love or material possession gladdens our heart lastingly. Appreciating this, the Buddha realized that all life is suffering. We never find complete satisfaction. As long as we strive, desire, we feel as though we were burning. Appreciating this, Plato spoke of the divine as the beyond, that toward which we are always moving with erotic love.

The second reality grounding prayer is precisely this presence of an objective, divine beyond. When we intend what is real, want to understand and make and commune with what is so, with the world both natural and spiritual that stands in front of us, often most alluringly, we go outward and enter something comprehensive. Ecologists speak of the natural, biological realms of this comprehensive something, this universe, as webs, systems, dynamic or interactive wholes. Physicists seeking a comprehensive, unified overview of the entirety of creation hope that an original big bang will explain all that followed.

Metaphysicians East and West, who have had to include spiritual realms, images and movements beyond the material ones germane to physics and biology, have tended to develop more abstract language. The *Brahman* or God that became their final candidate for the ultimate and whole was absolute, infinite, eternal. Negatives predominated. The source and content of the whole that the human spirit could intuit, the limitless correlative of the horizon opened by human transcendence, by the beyond, was "not this, not that." It was *nirguna* and *saguna*, on the side of no-thing-ness yet also positive being. Christian mystics have also spoken both negatively (apophatically) and positively (kataphatically). God is not like anything in human experience (because unlimited), yet God is also like everything positive in human experience (because the creative source).

People who analyzed religious consciousness therefore had to become quite sophisticated about spiritual movements, images of finitude and infinity, what human reason might infer legitimately and what logical steps became *faux pas*. They had to prefer, grant some primacy to, experiences of light and love, reason and spiritual movement toward the good, the intrinsically beautiful, the true, the unified, but they had also to recognize the limits of even these primal experiences, these apparently purest analogues for what ultimate reality is in itself. Darkness, silence, the overshadowing of human awareness by a divine cloud, pitched in to help in this work of chastening. Lao Tzu discovering that, while all others are clear, he alone is cloudy, confused, stands for the deeper personality, the person face to face with the term of the intentional journey (which is also the origin and foundation), the *Tao* that cannot be named.

Prayer is the outreach of the human person toward the holiness, the ultimate reality, of God, the beyond, the ineffable *Tao*. It is the acknowledgment, in reverence, that creatures are only wise when they estimate well the whole in which they move, the entirety or universe that is their habitat, and that praise of this whole, gratitude for it, worship of it, is the most honest of our proper human acts. Prayer reflects, expresses, actualizes from subjective awareness the bedrock, most basic fact about all creatures: we did not make ourselves, we do not explain ourselves, we are contingent, not necessary. Amusingly, we do not know the most basic things about ourselves: where we came from, where we are going, why and how it happened that we gained being, why, indeed, the world itself happens to be. To assert or assume or insist that the world has always been is no more justified, rational, compelled by either empirical facts or lucid reasoning than is the proposition that God has always been and chose at a given moment to bring into being other realities, existences limited and so not divine. None of us knows why there is a world, but any of us can feel a great wonder at the mysteriousness of our situation. Aristotle made of this wonder an incitement to philosophy, a life driven by love of wisdom. Christian masters of prayer have made of it an intuition that God is always greater, that we shall never understand, and so our growth, our beatitude, can be endless, if only we join ourselves to the endlessness of God, by letting God take us over in love.

The precisely incarnational refinements that come to Christian prayer through a creed that focuses God's actions onto Jesus the Christ are sacramental. Matter becomes a legitimate presence, vehicle, carrier of the grace of God, the help and divine life that God's interactions with us convey. Being human becomes a privileged locus in the economy, the ecology, of creation and salvation, because Christ reveals that being human is not only a coordination of matter and spirit but also a coordination of finitude and infinity, creaturehood and divine creativity. We do not understand how the unlimited God could take flesh, becoming one with it so intimately that, orthodox Christian theologians had to insist, the faithful could say that Christ was their God, or that God died on the cross. But that is the paradoxical, even scandalous Christian claim.

At prayer, facing God, trying to love God from their depths and through all their senses, Christians could be aware of much of this span of consciousness, reality, and language or of virtually none. They could pray as learned theologians or as simple peasants. The concepts in their heads were always second to the actual movements in their spirits, the stirrings in their minds and hearts. The metaphysics and Christology were realities of a second order, a notional realm, less crucial and substantial than the openness, or the sin, or the wrap-around-ache of the single, whole, embodied self. People could pray as quiet, careful interlocutors of God, or as suffering leaden lumps. They could pray alone or with others, in the fields or in the chapels, with elan and joy or with torpor, acedia, sadness. But any time that they tried to reach out to God, or to open their hearts to God's coming in, or to weep toward God in pain, or to remember the benefits of God, the goodness of Jesus, with gratitude, they were praying.

Through such praying, they were keeping their world going, sustaining the field of images, the network of discourse, on which their Christian sense of reality depended. To seek God or to open to God was to reaffirm the reality of God, to re-express their hopes that God was real, interested in them, connected to them. So reaffirmed, God might continue to be their rock and their salvation, making them fearless. Contemplated again as hanging from the cross, Christ might continue to be their loving savior, the proof that divinity so loved the world it did not spare its own son. The specific remembrance celebrated at the eucharist, the anamnesis of Christ's last meal and passover from death to resurrection, became the axis of communal Christian prayer. The celebration of Easter has always been the center of the official Christian liturgical year, the hub from which radiates everything else. Communion with Jesus, through immersion in the biblical images filling the New Testament and sacramental reception of loaf and cup, has been the most basic, trustworthy form of mystical union, humble as crumbs yet never to be plumbed, fathomed, fully appreciated. Eucharistic prayer is the most reliable and representative of Christians' formalized prayers, because the most acutely focused on the body and blood, the primitive human enfleshment, the Messiah and Logos of God.

Whenever Christians have prayed effectively, through any of these forms, they have moved out of the world that is merely factitious, only things and bits and stuff. They have affirmed, at least implicitly, that they were much more than their money or food or clothing. Since so much of what we experience at prayer is of our poverty and need, the significance of what we can possess, can store in our barns, shrinks considerably. Considering the lilies of the field, God's constant creation of the world in variety and beauty, we can feel our anxieties lessening, our trust in our Creator growing. The body is more than food. Our lives are more than clothing. Those who kill the body cannot kill the soul. No one can make us lie, deny the truth, stop loving. We have realms of freedom, prairies wide open for spiritual exploration, as long as we can think.

Prayer is thinking about God, thinking about the world, reality, in the light of God. Prayer is loving God, longing for God, yearning, suffering God's apparent absence. The pain of the saints is being without God, feeling delivered up to themselves. The realization of the saints is that hell would be being closed in on oneself, no longer ecstatic for God. The maturation of prayer tends to overturn the commonsensical assumption of the secular person, or of even the beginner at prayer. The challenge is not to prove the existence of God but to explain how there came to be a finite world, anything less than God. The good news is not that God will pluck us from terrible hellfire but that God is completely good and we can try, at least want, to love God mainly for God's own sake, caring less and less for the benefits such love might bring us.

As long use of the Psalms has taught contemplative Christians, the best states of soul are gratitude and praise. We are terribly short. God is wondrously long. We don't matter greatly, in the long view. God matters completely. Our greatest spiritual health comes from God's mattering completely for us, in our awareness, to structure our lives in the fullest realism. Our deepest and richest freedom is to live as the pawns, the captives, of nothing created, nothing less than God.

In Christian maturity, we would do this gracefully, not churlishly. We would do it sacramentally, with great tenderness for human flesh, animal vitality, the green goodness of plants, the mica shine of rocks, the undulations of water. But the best thing we can do to move toward any of such maturity, make any progress toward significant wisdom and holiness, is to challenge ourselves to make God be, let God make Godself be, real for us – not just a traditional word, however hallowed, but rather a wonderful, raging, quiet reality: the Other and Beyond defining what our awareness is for.

Study Questions

1 What are the implications of the requirement of Christian faith that people define themselves foundationally through their relationship with God?
2 What shifts in nuance ought to come to the phrase "women's work" when one subjects it to a feminist Christian analysis?
3 How valid do you find the claim that love is the crucial human experience and responsibility?
4 When we characterize the self, how ought we to strike the balance between its private and its public aspects?
5 What are the sins of the human self that you find most capital?
6 How useful is the staging of the female life-cycle in terms of the classic Greek triad of Virgin-Mother-Crone?
7 Why can prayer be the self's way to an ultimate freedom?

Notes

1 Frank Conroy, *Body and Soul* (Houghton Mifflin, New York, 1993), p. 408. See also Donald Hall, *Life Work* (Beacon, Boston, 1993).
2 See Eric Voegelin, "Universal humanity," in his *Order and History*, vol. 4 (Louisiana State University Press, Baton Rouge, 1974), especially pp. 316–36: "Question and mystery" and "The process of history as the process of the whole."
3 See Thomas Moore, *Care of the Soul* (HarperCollins, New York, 1992) and *Soul Mates* (HarperCollins, New York, 1994).
4 Ellen Gilchrist, *The Anna Papers* (Little Brown, Boston, 1988), p. 16.
5 See Valerie Goldstein, "The human situation: a feminine view," *Journal of Religion*, 40 (1960), pp. 104–17; Judith Plaskow, *Sex, Sin, and Grace* (University Press of America, Lanham, MD, 1980); Joann Wolski Conn, *Women's Spirituality* (Paulist, New York, 1986).
6 See Dorothy Dinnerstein, *The Mermaid and the Minotaur* (Harper and Row, New York, 1976). Note how the designation of the sexes continues to run toward these stereotypes in such recent good books as Hariett Doerr's *Consider This, Senora* (Harcourt Brace, New York, 1993), where the first woman we meet, the Senora, is charmingly vague, and Brian Keenan's *An Evil Cradling* (Viking, New York, 1992), where his male Muslim captors seem bound to treat their hostages brutishly.
7 Apparently Hindu females were not held to the same ideal life-cycle as males, though there is evidence that some young women studied with

gurus. See, for example, the questioning of the sage Yajna Valkya by the female student Gargi in the *Brihad-aranyaka Upanishad*. Concerning a recent female *sannyasin*, see Charles S. J. White, "Mother guru: Jnanananda of Madras, India," in *Unspoken Worlds*, ed. Nancy A. Falk and Rita M. Gross (Harper and Row, San Francisco, 1980), pp. 22–37.

8 See Christine Downing, *The Goddess: Mythological Images of the Feminine* (Crossroad, New York, 1981).

Chapter 7

THEOLOGY

GOD SO FAR AND YET SO NEAR

God So Far: Thinking Correctly about Transcendence

I take "God" to designate ultimate reality, the most real, and so holy, of the realities that we experience or think about. God is reality of an uncreated, necessary order, and therefore God is radically different from all created, contingent realities. Traditional Christian theological language has expressed this difference between God and all the creatures in the natural world, all the angels in the spiritual worlds that many peoples (Jews, Christians, Muslims, Hindus, for example) have accredited, by saying that God is the Creator. What does this mean?

It means that everything that exists comes from God, but God does not come from anything but himself, herself, itself. God makes the world, but there is no more reality after God has made the world than what God had alone before she made it. The mystery of creation is how creatures, finite beings, limited instances of existence like ourselves, come into being and stay there. The primal question is why there is something, rather than nothing, and the constant prod to raise this question is the manifest fact that we creatures move, change, are born and die. The grass withers, the flowers fade. Only the Word of the Lord, the realm of God, endures forever. This biblical conviction (Isaiah 40:6–8), with its mood of melancholy, runs deep in believers of all stripes. However much we praise the endurance of God, the divine reliability, we find sad the passingness of creation, the omnipresence of mortality.

To say that God is the Creator, existing beyond the divide of nothingness that makes creatures mortal, is to say that we do not understand God, cannot. Buddhists agree with biblical believers on this score. The "stream" of existence in which creatures find themselves is something that people must cross (through enlightenment), if they are to come to wisdom, fulfillment, salvation. The wisdom at work in Buddhist salvation is the *Prajnaparamita*: the wisdom that has "gone beyond" the stream of finitude and suffering (*samsara*). The horizon that one finds in the sutras of the *Prajnaparamita* literature stretches from an ultimate, absolute, nirvanic, God's-eye point of view. Generally, it arranges things so that all creatures, all items of sensible experience or conceptual control, are "empty." They owe their reality to the ultimate light, being, buddhanature in them. This buddhanature in itself is a whole beyond the grasp of human beings, present in samsaric beings but resident more radically on the far side, across the stream.[1]

The transcendence of God, God's always being beyond, being more, being "excessive," connotes the reasons for religious awe. Any experiential appreciation of the otherness of God, the beyondness, the totality, tends to stop the clatter of the mind, the wanting of the heart, the preoccupations of the self. On a cold, clear winter night, when the stars glitter like flakes of diamond laid out on indigo velvet, I may sense the unimaginable sweep of the universe, the billions of miles, the numberless galaxies, and so give up my mind. An impression of the divine endlessness, in-finity, may take up my soul, probably to let it go in the morning, send it back to the eggshells and coffee grounds. While it was gone, though, traveling the galaxies, I moved to the edge of the universe, where I saw and felt there was no end. I sensed that I could keep going forever, a spiritual arrow, and all my traveling was through heaven, the abode of the endless God.

Heaven is not boring (one hears lesser theologians worrying what the saved will find to do in eternity with God), precisely because there is never an end with God. Greek Christian fathers such as Gregory of Nyssa realized this and so spoke of a never-ending human maturation. We are bound to imagine the endlessness of God as a sweep like that of our physical universe, but without beginning or end – a tract with no term or borders or crossing guards. The realm of God, God's heaven, is the full extent of God, which is immense (not-to-be-measured).

The harder but better analogy comes from the nisus, the lift and drive, of our spirits: how we can think and love beyond and beyond. There is no end to our desiring to know, to understand. There is no term to our erotic love. Our spirits are quasi-infinite, able to make and become all intelligible things. The nisus that moves us beyond where we were yesterday is our human share in transcendence. Our destiny is heaven, nothing limited to time and space. The innermost coil of our being is a wellspring throwing us forward into God.

To be sure, "heaven" connotes other images (gardens, angels, liturgical songs), and they vary from tradition to tradition. The heaven that traditional Jews have imagined differs from that of traditional Christians and Muslims. On the other hand, the three sets of images that one finds in the Abrahamic faiths share much common ground, because all three consider God to be the unlimited Creator. For the moment, I only want "heaven" to connote the endless sufficiency of God, the was-is-will-be that never stands within time, that always is deathless, all-at-once, and full of bliss.

How do we know that the heaven of God, God's own manner of existing (totally) is full of bliss? We intuit and argue that this must be so. Ultimate reality, the fullness of being, the source of all creation, must be pleased with itself, replete with a proper self-love, for otherwise it would display some lack, some imperfection. If Genesis has the Creator pleased with what he makes, moved to say that it is good, how much more must the Creator be pleased with his own divine being, "complacent" in the highest of senses? This complacency is nothing narcissistic. It is simply an objective appreciation of an objective reality: God is perfect, a limited being would not be God.

The career of Jesus the Christ, his personal history, brings the question of suffering and evil into theology proper, the task of understanding the being of God, but we may defer this question to a later section of this chapter. Here the second capital point is that the farness of God that I am struggling to suggest also parses itself out as a moral transcendence. Just as God is endless in being, so God is endless in goodness, holiness, freedom that has no flaws. God does not create the world from any impure motives. God has no *libido dominandi*, no will to rule others and make them her slave.

The reason for creation, according to traditional Christian theology, is the goodness of God, God's desire to share the divine glory. God is good actively. Through creating, God diffuses the divine goodness, lets it go "out" to make other beings be. The being, the existence, of these other beings, such as our human selves, comes from God. The puzzle is how God "stops" it, so that it is the being of Denise or Sam, of Ike the iguana or Polly the pony. Matter is a puzzle, even a bedrock mystery (there is more there, in the rock, and it is there more densely, powerfully, and simply, than we human beings shall ever understand). Spirit is also a puzzle and a mystery: the flash of reason, the relations among being, love, and light.

The divine glory is the splendor, the glow, of the divine goodness. In Jewish theology, the *Shekinah* is God-as-lustrous, the *Kabod Yahweh* is God-as-glorious-and-dazzling.[2] A Christian theology of the divine glory, dazzle, light can draw from Johannine imagery. The second half of John presents Jesus as glorified, communing with his Father. Revelation brims with shining figures for the risen Christ, the first-born from the dead. This light expresses the purity of God, something elemental. Darker, and perhaps fuller, is the love of God, the warmth and will to do others good. Christian trinitarian theology has tended to associate the being of God with the Father, the light of God with the Word, and the love of God with the Holy Spirit, but none of these associations has been rigid. Thus Christians have also considered both the Word of God, incarnate in Jesus through Mary, and the Holy Spirit to be wise – the benevolent reason of God active in creation. They have made love the inmost substance of each divine person, as they have made love the orientation of each relation among the divine persons.

In creating the world, the Christian God moved from its own center and gave of its own substance. This did not move the divine center off course, and it did not diminish that endless substance. But creation did put into time the eternal divine love. It did express in space something of the unlimited divine light. How it did these things, we cannot say. We can speculate, though, that in making the world God did not work extrinsically. Despite the images of craftsmanship from the Bible, more of the divine substance came into play. God was not the aloof clockmaker that the Deists imagined. Rather, the being of the world, its standing forth from nothingness or mere possibility, its coming into reality, depended on an intimate communication. Indeed, that communication probably bore the imprint of Father-Son-Spirit. For a Christian theology of creation, the one God making the world is also trinitarian, is never not Father-Son-Spirit.

This means that the transcendence of God, all the limitlessness, all the existing beyond what creatures can know or be, is not at odds with personal communication. It means that nearness, immanence, intimacy, which we discuss in the next section, is not for God contrary to transcendence. God is not bound by the either/ors that we tend to need, our binary cast of mind. The closer we come to God, the more fully we seize our proper freedom. The more we run away from God, the less human we are. These convictions of the Christian saints offer stimulating hints about how God deals with creatures. If the dealing is in love, through persuasion more than force, by a drawing of the creature's desire, then "conservation" (keeping creatures in existence, continuing their creation) is like a friendship or a romance. God lives with creatures in a compact, a covenant, written on their hearts, in their bones, from the substance of their souls. God does not cease to be transcendent – other, beyond, endless, far. But this far of God is also a near. We bob on the farness of God like lobster pots on an eddy, like kites on a breeze. It is our home channel.

The religious conclusion that many Christian saints have reached is that God is always greater (*semper major*). If we feel tempted to despair, we have forgotten: Even when our hearts condemn us, God is greater. If we feel that death, or evil, or pain is bound to have the last word, we need to remember: they may well be limited. Only God is not limited. That is most of what the word "God" means in orthodox theology. God is one, sole, unique, absolute – free of all the conditions that limit creatures. Like to God is no other.

"Monotheism" ought not to be a fanatical effort to strip the world of idols so much as a hymn to this soleness of God. It ought to reside in an abnegation of imagination that refuses to let us settle for anything not always greater, not intrinsically beyond us and all other creatures. When we sing our most heartfelt songs to such a God, we move into an exquisite freedom. Nothing less than God is our master. Nothing in space or time can make us its slave. The transcendence of God writes us a *magna carta*, an emancipation proclamation. When we set our souls on the divine beyond, we leave the tyrannies of Egypt, enter upon the liberations of the desert.

God So Near: Thinking Correctly about Immanence

The Koran says that God is as near as the pulse at our throats. No scripture places more emphasis on the sovereignty of God, the transcendent holiness, so this affirmation of the intimate nearness of God that we find in the Koran confirms an important theological intuition. The people who experience God most intensely solve practically the apparent dilemmas confronting people who only deal with God conceptually, whose theology is principally a matter of trying to square traditional ideas. Experientially, God is the holy ground of everything, and perhaps one's own personal savior. In awe, one senses how different the divine holiness makes God. In joy, one senses that God has chosen to be God-for-us, a creative love intent on dealing with each of us personally.

Medieval Christian mystical masters, such as Meister Eckhart and the anonymous author of the *Cloud of Unknowing*, stress the Augustinian intuition that God is more intimate to us than we are to ourselves. We get our being from God. We only are, exist, because God says "Let them be." That we are means that God is at work in our deepest substance – wherever it is that the idea of us gains reality. So there is never a time, never a place, where we are without God, where God is not more of our reality than we are. As long as the word "I" or "he" or "she" makes sense, names something in creation to which we and others can point, or something in memory to which we used to be able to point, we know a personal place, a spiritual site, where God abides.

This interpretation of what it means for anything in creation to exist applies to rocks and trees, emus and tapirs, as well as to human beings. It makes God the inmost referent of anything, everything, that we can see or feel or know. The implications for a style of life more compatible with the ecological realities of our present earth than the consumerist style still favored in the First World make this ontological accent of medieval Christian mysticism acutely relevant. If we began to see all creatures as presences of God, we might deal with them more reverently. We would still have to work out what our relations with our sources of food, shelter, medicine, and other necessities ought to be. But we might go about this work less aggressively, better able to consider the common good of the ecological whole.

If everything is a presence of God, through God's grant of exist-ence, does it follow that nothing is peculiarly the presence of God, something that should summon us to worship (the cultus that we offer only to God, in recognition of the distinction of God from all creatures)? To worship a creature (a difficult task) is idolatry. Many people seem to preoccupy themselves with money or pleasure, power or looks, to the warping of their souls, but seldom have I heard a worldling say, with full seriousness, "My bank account is the holiest, most important thing in my world." A benevolent theology, as any professing to be Christian has to try to be (God is gracious, startlingly generous), can take this reluctance in the souls of the vast majority of people to make a finite good such as money or power absolute to be a sign of lingering health. The person in question has not become completely deaf to the hints of the Creator. Some sanity about the passingness of everything created, mortal, remains.

When they have pondered deeply about the immanence of God, the nearness, some of the best Christian thinkers have looked closely at pantheism. Impressed by the dependence of all creatures on God for their reality, such thinkers have wondered whether we shouldn't say that God is everything, nothing is not God. The problem with saying this, promoting pantheism proper, is that God is not the limitation through which creatures become partial presences of God. If God were everything, then everything would be unlimited, simple, one, seamless, as God is. Everything would be eternal, as God is. To claim that, in fact, creatures are all these divine things contradicts so badly our common sense, our daily experience, that no critical theologian, ruled by data and reason, can hold it.

Nonetheless, pantheism expresses a profound intuition. The reality of the world does not come from the world. The world does not furnish its own explanation. To want the world to furnish its own explanation, moral as well as ontological, is to opt for chaos and absurdity. If God is dead, a word empty of force because naming nothing real, then everything is permitted, and nothing makes sense. So people convinced that absurdity is not their fate think that God must be alive, indeed blazing with life, the ultimate force and source of all that lives. This is how pantheists think, except without the restraints that would make their thought compatible with orthodox Christian theologies – analogical explorations of God found healthy by the Christian community as a whole down the ages in view of the

Incarnation of the Word and the mainstream of Christian practice (both liturgical and ethical).

One position more acceptable theologically than pantheism on the relationship between God and creation goes by the name "panentheism."[3] Here the key notion comes from the tiny Greek word *en*. God is *in* everything, and everything is *in* God. Nothing could be without God, who grants it its being moment by moment. Everything that is has God as its final, only adequate, context, matrix, milieu. Creatures do not lose their identity, melting into the aseity (self-sufficiency) of God, becoming mere drops of being indistinguishable in the divine ocean. The real limits that make creatures what they are give them an existence that God does not swallow up. When they speak to God, creatures are not speaking to themselves. When God speaks to them, acts in them, God is not speaking to himself, acting on herself. How this can be so while we still say that God is the inmost reality of all things is hard to clarify, perhaps impossible. Much at these outposts of speculation about the being of God the Creator depends on a given linguistic frame of reference.

For example, a theologian may want to say at one moment that God (usually the Holy Spirit) makes the prayer of the believer, or at least carries the spirit of the praying believer, so that from one point of view God is praying to God. All the more so would this affirmation be appropriate if the Christian theologian were trying to clarify the prayer of Christ: the person incarnate in Jesus is divine, so (with proper cautions), we can say that in the prayer of Jesus, as in any of the other religious thoughts or acts of Jesus, God was, is, dealing with God. But we can, in fact must, also speak about the religious action of God in creatures as supportive rather than determinative.

We can do this, because Jesus and the other foremost Christian authorities have made individuals responsible for their salvation – their healing through the graciousness of God. Such authorities either have taught explicitly that human beings have considerable freedom to say yes or no to God, or have assumed this freedom when they preached or taught. It would make no logical sense to urge people passionately to amend their lives, leave their sins, and believe in the good news that Jesus preached if such people had no freedom to do this, could not change their minds, their hearts, their wills.

Christianity does not have a doctrine of *karma* like that of Hindus and Buddhists. It does not stress the predestined character of history so forcefully as Islam. Looking at Jesus preaching to the crowds, it says that human beings can perceive that nothing other than God can fulfill them, and so they can make themselves indifferent to everything less than God, free regarding all fellow creatures.

We human beings can also make ourselves indifferent to our selves, free regarding this closest fellow creature. In fact, we might summarize the goal of Christian asceticism as precisely to make God more real, significant, beautiful than anything in our own memories, imaginations, piles of possessions or hopes. We have noted the epigram of Augustine: sin is love of self unto contempt of God, holiness is love of God unto contempt of self. When we consider the intimacy of God to us through our existence, we can let our self-concern diminish, our appreciation of God increase, and so come into the liberty of the children of God. This has never been easy, so important does self-awareness seem to be to evolutionary survival, but in each generation Christian saints have kept at it, achieving notable success. The best of them have lost themselves in the wonder, the splendor, of their divine beloved. The best of them have become transparent to God, for God – presences of God truly beautiful.

When they have meditated on what it means to be an image of God, the signal Christian saints have stressed the "God" in this phrase more than the "image." Usually, they have not cared overmuch that they have not been able to get clear fully what it means to be an image of God, as no one else ever has. Their images, like their lives, their selves, their very beings, have been hidden in God. They have not known whether they were righteous, pleasing to God, or offensive. They have had to believe, down in the darkness where the intimacy of God to their selves created a cloud of unknowing, that God holds us in love, carries us tenderly, like a mother great with child.

Christian feminist theologies, constructions of what "God" may mean best, ought to underscore the shared, relational character that these ontological accents give to our dealings with God. If the reality is that God is always with us, has to be present if we are to be, then our relationship with God is constant, even constitutive of who any of us is. We are not autonomous, and the dealings with our children, our spouses, our colleagues, our friends that we treasure most find their most telling analogue in our dealings with the God who is, constantly, our source. Because God is also the source of all other creatures, we live, exist, move in ecological systems filled with the creative activity of God. These ecological relationships are not accidental to our definition as children of God but substantial.

Certainly, we cannot validly collapse our selves into any of these relationships. Always we remain somewhat distinctive, unique in our genes, our graces, our sins. But the core relationship that we have with God softens the hard edges that our distinctiveness can acquire, if we let it seize us and shape our decisions as though we were autonomous. Even if we wish it were not so, or deny that it is so, the fact, as Christian believers see it, is that our basic being, our most fundamental reality, takes shape as a reception rather than an achievement: both what we are and that we are come ultimately from our divine Creator.

Jesus: the Wisdom of God in Flesh

We have been speaking of God the Creator, who is both beyond all creatures and completely intimate to them. To speak of Jesus, the historical anchor of Christian faith and theology, we need not deny anything that we have said about God as the Creator. Indeed, we cannot deny anything expressed rightly, in orthodox fashion. The God whom Christian tradition credits with creation is the Trinity, the divinity that is both one in nature and three in persons. When God creates, the oneness is to the fore, but all three divine persons possess the divine nature, so Father, Son, and Holy Spirit are all implied in the word "Creator".

From the third century of the Christian era, when Greek Christian thinkers well educated in classical philosophy began to speculate boldly about the implications of the Christian scriptures and sacraments, Christian theology has struggled with the difficult question of how to relate the inner life of the Trinity with the work of creation and salvation.[4] The inner life of the Trinity is the active relationships characterizing the persons in their distinction as Father, Son, and Spirit. Let us summarize these relationships briefly.

The Son is all that the Father is, except that he is not the Father, the generator or speaker of an all-inclusive divine Word, but rather the generated, the spoken, the Word itself. If the Father is a limitless act of understanding, the Son is a limitless concept expressing this act of understanding. The Spirit is all that the Father and the Son are, expressing their perfect mutual love, except that he or she is what is breathed forth, not the one or two who breathe (Eastern Orthodoxy attributes the spiration of the Spirit to the Father alone; Western, Latin Christianity has the Spirit proceed from both the Father and the Son). The Father is unbegotten, the limitless point alpha in any geometry of the Christian Trinity. The Son is the complete expression of the Father, the comprehensive utterance. The Spirit is the full love of God, matched to the full divine knowledge and being.

Inasmuch as the Son, who takes flesh from Mary, is the Word of God, Christian theology has tended to think of him as a complete reason (*Logos*). Inasmuch as creation comes from God intelligently, reasonably, it occurs in the Son. Indeed, some Christian theologians have made the rational order of creation a subset of the eternal generation of the Son as the self-expression of the Father. Whatever the conceptual scheme, though, Christian theologians who thought hard about the *Logos* had to grapple with such New Testament texts as John 1:1–14 and Colossians 1:15–20.

As we have seen, both of these texts make the Word of God central to creation. Both also draw on the conception of the "Word of God" prominent in the Hebrew Bible. There neither the Word of God nor the Spirit of God has the clarity that Christian theology finally gave them as somewhat independent divine "persons" (the term is only analogous to what we mean by a human person, because all human beings are *limited* centers of awareness and volition, while the divine persons are unlimited).

Nonetheless, the authors of the Hebrew Bible recognized that religious experience of the Lord often took the form of hearing a command or a word of comfort. Another regular form of religious experience was of feeling the divine Spirit move in one's own human spirit. The prophet Ezekiel speaks dramatically of these experiences, but many other voices, beginning with Genesis itself, refer to the speaking of God and the movement of the divine Spirit. Thus the Christian conception of God as trinitarian was not completely novel, nor was the Christian sense that creation must have occurred through the speaking of God, the rational self-expression of God – in a word, through the divine wisdom.

We have seen the conception of Wisdom recorded in Proverbs 9. There she is the daughter or lover of God, playing before him at the dawn of creation for his delight. Jesus, whom Paul called the "power and wisdom of God" (1 Corinthians 1:24), is always in traditional, orthodox Christian theology both fully human and fully divine. As fully divine, the *Logos* like to the Father in everything but the relational position that we have mentioned (begotten, not the begetter), he can express the infinite, limitless knowing of the Father in such a way as to include all the intelligibility of creation, everything that can come to be. He is not merely playing before God at creation, his generation from and by the Father is the larger creativity of which natural creation is only a limited reflection. Taking Jesus the *Logos* incarnate in this way, some Christian theologians have made creation itself Logocentric, even Christocentric.

The humanity of Jesus, the enfleshment or incarnation of the *Logos*, suggests other ways in which for Christian believers God has revealed the divine wisdom. The life and fate of Jesus, his preaching the dawning of the Reign of God and suffering crucifixion, seemed to the first generations of Christians (those who composed or compiled the New Testament) the peak of what God could say through a human life. With the resurrection, the death of Jesus revealed most powerfully the sinfulness of human beings, their aversion from the light.

Bad people hate the light, because their deeds are evil. Good people come to the light, that their deeds may be seen in God. The light shines in the darkness, and the darkness has never overcome it or understood it. These are fundamental theses in Johannine theology, radiating from John's view that Jesus is the Word of God, the eternal divine light of self-understanding, come into flesh. As the first half of the Gospel of John makes clear, Jesus worked many signs that expressed his exceptional wisdom and power. These were all works of light, invitations to people of good conscience, who wanted to live in the light, to believe in the good news that God was offering the needy, mortal world divine life. The irony that flows so strongly through this gospel (see, for example, chapter 9, the dialogue between the man born blind and the Pharisees) is the product of the depressing experience that not even the divine light can win over people who have become warped in conscience, ideologues or legalists or slaves of some current political correctness.

At any rate, the full power and wisdom of the incarnate Word only appears in Revelation, where the risen Christ dominates. He is the first-born from the dead and Lord of all. He resides now in heaven, at the right hand of the Father, but he is active on behalf of his church, their champion against all their foes. When he rides out on his white horse to lay a scourge on such foes, his name is the Word of God (Revelation 19:13).

The author of Revelation is using a literary form ("apocalyptic") well-known to his Jewish contemporaries. In it God discloses what the future will be, usually to comfort his people, who are suffering persecution. The persecution of Christians by the Roman emperor Nero (37–68 AD or CE) may have been the occasion for the book of Revelation, but the book has served Christians of later ages as a treasure-trove of symbols for the life of the risen Christ.

For example, he is the lamb who was slain for the salvation of all human beings and so is worthy to receive power and wealth and wisdom and might and honor and glory and blessing (Revelation 5:12). He is also the dazzling Son of Man, the strange champion described in the book of Daniel (10:5–9) but described more fully at the outset of Revelation:

> I saw one like the Son of Man, clothed with a long robe and with a golden sash across his chest. His head and his hair were white as white wool, white as snow; his eyes were like a flame of fire, his feet were like burnished bronze, refined as in a furnace, and his voice was like the sound of many waters. In his right hand he held seven stars, and from his mouth came a sharp, two-edged sword, and his face was like the sun shining with full force. (Revelation 1:13–16)

The two-edged sword befits the status of the Son of Man as the Word of God. It cuts to joint and marrow, according to Hebrews (4:12), creating a crisis. People have to choose, for God or against. Again and again all four gospels make Jesus the occasion for a decision. People opposed to the revolution – personal, social, theological – implicit in the preaching of Jesus about the dawning of the reign of God find him a stumbling block, a scandal, long before his shameful death on a cross. Those among them most offended by his message, with its challenge to the status quo, turn murderous. They want to do away with Jesus, so that they do not have to deal with his demands. The evangelists see this reaction as a judgment on the world mired in the sin that began with Adam and Eve. In tandem with the encouraging positive response of some who heard Jesus, the willingness of a remnant to give him their faith, the reception that the Wisdom of God incarnate received becomes the touchstone of Christian realism. The fate of Jesus is the paradigmatic lesson, for Christians, in the moral transcendence of God.

God is light, in whom there is no darkness at all. God is love, the most creative of our human energies. God is life, completely full and unending. We human beings have an inclination toward the light. We find in love the best of our times. And we want life, both vitality now and union with God for eternity. But we cannot bear much reality. Our spirits are willing but our flesh is weak. Wisdom about our nature, our typical character, ought to include a significant caution about declaring us to be good. Protestants and Catholics have disagreed about the proper characterization of human nature, but no Christian family of churches (Protestant, Catholic, Orthodox, or, now, Evangelical) has overlooked the power of sin.

Sin is an aversion from the light of God, a flight from the love of God, a choice of a death among the fleshpots rather than a life gained by trekking through the deserts of penance and prayer. We are weak, easily mesmerized by baubles, willfully forgetful of the brutal fact that we are all soon to die. Christ, the wisdom and power of God, reveals what we are, the sin and grace in our lives, with troubling clarity. Jesus, like us in all things save sin, shows us in his wounds the depravity of our irreligion. So the wisdom of the *Logos* incarnate runs a full gamut. Everything that Christian believers want to say about right thought and right action ticks along unobtrusively in the message and work of Jesus of Nazareth, whom God raised from a terrible death to be the first-born of a new creation.

Last, can women subscribe to this Christian wisdom as fully as men? Why not? Much of it is generic, a challenge put to the experiences that all human beings have, as they go through life. Some feminist theologians think that a male savior cannot do the full job for women, while others so stress this generic quality of Christian wisdom that they lose the historical specificity of Jesus of Nazareth. Neither position is necessary. I believe that a theologian who denies that the Incarnation could have occurred in female flesh sins intellectually against the equality of women and men. But, granted the patriarchal character of history in the time of Jesus, I find the reality that *de facto* the Incarnation occurred in male flesh fully understandable. (The position espoused by Roman theology – the species of Catholic theology favored by the Vatican – to the effect that only males can represent Jesus the Christ in priestly functions – that a bodily likeness as male to male is necessary – seems to me highly dubious.)[5]

What I would have Christian feminists draw from the revelation of God available in Jesus is its counter-cultural quality. The values of Jesus are not the values of "the world," in any time. Inasmuch as women have lived on the margins of most historical cultures, denied official power and pressured to survive psychologically, sometimes even physically, by their wiles, we ought to be able to appreciate the freedom that the denial by Jesus of the going worldly values of his time opens up. We ought to see in the egalitarian cast of the ministry of Jesus his willingness to consort with all ranks of society, a good model for our own living freely, apart from stultifying conventions. The courage of Jesus, the fortitude of his wisdom, challenges our inclinations toward timidity, our fears of getting hurt, while the honesty of Jesus challenges our temptations to shade the truth, massage an ego, or forget a key fact. At the end of the day, Jesus responds as fully to the needs of women as to the needs of men. The light, love, and life expressed in the risen Christ of Revelation were as wonderful to Mary Magdalene as to Simon Peter.

Jesus: the Suffering of God

The life and death of Jesus involved considerable suffering. Christians believe that, as the *Logos* incarnate, Jesus was one person with two natures. The one person was divine, the second person of the Trinity, the eternal Son. The two natures were divine and human – Jesus was fully God and fully a man. Because the one person was divine, we may refer to the things that Jesus said and did, enjoyed and suffered, as acts, experiences, of God. Traditional Christian theology sometimes spoke of this freedom to attribute human experience to the divine Son as a *communicatio idiomatum* – a sharing of qualities from the two natures, based on the final unity of the ontological subject, the one divine person. One could say (ideally with enough explanation to avoid misunderstandings) that God died on the cross. One could also say that Jesus was always in union with the Father.

Now, before we take up the question of the suffering of God in Jesus, we need also to say that, as fully human, Jesus had what we now call a human "personality." The "person" at issue in the classical Christological confessions (for example, that of the Council of Chalcedon in 451) was not what we mean today by a personality. It was rather the bearer or recipient of the act of existence that finally makes a being be and shapes from within what it is, how it exists.

The implications of this distinction are considerable. For instance, in their portrayal of Jesus as fully human, the evangelists show him not knowing some things, having to learn other things, growing up as other boys did, feeling rejection and physical pain, and, finally, dying on the cross. None of these things fits with a strictly or solely divine being. As unlimited, absolute, God does not die, suffer any lack, find any positive future impenetrable. For Jesus to show such limitations reinforced the notion that he was fully human, a "person" or "personality" in the sense we give to those words in ordinary conversation today.

The most acute angle of this issue bears on the awareness that Jesus had of his own status. In the synoptic gospels he does not proclaim himself to be divine, and most of the claims we find there for his messiahship probably come from after his death and resurrection – are not sayings of the historical Jesus. In the gospel of John the "I am" sayings suggest that Jesus identified himself with the Mosaic divinity of Exodus (for instance, 3:14), but John is so highly structured and theological a work that one has to be cautious about taking the words of the Johannine Jesus as either solid history or flat declaration. Usually, the words of the Johannine Jesus are richly symbolic. For example, the words of address to God that we find in John 14–17 (the "high priestly prayer") seem to be more a theological portrayal of Jesus as already living in heaven (for many purposes, never having left heaven, inasmuch as "heaven" is primarily union with the Father), rather than preparing his spirit for earthly crucifixion.

So, whenever we take up the question of how the divine acted in Jesus of Nazareth, of what the divine Son experienced through the flesh taken from Mary, we delve into strict mysteries. Just as we cannot understand how the *Logos* could take flesh in the first place (how the infinite could let itself be contained by the finite), so we cannot understand what the *Logos* made of the experiences that came to Jesus in ordinary human fashion, through his senses and finite intellect. (The distinction that the Canadian theologian Bernard Lonergan makes, between oblique awareness of oneself as a subject and direct knowledge of oneself as an object, helps to suggest how Jesus may have experienced his own divinity. Lonergan would never claim, however, that even so sophisticated a theory of consciousness as his own draws the veil from the mystery of the Incarnation of the Word in Jesus of Nazareth.)

The plan of salvation chosen by God required the suffering of Jesus. The law of redemption that God established through the experience of Jesus was that suffering evil in love may reverse, overcome, the tit for tat, endless retaliation characterizing so much of human history. The divinity of Jesus shone most brightly for the Roman centurion whom Mark (15:39) treats as an objective, unbiased witness through his suffering and death. When the centurion says that Jesus was the Son of God, he speaks for the power that the innocent suffering of Jesus manifested. It was of such a purity, such an otherworldly character, that it brought the centurion to awe.

Let us meditate on this power of suffering, asking what it tells us about the Christian God. There is no doubt that God has power, unlimited power in fact, in the more obvious sense of the capacity to explode the atoms, fling the stars, get the amphibians crawling back to the sea. Jesus has a power to cure the sick, calm the winds, multiply the loaves, that strikes fear in the souls of onlookers. The Bible associates power with health, life, vitality, creativity, all of which it considers good, imprints of God. The Bible turns away from death, hatred, coldness, sterility, thinking them ungodly. Following this instinct, the early Christians rejected "patripassianism," the claim that the Father suffered with Jesus on the cross. The Father, standing most directly for the divine "monarchy" (oneness), could not suffer, because the Father, not incarnate, was unlimited perfection, as Greek Christian notions of divinity (total realization in act, no lack or taint from mortality) required.

Still, the Hebrew Bible is intrigued with characters such as Elijah, who finds God in a still small voice while hiding out from Jezebel, such as Esther, who becomes the King's concubine, so as to get his ear and save her people, such as Jacob, who wins through guile. Equally, the New Testament is intrigued by the rules of Christ's victory, which often seem paradoxical. Recall, for example, the first shall be last and the last first. Blessed are the poor in spirit. Jesus, the leader of them all, thought of himself as a servant, one who came to minister, not be ministered unto. Jesus, the Lord who would triumph in the resurrection, raising up in three days the temple of his body, comes for the synoptics in the conceptual clothing of the Suffering Servant of Second Isaiah and thought of himself as the Son of Man, a simple human being (as well as the splendid figure from Daniel), under way toward Jerusalem to meet his death. He had no choice in this matter, if we can believe the synoptics, and the suggestion of Peter that he avoid his fate struck him as Satanic. He was at war with Satan, was a strong man determined to tie Satan up and ransack his house. He was at war with a corrupt religious establishment that cared more about the letter of Torah, religious law, than the spirit, heaping up burdens where it should have been easing them. The sabbath was made for human beings, not human beings for the sabbath.

So the ways of Jesus were never the ways of the rich, the powerful, the esteemed. He was, in the striking phrase of John Meier, "a marginal Jew."[6] And he died as he had lived, scandalously, breaching many conventions. For a Jew to be strung up "on a tree," crucified, was accursed. For a Jew to be considered a criminal was a great blot. If we can believe the evangelists, the leaders of the religious establishment found Jesus guilty of blasphemy – making himself the equal of God. That was a capital crime, which Jesus was willing to commit rather than portray himself as the establishment pressured him to do.

The suffering of God revealed in Jesus stems from the waywardness of human beings. (We can leave to the side the question of whether there is a waywardness, a chaos or merely statistical order, in natural creation that puts it outside the peaceful divine control and in some way causes the Creator suffering.) A blindness of heart, darkness of character, even hatred of goodness makes some human beings oppose God, say no to the solicitations of God in their consciences. This is the mystery of evil, the surdity of sin. This is the height of irrationality, so commonplace that we cease to see its craziness. Bad people hate the light, because their deeds are evil. But why are their deeds evil? Whence comes the *fomes peccati*, the itchy will to sin? We do not know, and even the brilliance of the myth of the primordial sin that we find in Genesis does not give us an answer. We fear God, as well as love God, perhaps terrified that God will overwhelm us. We run from God, as well as toward God, because divinity is a mystery provoking terror, as well as great fascination.

Finally, feminist Christian theologians have special reasons to note the patience of God, as well as the patience built into Christian faith. Often the only reasonable course of action open to women in patriarchal cultures has been to endure, suffer, with what grace and indirect resistance to evil they could muster without being battered. Women can find it encouraging, therefore, to contemplate the patience of divinity itself, in both the crucifixion of Jesus and God's general dealings with history, both natural and human. This patience can indicate another reason to imagine God as a mother or sister or spouse wise enough to let the headstrong, the know-it-alls, get themselves into enough trouble, enough pain, to "come to themselves," as the prodigal son of Luke 15 does, and return home chastened, ready for instruction. The bruised reed God does not break. The smoking flax she does not quench. God is patient and merciful, long-suffering and abounding in steadfast love. She cares nothing for partial victories, temporary triumphs worked by threat or fear. She wants the whole mind, heart, soul, and strength, which people will only give when they have been persuaded, brought to a free gift of themselves in love.

The sufferings requisite for mature Christian faith include the endurance of conflict with the world, of embarrassment at one's own stubborn sinfulness, and, if we are fortunate, blessed, of anguish at separation from God. We have here, in space and time, no lasting city. We believe, according to the ancient Creed, in the Holy Ghost, the holy catholic church, the communion of saints, the forgiveness of sins, the resurrection of the body, and the life of the world to come. Our hopes reach well beyond anything this-worldly, tangible, able to fit into a security box at the local bank.

We believe in the forgiveness of sins: relief for the shame that our stupidity and selfishness cause us, pardon for the pains we inflict on others. We believe in the resurrection of the body: what Jesus gained through suffering can become our gain. We believe in the life of the world to come: if we have suffered for our faith with our eyes limited to worldly benefits, we are of all people the most to be pitied.

The full horizon that Christian faith requires, to make what sense of the grace of God that took sacramental form in Jesus it can, stretches to where Jesus ended, at the right hand of the Father. These images are not the psychic projections that Marxists and other followers of Feuerbach deride. These images are the fruits of Christians' long, intense meditation on the fate of Jesus, his sufferings and his triumphs. Inasmuch as women have had a full measure of suffering throughout history, and continue to have a full measure today, the patience of God, and God's reversal of the destruction implied in suffering, through the resurrection of Jesus the Christ, carry to women a message all too relevant. God knows our sufferings in all their details. God sees the victories and defeats we endure as we try to cope with our sufferings, small and great. God wants to wipe every tear from our eyes and make death be no more. All that is implied by the resurrection of Jesus, indeed trumpeted by Revelation.[7]

The Trinity: God as Father and Mother

In order to "locate" Jesus the Christ, the Incarnate Word, we have had to deal with the uniquely Christian view that God is a trinitarian community. If, as the Creeds say, the Word who became incarnate was, is, "God from God, Light from Light, True God from True God, begotten not made, one in substance with the Father, through whom all things were made," then to locate Jesus adequately one has to deal with the Father, his divine source and the God whom he worshipped through his humanity.

People not brought up on these creeds find the notion of the Trinity difficult, even incomprehensible. Thinking purely logically, they want God to be either one or three. One seems easier to handle, especially for Jews and Muslims, whose God is sole, unique, the only Lord they can accredit. But the Christian doctrine of God, for all its dependence on Israelite monotheism and Greek philosophy, has never been determined by pure logic. It has developed from a careful, at its best loving, study of how in the New Testament Jesus deals with God.

Without doubt, Jesus deals with God as though God were his Father. God is for him personal, absolutely trustworthy, intimate, never failing. Even in times of desolation, when he is tempted to feel forsaken, Jesus turns to his God, commends his spirit into his Father's keeping. If he, or we, ask this God for bread, we will not receive a stone. If we ask for an egg, we will not receive a scorpion. Nine times out of ten, ninety-nine times out of a hundred, we fail on the side of distrust. Looking at us, typical potential disciples, Jesus has to say, "O ye of little faith." The main argument of Jesus for trust in God proceeds *a fortiori*. If we, evil as we are, know how to give our children good things, want our children to flourish, how much more strongly must God, our heavenly Father, want our flourishing, want to give us good things.

From his trust in God, his Father ("Abba," "Daddy"), Jesus derives a distinctive freedom and authority. Onlookers marvel at the directness of his teaching. He does not argue from precedents, the consensus of rabbinic authorities. He argues, commands, from his own perceptions. The sabbath was made for human beings, not human beings for the sabbath, because Jesus finds it clear that God, his Father, wants the life of the sinner, not the sinner's perishing. The Law, the codes geared to sanctifying the sabbath, are only as good as what they contribute to the life of the sinner. Irenaeus, an influential second-century Greek Father, said that the glory of God is human beings fully alive. A sabbath law that got separated from serving the full vitality of human beings would not be holy but an idol.

The freedom of Jesus was as distinctive as the authority with which he preached. When Jesus consorted with "sinners," those whom the Law accounted unclean or retrograde, he broke the rules of propriety governing the rabbis of his day. When Jesus dealt freely with women such as Martha and Mary, accepting them as disciples, he again moved against the grain. Where did Jesus get such freedom of spirit? What made him think that what he said or felt moved to do could be more authoritative than longstanding traditions?

The answer that makes most sense is that Jesus found in his relationship with his heavenly Father a great sense of both freedom and power. Theologians might reason that the man Jesus experienced in human terms all that a member of our species could of the intimacy existing eternally between the Father and the divine Son. However, the evangelists appear to have worked from the other end, first describing how Jesus dealt with God (and with other people), then realizing that his ways made Jesus unique – surely the Messiah, perhaps considerably more.

Later Christian theologians took this New Testament patrimony to the bank, working out the terms for declaring Jesus to have been strictly divine: the incarnation of the *Logos*. What the Prologue of John, the famous hymn in Colossians (1:15–20), the dazzling visions laid out in the first chapters of Revelation, and other famous texts said with more or less clarity, the later conciliar theologians expressed beyond doubt: the God of Jesus is a community of three divine persons possessing one divine nature; Jesus himself is one divine person possessing two natures, one divine and one human.

In the Christian trinitarian understanding of God, the Father is the first person. For Augustine, who used a triad of memory, understanding, and will as an analogue for the three persons, the Father is like the nearly endless capacity of our human minds to delve into the past and call back experiences of yesteryear. The limitlessness of memory, the sense of being at the unbounded origin or bottom of the mind, recommended it to Augustine. Convinced that the biblical notion that we human beings are images of God is verified principally in our human spirituality, Augustine concentrated on attributes of mind and will.

Aquinas, who took Augustine and Aristotle as his prime mentors, refined this "psychological analogy." For him the Father was like an infinite act of understanding (insight), the Son was like the inner word or concept that an act of understanding generates (in this case, equally infinite), and the Spirit was like the (infinite) love that their mutual recognition of goodness might stimulate in the Father and the Son.

Whether as memory, unlimited understanding, or aboriginal paternity (generativity), the Father is the first person, the primary possessor of divinity, the source of everything either divine or human. Since designations such as these refer to realities outside of space and time, not framed by the limits ordering creation, what they yield is more unlike than like what the Father is in himself. We cannot understand how the Father can be both the source of the Son and the Spirit and their equal in the possession of divinity. The subordination of the second and third persons to the first is more conceptual than real. For our human need to put order into the divine relations, the Father serves as the foundation, the origin, the personal reality that is absolutely (unconditionally) ultimate.

True, the Father is paternal, generative, through relations with the Son and Spirit. They color how we think about the Father, what his absoluteness means, brings forth, shows of his character. But the generativity of the Father is so perfect that the second and third persons are as fully divine as he. They may be derivative, and he underived, but what he establishes through the relations constituting the second and third persons are perfect expressions of his unlimited divine light, love, and life.

Clearly, trinitarian theology involves hard work at the borders of human imagination. We must take our best perceptions of community and extrapolate them toward an asymptotic point where they would suffer no limitations. The psychological analogy orients us to consider carefully our centrally human capacities for knowing and loving. For example, when we understand something significant, a light dawns. We know why Archimedes rushed from the bath shouting, "Eureka." We also know that we tend to express our understanding – that it generates images and concepts spontaneously.

Grasp the reason, the logic, the order of a row of numbers such as 5, 10, 2, 0.2, 0.1, 0.5 and you will experience a minor insight, the flash of a 60 watt bulb. Extrapolate this flash, this act of understanding, so that it has no limits and you glimpse the light in which the Father dwells, which the Father is. Notice the connection between your act of understanding and the formula expressing the order of the row of numbers, the conceptual form into which the mind seems inclined spontaneously to render its act of understanding, and you will get an inkling of the relationship between the Father and the Son – between the infinite light of understanding that depends on nothing outside itself and the infinite Word that renders perfectly what the Father knows and is.

The formula rendering this little row of numbers is the relation between the new entry and its predecessor. The next number in the sequence would be 5: 10 is twice 5 (2); 2 is a fifth of 10 (0.2); 0.2 is a tenth of 2 (0.1); 0.1 is half of 0.2 (0.5); 0.5 is five times 0.1 (5). No world-class intelligibility is at stake in this example. At best it may furnish those who like puzzles an occasion for experiencing a small-scale insight. To repeat: the light of that insight, the illumination that comes when one understands, grasps the intelligibility of the sequence, is the experiential basis Aquinas offers for thinking of the Father as an active unlimited light. The relationship between the Father and the Son seems like that between our human insights and the formulas or concepts that we use spontaneously to express them. In the nature of the case (our finite minds dealing with an infinite divinity), this analogy is more unlike what the Father is in himself and how the Father relates to the Son than like them. But it gives us a clue, a hint, a suspicion.

If we entertain the understandable desire of feminist Christian theologians to imagine God, think about God, in feminine terms, we find that among human beings understanding, conceptualization, and love (we deal with the procession of the Spirit as unlimited divine love in the next section) are not tied to sex. Certainly social factors shape how we human beings tend to think and love, so that gender (sex as creating different images of the self and different social roles) is a factor in our intellectual activity. But women have insights much as men do, and women can express their insights much as men can. The successful performance of female scientists, mathematicians, linguists and the like shows that human intelligence has a central channel or panel that makes sex and gender subordinate to something common to women and men.

Whether we ought to consider this common something the image of God is another question, best reserved for another day of theological speculation. The point here is that it would change nothing essential in the psychological analogy to make the first person "the Mother" instead of "the Father." The mother could be unlimited understanding. The second person, either Son or Daughter, could be the unlimited Word expressing this unlimited understanding. And the Spirit could be the love of Mother and Child, the unlimited act of appreciation flowing from the mutual acknowledgment of the first and second persons that each is fully good, holy, beautiful, and so on.

If we deal more concretely with the generative overtones of the root metaphor (father–son) that governs traditional Christian thought about the first two divine persons, asking what would change were we to call the first person "Mother," we find that generativity can remain. A mother is the source of a child, the parent of a child, just as a father is. Indeed, the mother is this source, this parent, more obviously than the father. The patriarchal culture in which Jesus lived suggested that he call his parental God "Father." A matriarchal culture no doubt would have inclined him, or the female in whom the Word of God had taken flesh, to call this parental God "Mother." The core of the relationship would not have changed. Parenthood and generativity would be equal in both cases.

What, though, about the differences that might come from calling God "Mother" rather than "Father"? It is impossible to know what they would be, in anything like full detail, because they would develop slowly, through ongoing Christian prayer, ethical behavior, theological reflection, political activity, experience of family life, and so forth. If "Our Mother, who art in heaven, hallowed be thy name" became the first line of the most central Christian prayer, the one we call "The Lord's," Christian prayer might become slightly less formal, Christian awe might give way somewhat to quicker intimacy. This suggestion depends on an assumption that children, both male and female, tend to find mothers less daunting than fathers, fathers more commanding and aloof.

Certainly, the relationship between Jesus and his heavenly Father is warm, intimate, fully trusting. Nothing sexual or stemming from gender determines that the relationship between a child and a parent have this or that degree of warmth or formality. Still, overall, mothers seem to have more spontaneous and flexible relationships with their children than fathers do. If only because mothers carry children in their own bodies and nourish children from their own bodies, mothers tend to dominate the first years of any child's life, boy as much as girl. However complicated parent–child relationships become as time goes on, this original relationship, which the child can barely remember, seems often, usually, to remain a basis for mothers being less daunting than fathers, fathers being felt by children to be more formidable than mothers.

In my opinion, when one has gone across the major cultural systems that have developed in history, this is what one tends to find. The underside of the patriarchal arrangements that have prevailed in recorded human history is a closer association of children with mothers than with fathers. Indeed, "women and children" is often a compound class set over if not against "men."

For theologians free of the need to make God the most macho of male leaders, an intimacy with creatures based on the closeness of human mothers to their children could give the Creator more warmth, make the Creator more approachable, make easier the creature's sense of trust than has been true of the standard Christian imagery. It could make it more natural for us to think of the three divine persons as easy in their communal life, fluid, intimate, conversational, cooperative, mutually supportive. This is not to say that the presently dominant trinitarian imagery, Father-Son-Spirit, excludes these characteristics or inclines us to think that the divine persons do not enjoy such characteristics. It is only to say that, if (hypothetically, *ex suppositione*) women tend to develop communities, groups, circles of sharing where these qualities are more apparent than they are in groups of men, then thinking of the first person in the Trinity as "Mother" rather than "Father" could take us in the direction of imaging the entire common life of the three persons in more feminine terms (all the more so if we thought of the second person, the Word, as "Daughter").

Last, we should note the difference between convention and dogma (here taken in the positive, non-pejorative sense of doctrine that has been established authoritatively as official and obligatory). It is conventional in Christian discourse on the Trinity to speak of Father-Son-Spirit, but there is nothing in Christian dogma that forbids speculating about the fittingness of considering God to be "Mother" as well as "Father" (indeed, Pope John Paul I explicitly affirmed this fittingness, as have many Protestant feminist theologians), nor is there anything that forbids speculating about the likely consequences of such a consideration.

God is not limited by sex. In calling God our Father, we employ a metaphor (bound to be privileged, because used by Jesus) that compounds unlikeness to what divinity is in itself with (lesser) likeness. If we call God our Mother, we gain no greater likeness, but also no greater unlikeness. We speak less as Jesus did, but perhaps more as the religious needs of present-day women require. Overall, as children of God we have the liberty to imagine, reason, speculate as honesty and a strong desire to keep faith with Christian tradition dictate. Anything good, noble, true suggests what divinity is like. Motherhood can be good, noble, and true, just as fatherhood can. Motherhood is as valid an image for the generativity of God as fatherhood.

The Trinity: God as Inclusive Spirit

The third person of the Christian trinitarian divinity, the Holy Spirit, is the love proceeding from the mutual knowledge of the first two persons. For the psychological analogy that finds our human operations of knowing and loving to be the best expression of how we are images of God, the Spirit comes forth from the relationship of the first two persons as a breath of admiration, appreciation, warmth, love. One of the most endearing patristic figures for the Spirit is that he, she, it is the kiss of the Father and the Son. One of the best recent images, proposed by the German Catholic theologian Karl Rahner, is that the Spirit is "God given and received." To the Spirit we tend to attribute the work of sanctification. If Jesus, the second person incarnate, accomplished the work of salvation, the Spirit presides to the present day over the ongoing work of our taking grace to heart, becoming holy as the life of God displayed in the resurrection of Jesus invites us to become.

The Pauline figure of the Spirit moving in our depths, making our prayer with sighs too deep for words (Romans 8:26), has encouraged Christian theologians to ponder the primacy of the Spirit, the divine, in our sanctification. The stress of the classical Protestant reformers on the priority of grace, along with their intense study of the scriptures, made them take the gratuity of justification (standing before God as righteous, not requiring condemnation) as a standard theological assumption. Justification comes by faith, by grace, by the action of God, not by human works. It is the Spirit of God who makes people holy, not what people themselves can do.

Christians have seldom laid out precisely the relations between the work of Christ and the work of the Spirit. From New Testament times, the two works have spilled over any barriers erected to restrain them to nicely separated conceptual channels. The Spirit is the Spirit of Christ, as well as the Spirit of the Father. The Spirit descends on Jesus at his baptism, strengthening him for his ministry. It drives Jesus into the desert, for his boot-camp and first encounter with Satan. At Pentecost the Spirit descends on the first disciples, making them a full church. The growth of the church, as we observe it in Luke and Acts, is the work of the Spirit, the inmost pulse of the history of salvation. When Paul approaches Rome, Christianity has reached the center of what Luke imagined to be the ecumene, the whole inhabited world. All this is the work of the Spirit, of God in our midst, of the paraclete given by Jesus to continue the work of oversight, encouragement, guidance that he began with the disciples face to face.

Within the Trinity, the Spirit does not stand in a linear relation to the first and second persons, as though the divine persons were peas in a pod or three little piggies. The Spirit bends back, as it were, to encircle the divine whole (without limiting it) and so to effect what traditional Christian theology has called the *perichoresis* of the three. They dwell within one another. They overlap, copenetrate, suffuse one another. Take your best images for human communion – sexual union, the symbiosis of mother and child, the *homonoia* (like-mindedness) of friendship, whatever – and extrapolate them toward perfection. The oneness of mind, heart, affection that you find yourself appreciating comes to the divine persons, expresses itself, through their *perichoresis*.

The Latin translation of this Greek term, *circumincessio*, is more graphic. The divine persons abide around and in one another. The flow, the circulation, of the inner life of God makes the three persons concentric, coupled (trebled), like Russian dolls nested within one another, like lovers entangled in their sleep. Without destroying their relational difference, the three are partakers of one another, inseparable, equally stretched to an infinity both linear and circular, one God yet varied, full of color, spilling outside easy categories and so requiring us to employ social as well as individualistic images.

The "circulation" of the Spirit around, perhaps through, the personal realms of the first two persons makes love a divine medium, the fluid of the divine life (blood, lymph, bile – everything liquid in our human vitality comes to mind). The Spirit also tends to bear a feminine persona, in part because of its associations with creation and wisdom. As Genesis depicts creation, the Spirit moves over the primeval waters, like a bird brooding. The wisdom of God is the reason by which creation and salvation occur, the divine plan. Substantially, this reason relates to the *Logos*, the second divine person, who expresses the divine nature and consciousness (self-understanding) fully. Operationally, the unfolding of both natural history and the history of salvation (the crux of human history) comes under the guidance of the Spirit. According to the classical creeds, the Spirit is the Lord and giver of life, the wisdom that spoke through the prophets. What Jesus was for his disciples, the Spirit has become for those who deal with Jesus by faith, not having seen him in the flesh.

The Johannine stress on *abiding* in God, resting in the relationship with the Father, himself, and the Spirit that Jesus has established, suggests how the life of grace (divinization now, in time) relates to the life of glory (consummation, after death, in heaven). The substance of the communion with God that faith in Jesus makes possible is available now, through the work of the Spirit. As the lives of the saints suggest, the importance of God can increase more and more, the self-centered concerns of the individual decrease. At the extreme, where one can speak of sanctity in a formal sense (extra-ordinary holiness), the individual can resemble Jesus in defining herself, himself, mainly in terms of relations with God.

The Johannine Jesus (14:8–14) told Philip that anyone who dealt with him dealt with the Father: he and the Father were one (10:30). We may take this as an expression of the divine *perichoresis* in the psychology that John imagines the earthly Jesus to have enjoyed. Never separated from his Father, always led by the divine Spirit, the Johannine Jesus moves on earth as an emissary of heaven, his flesh the prime site of revelation. His works of healing become sacramental signs, testifying to both the goodness of God and the authenticity of his prophetic speech on behalf of God. His death becomes the great disclosure of how radically God has loved the world.

The glory of God comes into the world from the moment of the incarnation of the Johannine Jesus. Reminiscing, the beloved disciple recalls the impact that Jesus made on people like himself, pious Jews sensitive to the call of the God of Moses:

> And the Word became flesh and lived among us, and we have seen his glory, the glory as of a father's only son, full of grace and truth. (John [the Baptist] testified to him and cried out, "This was he of whom I said, 'He who comes after me ranks ahead of me because he was [in heaven] before me.'") From his fullness we have all received, grace upon grace. The law indeed was given through Moses; grace and truth came through Jesus Christ. No one has ever seen God. It is God the only Son, who is close to the Father's heart, who has made him known. (John 1:14–18)

So the distinction narrows between grace and glory, life with God now, in space and time, and divine life untrammeled in heaven. Inasmuch as the Spirit of God moves in the hearts of believers, they enjoy an abiding with God like the germ, the seed, of a heavenly exfoliation. The seed will only burst into full flower after death, when the constraints of space and time have fallen away. But the life of God coloring, taking up, the inmost existence of the earthly believer is the same life that the 144,000 of Revelation express in their worship of God with unending hymns of praise.

Because the Spirit of God, the third person of the traditional Trinity, is not tied to a historically male personage as is the second person, feminist Christian theologians have been attracted to the project of thinking constructively about the third person as a feminine dimension or force in God. I find this project both praiseworthy and, frequently, simple-minded.

On the one hand, a praiseworthy desire to give women a rich sense of what their being images of God means makes this project praiseworthy. This same desire has led feminists to ponder the implications of calling God "Mother," and it has led to reflections on the feminine characteristics of the Wisdom of God incarnate in Jesus. For the third person, such a desire has stimulated efforts to imagine the Spirit as a fertile, supportive divine presence carrying forward both the creation of the world and the sanctification of human beings. There is much, then, to praise in recent feminist thought about the divine Spirit.

On the other hand, the rules governing all orthodox thought about God, constraining all images and concepts, apply to the divine Spirit. It does not bring the Spirit deeper into our control to imagine her as female than it does to imagine him as male, or to imagine it as impersonal. The Spirit is as much divine, unlimited and sovereign, as are the first and second persons. The key attribute of the Spirit, determined by the Johannine Jesus when he called the Spirit our paraclete, is the support of divine life in us. For the Christian, this divine life comes through faith in Jesus the Christ, and it remains the substance of the gift that the Father has offered to all human beings, through Jesus and in their Spirit. (Eastern Orthodoxy intuits that the Spirit proceeds from the Father, and so implies, logically, that the priority of the Father extends to both the love circulating within the Trinity and the work of sanctification going on in our human realm). Nothing in this substance changes if we make the Spirit feminine.

This attribute of supporting divine life in us, and the other works of the Spirit, fit well with a gentle, delicate feminine persona, but they also fit well with a powerful, courageous male persona. The Spirit is both delicate and explosively powerful. No stereotypes serve pneumatology (study of the Spirit) well, because the Spirit, like divinity in general, is the ground and source of creative beings, the truly prime analogy or fontal archetype. It can never become second to a created instance that would be, in itself, more illuminating. We may find a human analogy useful, but we ought always to remember that our analogies fall far short of what the Holy Spirit is in herself.

The Spirit is intrinsically mysterious, not even given to us in embodied form, as Jesus gives us the Word, not even given to us as an Image of God (the patristic theme that the Incarnate Word is the prime icon of the Father). Such figures as we have – a dove, tongues of fire, seven spirits before the divine throne, a divine breath carrying love – illumine little. They remind us of the gentleness of the divine operations within us, which all masters of discernment underscore. They suggest the burning purity of God, even in our midst, our impure hearts. They remind us that before God, and in the midst of the church, the Spirit makes present the fullness of divine spirituality (seven is the apocalyptic number of perfection, completeness). And they tell us that all that God is comes to us on a breath of love caressing our cheek, consoling our heart.

At the end of any faith-filled, traditional considerations of the third person, or of God as trinitarian, or of the Christian divinity as incarnate in Jesus, or of the one God as near and far, our tongues should stop, our minds shut down, our hearts strip away all desire other than a great longing for worship. God is too much for us, on every side, in every way. The Spirit helps us to worship this God always greater, taking up our fumbling efforts and somehow making them equal to what God deserves.

The mystery of God, whether one or three, whether outside of time or enfleshed in Jesus, knocks us on the head, kicks us in the teeth, and seduces our hearts with an incomparable beauty, sweetness, purity. Christians do best to follow the counsel of the Johannine Jesus and abide simply, lovingly, in the grace of God, the Spirit of

Jesus come through faith. The more they inform themselves about the prayer of the foremost Christian saints, the more fitting such a simple, self-abandoning contemplation will seem.

Perhaps the major crisis in Christian faith today is the illiteracy of most believers. They know barely a fraction of the spiritual history, the internal dramas, of the great cloud of witnesses that has preceded them. Seldom have they put themselves to school ascetically, for the reformation of their character. Usually their greater effort has been to put themselves to school intellectually, in pursuit of some worldly competence.

It is not surprising, then, that talk about a mysterious God, a trinitarian community of life, light, and love that makes it the sole fullness of reality, strikes them initially as strange, even absurd. They have no language, no training, equipping them to handle this analysis, this theology developed from the New Testament. Nonetheless, the reality remains, active for their transformation. God does not require our acknowledgment, either to be God or do us good. No matter how thick our ignorance, how perverse our resistance, God is always greater. Indeed, it is hard to escape God, thank God.[8]

Study Questions

1   Is a limited, finite God a contradiction in terms?
2   What is the problem with turning the immanence of God into pantheism?
3   Does the Christian view of the Incarnation and the divinity of Jesus make a radical Christian feminism impossible?
4   How ought Christian feminists to understand the crucifixion?
5   Describe a Christian Trinity that made the first person God the Mother.
6   How adequate would it be to describe the Holy Spirit as "God given and received"?
7   Why is (or is not) the major crisis in Christian faith today the illiteracy of most believers?

Notes

1   See Tadeusz Skorupski, "Prajna," in *The Encyclopedia of Religion*, ed. Mircea Eliade (Macmillan, New York, 1987), vol. 11, pp. 477–81.

2 See in *The Encyclopedia Judaica* (Keter, Jerusalem, 1972) the articles "Shekinah" (vol. 14, pp. 1349–54) and "Kabbalah" (vol. 10, pp. 515–16).
3 See Charles Hartshorne, "Pantheism and panentheism," in *The Encyclopedia of Religion*, vol. 11, pp. 165–71.
4 See Catherine Mowry LaCugna, *God for Us: the Trinity and Christian Life* (Harper San Francisco, San Francisco, 1991).
5 On feminist revisions of Christology, see Maryanne Stevens (ed.), *Reconstructing the Christ Symbol* (Paulist, New York, 1993). On feminist revisions of Christian theology as a whole, see Catherine Mowry LaCugna (ed.), *Freeing Theology* (Harper San Francisco, San Francisco, 1993).
6 See John Meier, *A Marginal Jew* (Doubleday, New York, 1991).
7 As landmark studies of New Testament Christology, the two volumes of Edward Schillebeeckx, *Jesus* and *Christ* (Seabury, New York, 1979, 1980), remain extremely significant.
8 On the Holy Spirit, see Yves Congar, *I Believe in the Holy Spirit*, three volumes (Seabury, New York, 1983).

Chapter 8

PRACTICE
ETHICS AND SPIRITUALITY

A Christian Feminist View of Ethics

In a recent study,[1] I analyzed some current Christian feminist works on ethics, concluding that the major lack was neglect of traditional Christian theology. Most of the works did not deal with the ethical implications of a traditional, high Christology – with the longstanding Christian conviction that ethics, behavior, living the good life is an imitation of Christ. To launch this opening description of how I think a constructive Christian feminist theology ought to deal with ethical matters, let me develop the notion of "imitating" Christ.

The most explicit New Testament text is 1 Corinthians 11:1, where Paul says, "Be imitators of me as I am of Christ." The apostles, among whom Paul counts himself because of his encounter with Christ during his dramatic conversion (Acts 9), mediate to later Christian believers the ways and means of Christ. Jewish in their religious formation, they know that masters teach by their entire bearing. How Jesus reclined at his last meal with them gave the apostles a lesson in intimacy, just as surely as his washing their feet gave them a lesson in humility and service. The ministry of Jesus was a teaching conveyed by deeds, gestures, looks, and silences, as much as by words. The rhythm that Jesus followed of immersion, to help sick people (sheep without a shepherd), and withdrawal, to pray in lonely places, became a paradigm for general Christian living. The wandering of Jesus, his having during his public years no place to lay his head, impressed on the Christian imagination the freedom from possessions, local neighborhoods, even blood relatives that the life of faith ought to inspire. In every way, the Incarnation implied that the man Jesus was the living exemplar of how God wanted human beings to live.

Clearly, the imitation of Christ cannot be slavish, a matter of replicating physical details. In the first place, we know few of these details: how Jesus chose to dress, wear his hair, eat, amuse himself. In the second place, times change, customs vary, each new historical age requires a new cultural adaptation, translation, of what the good news means. The Christianity of second-century Rome is bound to differ from that of thirteenth-century Paris or twentieth-century Manila. Any imitation of Christ worth taking seriously has to penetrate to something substantial underlying the accidental variations that historical epoch and geographical locale are bound to introduce.

The New Testament supplies the substantial picture of Jesus on which all later generations have had to rely. That picture makes it clear that Jesus dedicated himself to carrying out what he thought was the Father's will for him. The crux of this will was his preaching the good news that the Reign of God was dawning. Now was the hour of salvation, the exceptional time of grace. Slowly, the man Jesus realized that fidelity to the will of the Father might cost him his life. At the end, when crucifixion was imminent, he kept faith with the Father by commending his spirit into the Father's keeping. By then he was living far outside worldly values, concentrating only on pleasing God and providing as best he could for his followers.

The resurrection of Jesus, vague and mysterious as the New Testament makes it, was the Father's seal ratifying the way that Jesus walked. The resurrection was much more than a legal ratification, of course, demonstrating for believers the power of God to inaugurate a new era, a new creation, in which divine life would limit, indeed defeat, creaturely death. But for people asking whether the way that Jesus had walked, the good news that Jesus had preached, had the approbation of God, the resurrection supplied a precise affirmative answer. Jesus had pleased God so fully that God took the unprecedented step of rescuing him from death publicly and establishing him in heaven. Without the resurrection, the career of Jesus might still seem noble, but we would have to speak of it as a tragic tale: heavenly ideals brought low by human baseness. The resurrection overturns all this negativity, making the story of Jesus a comedy: something at which God smiles. Inasmuch as the story of Jesus becomes the narrative framework for any Christian's self-understanding, any Christian's life can also be a comedy: a playful passage through space and time in trust that a good God will give the passenger a grand finale.

The imitation of Christ crucial to a precisely Christian ethics depends on our making Jesus the unique, nonpareil revelation of God, and on our accepting the resurrection of Jesus as a definitive triumph. If we cut out of the Christian creed the articles proclaiming the divinity of Jesus the Christ and the resurrection of their bodies that his resurrection invites all believers to hope will be their own destiny, we eviscerate Christian faith beyond recognition. In consequence, we eviscerate as well the engine, the powerhouse, of a distinctively Christian ethics. Behavior follows upon being. If Jesus was not divine, then the things that he said, the works that he worked, had no unique authority, were not revelation not available anywhere else. Similarly, if the resurrection of Jesus is only a myth, nothing realistic grounding how Christians ought to lean into their own futures, then Christian ethics ought to content itself with a this-worldly horizon, one idealistic but finally tragic.

In my opinion, Christian feminist theologians inherit the entirety of this foundational view of ethics, both the demands that it makes and the privileges that it confers. My sense of the relations between the terms "Christian" and "feminist" will always give the first precedence over the second, because the first is the basis for everything transcendent in the claims that Christian feminists have to adjudicate and ought to promote. Without Christ, there is no trinitarian God, no gracious offer of divinization, no salvation from the radical sin implied by the anthropology of the Bible, no incarnation of the Word of God that makes history, human being in time, the foremost revelation of what ultimate reality is like, of how the goodness of God works for our wellbeing.

Compared to the heavenly life that Christian faith promises, not as pie in the sky but as a consequence of the resurrection of Jesus, any this-worldly fulfillments or ameliorations that feminist thought or politics can hope to accomplish are minor. The problem with many present-day feminist Christian theologies and ethical programs, as I suggested earlier, is their neglect of what ought to be their powerhouse. They try to make do with the *eros* of sisterhood, or with rage at historical injustices. These can be significant sources of energy and insight, but compared to the precisely "supernatural" (for theologians the word implies not something occult, rather our being lifted beyond our just deserts, by the grace of God – our being invited to partake of the deathless divine nature) benefits of Christian faith, I find that a secular feminist program pales to distinctly secondary status.

I also find in orthodox Christian faith a brand-new, much fuller basis for sexual equality. The life of God is not determined by sex or gender. The goodness of God allows no vicious discriminations. The more fully we imitate Jesus in living outside our own selfishness, living by the power of God's Spirit to transform our space and time, the less sexist and more egalitarian we ought to become. What matters is how a given person, female or male, acts and is treated. Stereotypes recede in significance. Political correctness and ideological cant tend to shrink. For the Spirit leads us to the elementary wisdom that people are richer than labels, and then to the intermediate wisdom that we can work doggedly at structural reform without becoming single-issue maniacs, lobbyists with tunnel vision.

If we imitate Christ, we make God our prime treasure. Better, we let the reality of God, the goodness and love of God, take over our hearts. This begins in faith, and faith must always carry it forward, but as we live our way into it more deeply, the reality of God produces its own warrants, proofs, evidences. These are evidences of the efficacy, the good results, of loving outside, beyond ourselves. We cannot prove that our God is fully faithful, any more than we can prove that our spouse or friend or child will never let us down. But we can commit ourselves to the relationship with our mysterious God, the love, reasonably, with a confidence that is not foolish, because year by year we find it good to live that way.

If intimacy with God, on the model of the intimacy of Jesus with his Father, becomes our goal, the treasure around which we at least want our life to circle, then our behavior, how we treat other people, think about other people and the natural world, evaluate money and status, and so on ought to reflect the holiness of God, the warmth and light of the divine love. No doubt we shall fail regularly both to achieve an exceptional union with God and to manifest in our behavior an exceptional goodness, but when we think ethically, about how we ought to behave, the life of God will be our beacon and touchstone.

The briefest summary of Christian values appears in the twofold commandment that Jesus left. His followers are to love God, with their whole minds, hearts, souls, and strengths, and they are to love their neighbors as themselves. This program comes from Deuteronomy and other sources bred into Jesus as part of his Jewish heritage. Scripture scholars debate what distinctive overtones Jesus may have placed upon it, but apart from this debate it seems clear that Jesus wanted love to be the basic disposition of his followers. The Johannine theology says that God is love (1 John 4:8). Certainly, God is other good things – light, life – but traditional Christian theology accords love primacy of place. Love is the best "explanation" of what moves God in creation, salvation, conferring heavenly life. Love is the best explanation of how the divine persons relate to one another. Among us human beings, love offers the best chance to soften our hearts, convert us from selfishness, bring about forgiveness and new beginnings. We feel most fully alive, reach the heights of wellbeing, through falling in love. We depend on the tough, practical love of members of our family and friends to get us through hard times.

What does the primacy of love in a Christian scale of values imply for a Christian feminist ethics? Perhaps that feminists trying to imitate Christ ought freely to explore the wisdom that women's experience of love makes available. For, even if we discount the stereotype that assigns women a larger portion of (emotional) love than men and a smaller portion of (sober) reason, we have to note that women's relations with children, and perhaps also women's culturally conditioned experiences of romance, incline many women to stress emotional support, tenderness, considerateness, and other forms of warmth or interest that carry significant doses of feeling more than many men do. Love is both rational and emotional. Love both stems from knowledge and creates a unique knowledge of its own.

We see those whom we love differently than we did before we fell in love with them, and we expose ourselves to them more nakedly. The Bible speaks of Adam's "knowing" Eve when it wants to designate sexual intercourse. Medieval Christian theologians spoke of a "connatural" knowledge stemming from intimate love, whether that of human lovers or that joining the soul to God. The Spirit of

God, the eternal love circulating in the Trinity, is full of such a connatural knowledge. Father, Son, and Spirit are transparent to one another, all for one and one for all. The best feminist circles verge on a connatural love, as over time what began as a group becomes a community.

Women are not necessarily better lovers than men, but many cultures place fewer inhibitions on women's freedom to express their affections, and their sorrows, than they place on men's. This could mean that a Christian feminist ethics encouraged women to express wholeheartedly their love of life, their trust in God, their being moved by the sufferings of the poor and sickly. It could mean that the willingness of Jesus to deal with all strata of the society of his time, to break many rules of propriety, and to oppose what he considered an irreligious power structure came into women's minds and hearts as a liberating heritage.

Jesus had little concern for his social image, what others thought of him. Knowing what was in people's hearts, he realized that human applause is usually a mixed blessing. He was no neurotic, only happy when people attacked him, but the prime motive of his action was never human respect. The prime motive of his action was love of God and love of neighbor. What Christian feminists most need to imitate is this passionate twofold love, adapting their behavioral expression of it to the range of possibilities open to their gender in their particular locale, and then perhaps transcending that range – acting as free spirits able to leave many local restrictions far behind, able, in the spirit of Augustine, to love and do what they will.

Community as an Ethical Touchstone

When we ask whether a certain course of action or policy is wise, by the criteria of a Christian feminist ethics, we may usefully employ as one of our touchstones how this course of action or policy is likely to affect our community. As well, we ought as a matter of course to ask how it seems to square with traditional wisdom – how Christian communities have thought about such matters in the past.

The longstanding rules for discerning the spirits at work in the hearts of individuals stress that the key pattern is what happens over time – the "fruits" of which Jesus spoke (Matthew 7:16). If an individual is becoming more honest and loving, is ringing truer and truer, then we can assume that the Spirit of God is at work sanctifying her. The analogy for communities is easy to develop. What have tax policies like the one proposed done for or to other communities that have put them in place? How has a lottery or venture in legalized gambling worked out? What have women's groups, social welfare agencies, and involved churches to say about legalized prostitution? What programs to get addicted pregnant women off drugs have done the most to minimize damage to both the women and their fetuses? And, more subtle but equally important, what has been the impact of a given policy on the ethical atmosphere of the communities affected most directly? Has it lifted their sights, encouraged personal responsibility, brought people together, or has it encouraged license, cynicism, private profiteering? These are the sorts of communitarian questions that an astute ethicist asks.

In the nature of the case, many of our judgments about particular situations will be less than crystal clear. But we have to make such judgments if we are to act responsibly, and if we pay close attention to actual, empirical realities, we can usually avoid major mistakes, encourage obviously good programs. For example, the Planned Parenthood organization in my former city does marvelous work in such areas as counseling about birth control, prenatal care, and what it calls "well baby" care. It offers counseling about abortion but it does not run any abortion clinics. The new clinics that it has opened are located in the midst of poor neighborhoods, to make coming to them as easy for the poor as possible. In view of the far-reaching debate about US health care that came to a peak of intensity in 1994, when the Clinton administration submitted its plans and various people responded with various alternatives, my local Planned Parenthood group has been making all the contacts, developing all the ties, it can to legislators and others who will determine which "providers" of health services will flourish in the future. Most admirable in this realistic political involvement has been the clear note that the leaders of the local organization have struck of not seeking the simple survival of their own operation anywhere nearly so centrally as the protection of their clients, the poor, to make sure that they do not lose access to health care.

Family planning, to say nothing of abortion, is a tangled matter. Is sterilization moral in the light of a Christian view of the body? What circumstances might justify terminating life in the womb? All things sexual seem a special bugaboo in my Christian tradition, Roman Catholicism, but ethicists working out of most other traditions can also find these questions difficult, no place to exhibit a simple mind. The same is true of questions bearing on the other end of life, questions of euthanasia. Traditionally, Christian ethicists did not hold people to "extraordinary means" of prolonging life. Is openended use of a respirator to sustain bodily life, when there is little sign of ordinary mental activity – conversation, work, prayer – still an extraordinary means, or has the widespread availability of such technology rendered it quite ordinary, in the sense of something, a recourse, that all caregivers ought to employ?

And what about the right to suicide? Increasingly, this is a question meeting with an affirmative answer: people ought to be sovereign over their own destinies, especially people in pain. Does this trend reflect a growing godlessness in Western cultures, or does it suggest a more merciful view of God than what prevailed in many past ages, or a more adequate view of the autonomy that God has given to human beings? Traditionally, the prime theological stumbling block to suicide was the judgment of believers that no creature is sovereign over its destiny. The time and manner of our death by right belong to God, not to ourselves, because in the final analysis we belong to God, not to ourselves. (If we belong to ourselves, then what we may become stops at incapacitation or the grave. If we belong to God, we can hope for grace and glory, divinization and heavenly bliss.)

Add economic considerations (the cost of terminal care that does not have much likelihood of restoring a patient to normal functioning) and the social, communitarian aspects of medical questions such as these become even clearer. What has widespread abortion done to societies such as the Russian, the Japanese, the American? Has it cheapened life, contributed negatively to our view of children? What does the experiment with legal suicide going on in the Netherlands seem to be suggesting about the social impact of such a policy? Certainly, we have to study cases such as these with a keen awareness of the conditions peculiar to each culture. But health care and other key aspects of any community's efforts to serve its citizens well now reveal themselves to depend considerably on ethical choices. If only in our budgets, we say through our programs for educating our children, caring for our sick and elderly, responding to crime, supporting the arts, and the like, what we value most, how we think about the good human life.

Ethics ought to be reflection on the good human life (on what the *ethos* of our group makes ideal), in the light of a sense of how life hangs together, what human time is for. In the case of medical care, too often technological issues dominate the horizon and deeper questions of meaning take a back seat. Recently the editors of the American weekly *Commonweal* referred to some work of my husband to make this point:

> In speaking on "A Theology of Illness," John Carmody observes that "illness is . . . something extraordinary, because illness strips human existence to the bone." "It is," he says, "as much about why this is happening to me, or why someone I love is in peril, as it is about what is happening or how we got to this pass." . . . In the midst of the health reform debate, the words of a man suffering from terminal cancer are a sobering reminder that illness, by which he means "the experience of disease – the full impact, physical and emotional, spiritual and social" – is always a larger subject than the medical means we have devised to treat the diseases that make us ill, the diseases that finally take us from life. Finally each of us will die no matter the state of medical progress – or heath-care reform.
>
> Why illness? Why death? Why *this* death?
>
> It would be foolish to imagine that the larger meaning of illness, of the kind Carmody elucidates, could make its way into the polling and posturing that go with the legislative debate on national health-care reform. Yet this larger meaning is implicit in questions about the limits to medical intervention and limits to the provision of health-care services. They are implicit because there are diseases, or stages in the course of a disease, for which there is no medical remedy, and others for which the cost of treatment would be simply prohibitive. It is partly because our society is unwilling and unable to set limits – even in instances where treatment is clearly futile – that medical care costs have risen and, in some measure, created the crisis that health-care reform is trying to relieve. Isn't this because we cannot ask why?[2]

I would have Christian ethicists stand out for their ability to ask why, and for the perceptiveness of their further questioning. I would have Christian feminist ethicists do this with a special concern for what women's experience has to offer, what the needs of female patients suggest about a sane view of living and dying. If women as a group live longer than men, then care of the elderly ought to open itself wide to the experience of perceptive elderly women and those who work with them. If women not only bear all the children but supply the vast majority of neonatal care, then the needs of such caregivers ought to bulk large in the programs that we design for our hospitals, the public financial supports we extend to new mothers, the policies about maternity leave that we encourage our business firms to embrace.

Ethics does best when it stays close to the ground, knows well the smells and tastes of local neighborhoods. Certainly, understanding comes from the creative friction between such empirical data and penetrating views of how human beings tend to thrive. Obviously, the mere gathering of data does little to advance such understanding. But neither does an abstract, deductive ethics that has no solid footing in present-day experience. Because men so frequently have run the institutions determining such matters as health care (hospitals, state and federal legislatures, insurance companies, research laboratories), the experience of women has gotten short shrift. This has been true even in such areas as obstetrics, neonatal care, and gerontology. Women have not been studied as intensively as men. When it has come to American research on smoking, heart disease, and other pathologies common to men and women, most of the trials have concentrated on men. Recently feminists have organized successful lobbying for more research on breast cancer, but this has been an uphill fight. The patriarchy slanting most large societies to this day has made women less visible than men, in sickness as well as health. Women have given care more generously than women have been cared for.

All this is grist for the Christian feminist ethicist's mill. Contributing to a just resolution of the problems, the biases, evident or implied in health care, as in other major social areas, is much of the reason why such an ethicist ought to set up shop. Perhaps the distinctive contribution, though, would be to keep the pressure on to open the discussion to deeper questions of why. Why are we here upon this planet? What are our ecological responsibilities? What is our destiny, the source of our dignity, the reason we ought not to abuse other people? Too often secular, pluralistic cultures shy away from questions such as these, finding them both intractable and embarrassing. Yet one has to be obtuse to suffer a serious disease and not raise them, as one has to be obtuse not to see the disproportionate damage that the neglect of them does to women. Only when a culture looks beyond its traditional patriarchal biases to a deeper reason for valuing females as much as males has it any chance of either serving the female half of its populace adequately or drawing forth the full creativity of that half.

The Pauline reason (Galatians 3:28) is that in Christ there is neither male nor female, as there is neither Jew nor Greek, slave nor free. What we hold in common, our basic humanity, is more significant than our sexual or ethnic or social differences. That may seem a mild enough proposition, but if one applies it to many social situations today, it becomes an axe sharp enough to cut through many diseased roots.

Love as the Power of Persuasion

If we take up the question of how to motivate people to ask the question why, or to treat women justly, or to reform health care so that poor people do not fall through the cracks, we come into the central matter of motivation. All the analysis in the world will go stale if we cannot get people to study it, take it to heart, and reform their lives in consequence. Certainly, we have to win minds if we are to move people to embrace what we consider wise programs, truly humane values. But we also have to win hearts, galvanize emotions. And we have to do this for the long haul, something more lasting than the revivalist's week-long crusade. The power that God herself seems to favor is the persuasive force of love.

God uses the entirety of our lives to educate us. Each day all that we experience tells us what it means to be human. People dominated by their sensual appetites, living in the cave that Plato depicts in the *Republic*, judge their experiences largely in terms of bodily pleasure and pain. People exposed to high culture through a good education may long for experiences of beauty, contact with grand ideas, consorting with the classics. Religious people, educated in the spiritual classics, tend to interpret their experience in terms of the canonical, scriptural depictions of the holy life dominating their culture. Traditional Jews tend to think in terms of the rabbinical ideals laid out in the Talmud. Pious Muslims look to the Koran and the traditions (*hadith*) about Muhammad. Buddhists study the sutras of Gautama. Hindus revere the *Vedas* and the *Bhagavad Gita*. Chinese favor the Confucian classics such as the *Analects*, and Taoist scriptures such as the *Lao Tzu*.

For Christians, the Bible is the comparable source of wisdom about the good life and the ways to persuade people to seek it. While the Bible is not a simple book, the various works composing it agree in making God the crucial factor. Serving the law of God is the main responsibility of a biblical Israelite, while following Christ by obeying his commandment of love is the axis of biblical Christian responsibility. If we reflect on how the New Testament presents Jesus at work preaching the good news of the dawning of God's reign, healing the sick and raising a Lazarus, we gain a clear focus on the practical implications of love.

Jesus speaks about the dawning of the reign of God in vivid, memorable terms. The reign or kingdom develops or works humbly, as a mustard seed does in becoming an impressive bush, as yeast does leavening a bowl of flour. Wise people would sell all that they had to come into the kingdom, thinking it comparable to a treasure hidden in a field, to a pearl of great price. The consummation of the kingdom may come swiftly, like a thief in the night. It may occasion such conflict that people will ask the mountains to fall on them. It can set brother against brother, sister against sister. It is a matter of the spirit more than the letter, of interior cleanness more than exterior polish. Who are the favored, the heroes of the kingdom? If we hear the beatitudes clearly, the favored are the poor, the meek, those who mourn, those hungry for righteousness, those persecuted for the sake of God and his Christ.

Jesus lays out this impressive array of figures for the reign of God, letting it make its own impact. He knows intimately the import that it carries for converting the minds of his listeners and engaging their hearts. The kingdom is what they most long for. It is the right state of affairs, the full dominance of justice, that their prophets have led them to expect in the messianic age. When God's anointed leader (*Christos*) has arrived, things will be as they ought to be, worthy of the covenant between Israel and its Lord. No longer will foreign rulers humiliate Jews and threaten to pollute their religion. God will be in high heaven and most will be right with the world. Jesus tells his listeners that this messianic time has arrived, though not in the garb that the more triumphalistic among them expected.

For Jesus the Christ, the Messiah, is not a political or military figure, not a contender for worldly power. At the very outset of his mission, when Satan comes to test him, he makes it clear that he does not care for the kingdoms of this world, where Satan has great influence. He cares only for the kingdom of God, the will of God, the life of God that can heal all sickness, bodily and physical, that will wipe every tear from the eyes of the poor, the suffering, the dispossessed. The basis of the conversion that Jesus seeks, the community that Jesus builds, is not main force but humble, ministerial love. Though at times the evangelists portray Jesus as threatening his listeners with disaster if they reject the opportunity he is presenting to them, the stronger motif is that Jesus makes his presentation, preaches the good news, as though the kingdom were a free gift. Jesus is not interested in compelling people into faith and acceptance of God's rule, bullying them. He wants their allegiance to come from the heart, their service to brim with love.

So Jesus goes out of his way to show his listeners love. As he treats them, so should they think about God, so should they treat one another. From the beginning of his ministry, Jesus labors to fulfill the text from Isaiah that Luke treats as an overture: "The Spirit of the Lord is upon me, because he has anointed me to bring good news to the poor. He has sent me to proclaim release to the captives and recovery of sight to the blind, to let the oppressed go free, to proclaim the year of the Lord's favor" (Luke 4:18–19).

The year of the Lord's favor was the jubilee, the seventh of the seven sabbatical years when the land was to lie fallow and people were to forgive those indebted to them (Leviticus 25). The service of the poor and the sickly stressed in the first verses makes the ministry of the one led by the Spirit of the Lord distinctive. The kingdom of God is a force, a realm, of freedom, liberation. Everything that oppresses the human spirit, or crushes the human body, is alien to the reign of God, aligned with the enemy. God wants the life of the sinner, not her death. God makes her sun to shine, her rain to fall, on just and unjust alike. And God cannot ignore, will not abuse, the freedom of human beings. The closer they come to God, the more their freedom will expand. But God cannot compel them to say yes to the hands they have been dealt, the lives that time has meted out to them. The only relationship that God desires with human beings trades in free, uncoerced love.

The victories that we win by force, manipulation, anything other than honesty and love, are pyrrhic, barely worth the ink we spill in writing them up for our diary. Jesus lets the gospel be its own advertising. He lets his works of healing speak for themselves. There is no hyperbole in the ministry of Jesus, no inflation or pandering to the curiosities of the crowd. Indeed, Jesus finds that he must lay suffering before his disciples, make it clear that night will have its day. His face is set for Jerusalem, the city that he thinks has slain the prophets before him. And the servant will not be less than the master. What the master experiences the servant will be hard-put to avoid. Any disciple who follows Jesus in speaking the truth, serving the prophetic Word of the Lord, will arouse hatred among people closed to God, hunkered down in this-worldly values.

How does love work its persuasion? By opening new vistas, in which our spirits delight. By nourishing what is best in us, stabilizing our creativity. Jesus calls people out of their dead-ends, their spiritual depressions. The first hallmark of the good news is that it cheers people's hearts. Those sitting in darkness see a great light. Those discouraged, persuaded that they will never find the treasures their spirits desire, find powerful reasons for hope. Jesus brims with conviction, because he and the Father are one. The substance of all godly reign, all salvation, all elevation to heavenly life is divinity itself. Inasmuch as Jesus brings the power of God, is the Word of God incarnate, union with God through faith in Jesus gives people the essence of what they have been made for.

Christian theology boils down to compact phrases such as Karl Rahner's "God gives himself." In the trinity, the three persons give themselves, creating a perfect community, a transparent *perichoresis*. In the Incarnation, the three give the second person to the world. He takes flesh from Mary, making her the *theotokos*, the bearer of God, and placing in history the divine *Logos*, with ripples, ramifications, ever after. And in grace, the third of the cardinal Christian mysteries, God gives to human beings her own deathless holiness, in the measure that those human beings can receive it. It is the nature of

God, then, to be giving, generous, love flowing out to make life, heal life, elevate life to its purest reality, where it becomes holy.

The implications for a Christian ethics are obvious. As God is, so ought we to strive to become. We ought to give ourselves. Generosity ought to become our password, our motto. Whatever sun and rain we control ought to shine, to fall, on just and unjust alike. Whatever power to save, to heal, to console we enjoy we ought to spend gladly on little children, people abandoned in asylums, the poor of the Lord. Women have been signal self-spenders, so much so that many analysts caution women not to love too much, to be sure that they love themselves, to avoid giving themselves dry, burning themselves out, ending up with no self. This is valid enough advice, justified by ordinary observation. Stereotypically, many women do seem to develop lives in which they are spilled out like water, a dribble here, a dollop there. Still, the valid Christian feminist alternative is not narcissism: "I'm worth it," "It's my turn." The valid Christian feminist alternative is a deeper entry into love, where loss of self goes below stereotypes, indeed may contradict stereotypes, and finds more than compensating fulfillment in the love of God, the plain respect and appreciation of the Christian community.

The persuasion worked by the saints, from Francis of Assisi to Dietrich Bonhoeffer to Mother Teresa, is the goodness that love makes shine in their lives, from their selves. They endure suffering better than the rest of us, with more peace. They enjoy the gifts of God more simply. For the glory of God held out to them, they submit to the nails of the cross. In the best of cases, they strike us as being more human, better exemplars of the potential encoded in our kind, than we or others at our level. They may be gifted or not, effective or not, but God has molded them to love. Their hearts are not hard, their judgments are kind. If Christian (or Muslim, or Jewish, or Buddhist) traditions can produce humanity such as theirs, we have to admire such traditions greatly.

Women and Scandalous Poverty

It is commonplace to observe that the poorest of the poor are women (and the children for whom women supply most of the care).[3]

Women head the great majority of so-called "single parent families." Most of those living below the "poverty level" that developed countries such as the US use to estimate basic needs are women. A Christian feminist ethics finds this phenomenon leaping off the page, begging analysis and redress.

The poverty of women combines two major injustices. First, it expresses the general inequity in the distribution of wealth around the globe. Second, it expresses the historical subjugation of women to men in patriarchal societies. Let us examine these two injustices.

For some of the most eloquent church fathers, the goods of the earth come from God for the benefit, the welfare, of all the people of the earth. God is the great landholder, stockholder, owner. Our rights to ownership are only partial. Always, the rights of other creatures, often expressed as "the common good," limit what we can rightly claim from the earth. Thus, the fathers and later Christian ethicists tended to say that the needs of the many take priority over the wants of the few, and that no one has the right to luxuries as long as anyone lacks necessities. Such sayings are not direct inferences from the idyllic picture of the Christian community that we found in Acts 2, but they square well, cohere, with the primitive communism described there.

Traditionally, Christian spiritual masters have found wealth at best ambiguous. For example, Jesus said that it would be easier for a camel to pass through the eye of a needle than for the rich to enter the kingdom of heaven. Relatedly, he told the rich young man who wanted to be perfect to sell his goods, give the money this generated to the poor, and come to follow him wholeheartedly. In both cases, the implication is that wealth tends to tie people down, give them more interest in this-worldly things than is good for their souls. Dives, the generic rich man who refuses to help the diseased Lazarus (Luke 16), ends up in hell, reproved by father Abraham. Ironically, Abraham says that even if someone rose from the dead, worldlings would not heed him. Thus evangelical poverty, the freedom from wealth that the New Testament promotes, became one of the three vows constituting the "religious" life that developed out of Christian monasticism. With chastity and obedience, evangelical poverty expressed the consecrated person's dying to worldly values, going to ascetical war against a possessiveness that tends to denature people, warp their minds and close down their spirits.

If we step back from the ways we have become habituated to and consider the relative wealth of the nations, the disparities are striking, indeed numbing. Citizens of so-called First World countries use far more of the goods of the earth, on a per capita basis, than citizens of Second and Third World countries. Citizens of the United States alone use about 25 percent. But have North Americans, Europeans, and Japanese any valid claim to special status? Do they stand higher in the sight of God, stand singled out by history as more admirable? Economists and politicians seldom ask questions such as these, any more than people concerned with health care ask why sickness occurs or what it says about human limitations. It falls to people on the margins of secular culture, people without a vested interest in the current political or economic arrangements, to cry out that the emperor has no clothes – that, objectively, the current patterns are mad.

The best arguments on behalf of the current economic patterns tend to be two. First, by a combination of historical accident and personal talent (education, drive), the countries of the First World have risen to the top, earned their lion's share of the world's wealth. Is this so? Well, the history tends to be tangled, much of the wealth of the First World countries being gained by brutal conquest and colonial occupation. The drive tends to be something whose goodness Christian ethicists must qualify. Rarely has it been anything like a pure love of God and neighbor. Rarely has the padre wielded more influence than the conquistador. (Indeed, often the padre has been imperialist in his own sphere, bullying natives toward conversion.) Drive to accumulate wealth or power, to build oneself a fine castle or trumpet a great name, is less the service of God than of mammon.

Christian feminists have special reasons for criticizing the will-to-power evidenced in so many chapters of the rise of the West to world dominance. The mentality at work has been distinctively male, macho, patriarchal. The blood shed, the wailing provoked, have blighted millions of women's lives. Unrepresented at the councils of war, underrepresented at the councils for peace, women have had their history parceled out to them by men. Seldom has that history been the story they would have written, had they enjoyed the chance. Seldom did it embody, even aim at embodying, what women conceived to be the good life and wanted for their children. Again and again we find men asking women to applaud their bloody exploits and women unable to muster more than a sickly smile. Such women have been supporters, even camp followers, because loyalty to their fathers or husbands or sons demanded that, or because bare survival made it necessary. But in their feminine circles, as in their dreams, they longed for what Paul (1 Corinthians 12:31) calls a more excellent way.

The second argument on behalf of our current patterns of distributing wealth is that all ways are bound to be imperfect, so the current ways are as good as any. Citizens of the First World countries may not be especially virtuous, but we can find slaughter and corruption in Africa, South America, the Indian subcontinent, and eastern Asia. Wherever we find human beings, their humanity is imperfect, venal, self-serving, even murderous. If anything, biblical ideals, the legacy of traditional Judaism and Christianity, have given the West a view of the individual human being, leading to a view of human rights, considerably in advance of what the rest of the world recognizes.

Moreover, this argument goes, the best systems for generating wealth and so helping the poor are the capitalistic ones developed in the West. Though environmental considerations ought now to play an important role, making nature a "commons" with rights to protection from economic exploitation, the historical fact seems to be that socialist systems seldom spark the incentives necessary to get citizens to labor energetically. Without the prospect of personal wealth, quite concrete material gain, most people will not exert themselves, work at anything like peak capacity. Jesus reminded us of some eternal truths, but his views were hopelessly idealistic. On a day-by-day basis, the only way to get maximal output from one's workers is to reward them with more money.

We can find the rebuttal to this argument right where the proponents of it are most disparaging. For Jesus life is more than food, the body more than clothing. Intimacy with God is a treasure beside which material wealth is as dross. The nonprofit goods of prayer, serving the poor, enjoying a loving community, creating artistic works of beauty, and discovering the secrets of nature far outweigh the goods of material production. We need not, ought not, to disparage the goods of material production. Business, money, and banking have their rightful place. But that place is not the top of the list of admirable or most important human occupations. Wealth ought to serve human wellbeing, not render human wellbeing more difficult. Wealth ought to bring relatively equal benefits to all the people who contribute to creating it, not separate them into classes nearly bound eventually to collide.

Christian feminist ethicists, mindful of the predominance of women among the lower socio-economic classes, ought to be radical in these traditional ways, revolutionary against the values of the world, with a special energy. They need not take up arms or overlook the benefits of political stability, even in unjust circumstances, but they ought to keep up the pressure for thoroughgoing reforms. The common good ought always to bulk larger than private interests. Doing business in the light, without shading or murky dealing, ought always to be the Christian way. Unfortunately, Christian feminists often have to pressure their own churches for economic as well as political justice. When church-related hospitals and schools pay their personnel (most of whom are women) disgracefully low wages, or even pressure them not to organize into labor unions, Christian feminist ethicists ought to cry foul, strongly and loudly. When churches deny women equal access to power, leadership, ministerial service, or career opportunity, Christian feminist ethicists ought to stand in the front lines of those calling the current leaders to account, reminding them of how Jesus regarded the Pharisees.

The scandalous, disproportionate material poverty and political powerlessness of women in the majority of countries bespeaks the ongoing influence of sexism, as the parallel poverty and powerlessness of blacks in First World countries bespeaks the ongoing influence of racism. Both sexism and racism are sinful – expressions of the deep wrongness lodged in the human heart, expressed in all human institutions like the smudge of a dirty thumb. Christian ethics ought never to be naive about human sinfulness, and it never will be, as long as it contemplates the fate of Jesus, its main exemplar. It was not accidental that the power blocs of his day determined to do away with Jesus. It is not accidental today that those profiting most from the status quo are most determined to preserve it.

However, the amazing changes in the former Soviet Union and communist bloc, along with the victory of Nelson Mandela in South Africa, remind us that we also ought never to short change the Spirit of God. Who would have thought that apartheid would come apart so quickly, or that Marxism-Leninism would in two years become a paper tiger? Yes, the new regimes that have arisen in the post-colonial era have not been simon-pure. Often they have done little dramatic to make the lives of women better. But sometimes they have been victories for the light, and we should celebrate such victories whenever God gives them.

Christian Feminism and Sexual Ethics

We have considered the basic orientation of a Christian feminist ethics, the communitarian cast that many women would like to give it, the central place of a love persuasive in its power to create rich humanity, and the bellwether problem of poverty. I assume this background in approaching the topic of sexual ethics. Crucial for any successful approach to such diverse issues as homosexuality, contraception, abortion, divorce, and adultery is a healthy, balanced religious horizon. Often the details are far less significant than the basic attitudes. Regularly the views of women reflect centuries of patriarchal subjugation, eons when relations between the sexes have been tilted, troubled. A Christian feminist ethics begins with the assumption that sex is a direct entailment of our basic human composition as embodied spirits. As such, it has to be thoroughly good: willed by God, blessed by God, taken up by the Incarnate Word as surely as he took up vision and the need to eat. Sex is no more problematic, on the basic theological level, than any other essential human characteristic and activity. Eating, drinking, sleeping, defecating, working, playing – all may be graceful or awkward. The same with sex. If at times sexual passion is among our most powerful drives, that does not make it unique. The artistic drive to create, or the scientific drive to know, or the religious desire to pray can be just as powerful. If sexual passion can throw us off balance, so can a passion for money or political success.

The conjunction in sexual interaction of the mechanism by which our race reproduces itself and the most intimate of our loves makes sex both fascinating and volatile. But nothing makes sex either uniquely holy or uniquely dirty. Moreover, women are neither more sexual than men nor less. Sometimes women appear to be sexual differently, but this difference is always contained by the common orientation of both sexes to reproduction and erotic pleasure. Men and women have to get along, cooperate – minimally, if human existence is to continue, generously, if human existence is to thrive.

This view of sex is heterosexual, in the sense that it follows Genesis in making humanity male–female, in finding the image of God to subsist in the conjoint humanity of female–male. The significant fraction of the population that is homosexual (attracted to the same sex) does not alter this view. In my opinion, both Christian theology and culture at large ought to reflect the relative proportions of heterosexuals and homosexuals. The prevailing suppositions and provisions therefore ought to be heterosexual. But people oriented homosexually ought to be free to make their orientation public, free to express it.

All human beings long to be publicly what they find themselves to be in their heart of hearts. No human beings endure well a serious clash between social persona and private self. I think that homosexuals are held to the same standards of fidelity and chastity as heterosexuals, and I find promiscuity repugnant in both groups. But the biblical condemnations of homosexuality cannot stand up to either present-day empirical data or a properly kind, generous reading of what the Christian God makes of our *de facto* sexual orientations.

When we move from orientation to practice, we ask primarily how Christian feminist attitudes ought to regulate activity between the sexes. Christian faith imposes the obligation to love one's neighbor as oneself. This vetoes any regard of a sexual partner as merely an object of pleasure, something to use. Feminism imposes the further obligation to honor women as the full equals of men in the possession of human dignity. This means that women's sexual ways and needs ought to receive attention equal to those of men.

Especially important among the needs of the race overall is rational, responsible exercise of human fertility, the consequence of which occurs right in the middle of women. To conceive a child irresponsibly is a major ethical failing. Because women bear the greater share of the consequences of conception, women ought to have the greater say about whether to have a child and when. But men contribute 50 percent of any child's genetic endowment, and the willing collaboration of two parents is the best overall recipe for the happy growth of any child. Fatherhood is not a trivial vocation.

Women who equate parenthood with motherhood do their men, their children, and themselves a significant disservice, going against the grain that God has set up.

Responsible conception implies intelligent family planning and so contraception of some sort. To make abortion anything like a standard contraception seems to me mentally diseased, for no people morally healthy kill their own young. The argument that life in the womb is not human reeks of speciousness. What a pregnant woman carries and would bring forth is never a cabbage. Special cases, such as carrying a defective fetus, or experiencing a pregnancy that puts the mother's life at risk, deserve special, non-doctrinaire responses. The rights of the fetus are never the only rights to consider. But ontological considerations, considerations of the common good and the common responsibility of the wider society, suggest that we miss the actual reality of a pregnancy if we make terminating it purely a private decision (all the more so if we make it only the decision of the mother).

The key ontological consideration is the relative goodness of being and being well. The bare being of a healthy fetus ought to weigh more heavily, appear as a more basic good, than the being well of its parents. In other words, though financial burdens merit consideration, especially when the mother is poor, they cannot in a rightly ordered analysis become more important than the right of the child to survive, the right of God in giving life to be honored. Thus the casual abortions of the affluent are mortal moral failures.

The rights of society at large, and its obligations, come into play when we recognize the possibility of adoption. Though recently this whole issue has become complicated through technological innovations allowing surrogate motherhood (the capacity of one woman to carry the genetic child of another woman and bring it to healthy birth), the main lines of a Christian ethical approach to adoption remain clear. A child is not simply the property of its biological parents. If only because that child will draw upon the resources of the community at large for its schooling, housing, medical care, even feeding, it is from the outset part of a commons. Should there be people in the community who desire children, and would be good parents, it makes no sense to abort healthy fetuses as "unwanted." Whatever the difficulties that adoption may entail, they pale before the moral errors of unnecessary abortion.

Divorce has become common in Western societies, though not completely easy. Divorce represents a failure of some sort, more or less profound. Few people who have gone through a divorce count it a good experience. In the healthiest cases, the parties admit their mistakes, confess their sins, and move along, humbler and wiser. They should not find their religious communities singling them out as special failures, any more than alcoholics or drug addicts should. We have all sinned and fallen short of God's glory. The message of Jesus stressed mercy, understanding, encouragement. None of us can read the conscience of another. All of us depend on the mercy of God, are saved only by grace. So though divorce is certainly undesirable, it is no unique failing. All the more so is this the case when most of the reasons for the divorce – infidelity, for example – gather at the door of only one of the spouses. The spouse who has been faithful, relatively innocent, is bound to feel wounded, maybe even feel guilty, but Christian wisdom suggests that friends ought to help her or him to stay level-headed.

I do not consider rape to be primarily sexual, though of course it expresses the sexual outlook of both the rapist and society overall. The desire to subjugate a weaker, more vulnerable person seems to be more important than sexual desire in a narrow sense. The vast majority of rape victims are women (apart from in prison, and perhaps gay circles, few men suffer rape), so rape ought to be a concern of all Christian feminist ethicists. Primarily, they ought to take aim at the cultural conditions that make many societies tolerate rape. These include a support of machismo and a tendency to blame the victim.

Machismo – the preening of men, and the assumption that society ought to indulge the male ego – smacks of emotional retardation, something we only put up with in adolescents because we hope they will grow out of it soon. A tendency to blame the female victim flourishes in patriarchal societies, which regularly cast women as seductive and deal with male guilt dishonestly. Rather than face their own responsibility, many men in patriarchal societies excuse abusing women sexually by saying that the women asked for such ill-treatment. Virtually never is that the case, as all honest people know.

Finally, what ought a Christian feminist interested in the moral life to make of the louche, self-indulgent use of sex that has become part of the good life that the advertising industries tend to lay before us? I believe that Christian feminists ought to regard such a use of sex, by either women or men, as significantly stupid and sinful. The pleasure that is right and healthy is that which follows upon the proper use of a human faculty. For example, to gaze upon rolling hills at sunset, or to smell fresh flowers, or to cuddle a clean infant, or to solve a mathematical puzzle, or to make love to a beautiful beloved, brings healthy pleasure. The pleasure is part of the process, but we throw the process off course, subvert it, if we make the pleasure the predominant goal. Thus, to divorce the beauty of a lover from her or his total personality, and then suborn that beauty into the service of one's own sexual hedonism, is to pervert the sexual interaction.

Between human beings, sex is never a purely physical interaction. It ought never to be mere breeding or physical release. Sexual interaction is a form of communication, ideally nonverbal because the word it desires to express is simpler than anything that can be spoken on the air, rounder and wholer. Pauline theology has the lovely notion that the body of the lover belongs to the beloved, and vice versa. In marriage, the spouses worship (venerate) one another through their bodies. They offer one another rest, repair, forgiveness, renewal, nourishment in love. The nuptial symbolism in the Bible, and in Christian mysticism, makes marriage a prime analogy for both the union of Christ with the church and the union of the individual soul with God. Earthy, humorous, very human, a sexual love inspired by Christian faith is thoroughly sacramental. In a time when much conspires to make interactions between the sexes disastrously reflexive, I would have Christian feminists champion simple common sense and support the free, happy coupling of men and women dizzy with love, drunk like the lovers in the Song of Songs, that ripens this sacrament to full fruitfulness. Today we have too many people pinched, crabbed, unable to love one another playfully. We need more people who can relax and celebrate a splendid gift of God gratefully. I would have Christian feminists recruit and train such people, largely by the example of their own erotic freedom, recalling Paul's wonderful line, "For freedom Christ has set us free" (Galatians 5:1).

Ethics and Spirituality: the Case of Ecology

Ethics concerns our actions, our practice, and our practical thought: what we believe constitutes or characterizes a healthy faith, tradition, way of life. Spirituality concerns what we think and feel about ultimate things, how our religious experience unfolds, where we find meaning to be most beautiful, what we find through prayer and service of our neighbors. Ethics and spirituality overlap, inasmuch as what we do reports back to what we think and feel about meaning and beauty. Equally, where we initially look for significance, the outposts to which we first march when we want to find God and serve her, shape the ethical questions we encounter. Consider, for example, the case of ecology.

Most people who have paid attention to the reports on the state of the earth that have in the past fifteen years become a steady stream recognize that the way of life developed in the industrialized nations may well be proving lethal to nature and so to ourselves.[4] Nature is the matrix, the mother-ground, of all our human culture, no matter how rarefied. The professor of theoretical physics or pure mathematics has to eat, breathe, clothe herself, deal with sex, recognize trees so that she doesn't invite them to faculty colloquia. The mother playing with her newborn child, counting his perfect little toes, is short changed if she cannot place herself on the broad stage of nature's fertility, does not see herself as kin to all other creatures pleased to have brought forth new life.

If ethical implications fan out from the embodiment of even our most cerebral fellow-citizens, their roots in material nature, parenthood sends out more intense ripples. We take on responsibilities in the very act of bringing forth new life. We bear responsibility for the earth *because* we bring forth new life. Generation after generation, children and the habitat within which they develop focus the work, the worry, the planning of the middle generation, their parents, as a happy burden of responsibility. Increasingly, that habitat comes under assault, as toxic wastes or high voltage wires threaten the genes of our children. The lakes sicken, the oceans nourish far fewer fish, the forests and jungles retract, shrink, house fewer and fewer species. This is our world, the estate over which the Lord asks us to be good stewards, and it is the legacy we shall pass on to our children.

Perhaps the degradation, the murder, of this world would begin to change, were we explicitly to link our generativity (the great concern of our middle years, in the late and lamented Erik Erikson's view of the life-cycle) with the fate of the earth.

Feminists tend to see the degradation of nature as an extension of the degradation of women. Pictured as a female, mother nature is exposed to the will to power, the itch to dominate, of developers, laywasters wearing military uniforms, farmers pressured by giant conglomerates headquartered in skyscrapers with sealed windows, no air that is not artificial. The number of human beings who live with the land intimately, who sail the waters like a childhood friend, diminishes with each generation. Good as the programs for educating children about environmental issues can be, they are bound to seem extracurricular or recreational compared to the life on the land that Wendell Berry, for example, has described in his novels and essays. Presently, the heart of the curricula obtaining in American educational institutions is the skills that will serve the great machines for making money. Both human beings and physical nature are supposed to bend to this central cultural imperative. For the Christian feminist, this priority, this scale of values, is radically wrong, the service of mammon. It puts a blight on the future of all the infants playing on their mothers' bellies. It threatens to pollute their souls as well as their genes.

The alternative is not a return to primitivism (the relations with nature that obtained before human beings had high technologies), even if that were possible. The alternative that I see as most compatible with a Christian feminist ethics and spirituality is a love of the earth that stems from viewing it as the creation of God and realizes that unless we are at home with mother nature we are short changing the Incarnation.

The Father of Jesus is not the creator of human beings alone. All that lives and breathes, indeed everything that takes up space, comes from the hand of God, depends on God's constant grant of existence. For her own good reasons, God chose to make us material and mortal, part of a universe developed from a few primary elements, one phase in a long story of evolution. "Natural history," as we sometimes call it, is our prehistory, and also the history of a contemporary system we share with millions of fellow creatures. We may be the mind of creation, the place where evolution became aware of itself, but this does not take us out of creation. We live within various niches, micro-zones, giving and taking influences, some benign and some malign. Until we find the proper balance for our interactions, we are more a menace, what Loren Eiseley called "the lethal factor," than good citizens, fellow creatures about whom the rest of creation might feel proud.

In the past, nature provided an easy egress from this-worldliness. Contemplating the stars, many human beings left the confines of their workaday lives, traveled out to divine mysteries. Contemplating the sea, an equal number recognized the flux of time, the constancy of its variety. Nature seemed to care little for petty human troubles, human triumphs sure to be short-lived. These natural contexts, this nearly unavoidable contemplation, helped to keep human beings balanced. Time and tide waited for no man, left no woman exempt. The birth of a child embodied the defeat of death for another generation, but all parents knew in their bones that it symbolized another stage on their own life's way to death. Just as burying a parent was for children a rite of passage, a parallel to the mystery that the parents went into the earth to meet, so beholding a newborn child was a threshold, a liminal time when the flux broke open and the wonder of their passage to death caused the reflective to take a deep breath.

We need nature for this kind of mental health. Certainly, nature does not exist only to fulfill our needs, even the most elevated and nonexploitative. But brother sun and sister moon ought to be our benefactors, as we ought to do well by sister stream and brother wolf. The new environmental ethics, the earthy spirituality requested by the third Christian millennium, ought to trade in reflections such as these. How can we make our symbiosis with the natural world, its serving as our matrix and our serving as its reflective awareness, more congenial and mutually beneficial than it has been since the industrial revolution? Where can we find the wisdom to place the proper limits to our economic growth, to our development of natural resources?

One place that Christian feminists ought to visit in such a search is the traditional doctrine of creation, updated to characterize all the species of the earth, the universe, as offspring of God. If all good things come down to us as gifts from a Father of lights (James 1:17), they also all come forth from the womb of our divine mother, God the fertile, the ever-renewing.[5] The traditional Christian doctrine of creation is susceptible of faithful interpretations that make God the material source of all that lives, moves, has being. Consequently, creation is also susceptible of interpretation as a grand family affair.

Ignatius of Loyola concludes his *Spiritual Exercises* with a *"contemplatio ad amorem"* that depends on the text from James. Purified, exercised into holy spiritual shape, the graduate of Loyola's regime sees the world as a thesaurus of graces. Whatever is true, good, noble comes from the hand of God. Before, to the side, behind, the goodness of God prevents us – goes ahead, prepares a place. Every above to which our spirit aspires, moving up toward the light, is a locus of divine brightness. Every below to which our spirit descends, in search of its unfailing ground, can be a stage of a holy unknowing, our putting off now this and now that false god. A renewed Christian doctrine of creation could repristinate these traditional instincts of the saints. For such saints (Ignatius, Francis of Assisi), the world became congenial, the forest became an oyster, because everything belonged to their God.

Let the one God become the mother of all living things, the wisdom of the necessity that gives birth to human invention, and the world can become your oyster. Let the playfulness of the creator and his nymph-like companion invite us to see creation from nothingness in time as a program of dances. Waltzes and sarabands, foxtrots and mazurkas – the tempos vary, the steps repeat and repeat until they become new. Some of this ballet of creation is flux and some is military order. Some is ragtime, Scott Joplin at the front of the bordello. Other movements, songs, orchestrations appear in the recitals of the whales, the close formations of the anchovies, the cheerleaders' sways of the giant kelp. The limits of our symphonies, our musical interludes, our long-playing tapes, are the limits of our imaginations. The lyrics of God are as clear as the ears that we attune, the hearts that we unharden.

We need to love the earth, much better than we have for the past century. That is the main command that any ecological Christian ethics or spirituality is bound to lay upon us. We need to treat the earth, the universe, as our neighbor, a family of creatures God wants us to love as we love ourselves. Such a love will not solve simply, at a stroke, the problem of how we are to use natural resources wisely. It will not absolve us from hard thinking about our diets, our manufacturing, the creature comforts we really need. But it will give us a better horizon than the exploitative one we have tended to favor recently. It will place us alongside the Creator of us all, who sees that we are all good, and make us less at odds with her constitution of the world.

God has not made the world for abuse, improper consumption or development. God does not see the rock face of "El Capitan" in Yosemite Valley as a blackboard for our graffiti. God smiles at the otters sporting off Point Lobos. The *crème de menthe* surf swirling off the Irish coast near Sligo on a windy day, nourishing the imagination of a Yeats, strikes the Creator as a holy liquor. "Drink up," the divine provisioner tells us. "Take your delight here, where the nectar will not shame you."

The trouble with most recent eco-spiritualities, including many that have come from eco-feminists, is their thinness. The majority do not find creation to be a profound mystery, something to contemplate with more silence than political ambition. Ours is not an ontological time, attuned to the wonder of being. The fluid being of the seas, like the rocky being of the mountains, or the darting being of the hummingbirds, makes no profound impact. Until it does, we shall not estimate nature rightly, nor move though nature with appropriate grace. Until the winds are again the breath of God, and the stones God's skeleton, we shall stomp on the earth with army boots, instead of walking unshod for reverence.

Conversion: Prayer and Social Justice

Assuming a good formation in Christian faith, basic doctrine, those trying to educate Christian feminists to a mature imitation of Jesus do well to concentrate on spirituality and social service. These two poles of Christian spirituality apply well the twofold commandment of love that Jesus made the center of his religious program for his followers. But neither pole will glow attractively until people have had the change of mind (*metanoia*, conversion), the repentance and belief in the good news, that the Markan Jesus demands at his first ministerial appearance (1:14).

Taking to heart the good news of the dawning of the reign of God requires a shift from worldly values that makes it possible to follow Jesus in living eccentrically, outside of one's self, with God, in love, for service. Jesus is the prime exemplar of such living. His overriding passion is the will of his heavenly Father. He spends himself night and day making known the Father's offer of a time of great opportunity (*kairos*). His parables, cures, prodigies multiplying the loaves and fishes or casting out demons into swine are so many signs, evidences, of the authenticity of his mission. If people will not believe what he says, let them believe his works. His works demonstrate the power of God flowing through him. They show the advent of salvation, radical healing, in his contemporaries' midst.

The individual who repents, is converted, experiences a sea-change. The same elements appear in her life, dominate her awareness, but they have fallen into a new configuration. Now they radiate from a center of commitment to Jesus. Now the horizon in which the person locates them stretches endlessly into the heaven of God. These realizations may not all come at once, but they arrive in germ from the start with the shift, the changeover, that inaugurates the conversion.[6]

Usually the formalization of the conversion, the person's bringing to consciousness the change that has occurred, comes after some months of subterranean struggle. Often the convert has been unhappy with his life, felt that he was going nowhere and his days were empty. This has primed him to look for a more meaningful explanation, situating, of his share in human time: why we are here, what we are for. The more persistently one keeps at such questions, the more explicitly religious one's quest becomes. Indeed, simply ask four or five questions in a line, four or five whys, and you are bound to come to religious or ontological wonders: where did we come from, why are we made the (imperfect) way that we are, what is the end, the goal, the final cause that might orient our behavior wisely?

Christian conversion takes the form of finding Jesus and the religious program (doctrine, worship, ethics) of his community to be a good answer to the generalized question of what human time is for, how human beings ought to live. Christian faith says, elementally, that human time is for the enjoyment and service of God in God's world – for the love of ultimate, fully holy reality that worshipful prayer accomplishes and the helpfulness, the practical love, that service of one's neighbor channels. Using their time for these things, human beings will experience grace now, in time, and glory later, in heaven. Doing this, their sufferings can seem meaningful, the desires of their hearts feel increasingly right and good, their spirits take satisfaction in the evidence that they are doing worthwhile things with the opportunities that God gives them.

Not all conversions last through a lifetime. People can become disillusioned with the Christian community, disaffected from Christian faith, disappointed with their own moral performance, and decide that honesty requires them to call themselves former Christians, or current agnostics, or, in a few cases, atheists. Still, many converts (or people who grow up as Christians but only find the inner significance of their faith through something akin to a conversion experience) do move ahead into a mature, ongoing love of God and love of neighbor. Many who repent and believe in the gospel, again and again, do find the yoke of Christ to be easy and his burden light. For them, the centrality of prayer and social service is obvious.

Prayer is address of God, intimacy with God, person to person exchange from the heart. The best analogies come from the communications in our human relationships, especially those rooted in love: friendship, romance, dealings of parents and children. These exchanges require words, but as they develop much is elliptical, tacit, a matter of a wink, a nod, a shrug. The better the people involved know one another, the fewer the misunderstandings, the more the laughs. Old spouses sometimes get scared at the ease with which they finish one another's sentences. Scholars who have loved a field of study for decades can verify the Latin dictum, *Ex pede cognoscit Herculem*: He can recognize (a statue of) Hercules from his toe.

This "connatural" knowledge develops in prayer, if prayer is regular. We come to find the mystery of God, the silence and darkness, familiar. The icons we love, the biblical passages we consider our favorites, become part of our personal art gallery, texts that anchor our mind. For example, at the foundations of ethics I ponder regularly the Johannine judgments that bad people hate the light, because their deeds are evil, while good people come to the light, that their deeds may be seen in God. One can apply these dicta simplemindedly, or use them unkindly as clubs. But one can also love them freely, liberatingly, self-critically, seeing that they express a profound insight.

When we move toward the light, love the light, we ask ourselves to make our motivations patent to God and other people. We say that we want to be honest, transparent, without guile. When we do not move toward the light, but run like rabbits from engagement with issues that will challenge our honesty, we can be sure that something is tainted in our motivation, rotten in our Danish soul.

One cannot pray well and not love the light. Dishonest prayer is a contradiction in terms. This is not to say that many religious officials do not pray glibly, from habit, as practiced public performers. But it is to say that experienced listeners know when public prayers are prefabricated, routine, something much less than the overflow of a mind focused on God, a heart asking to be converted again to the values of Christ. Honest prayer is not smarmy, doctrinaire, pious in a pejorative sense. It is free, fresh, sprung from the heart in wonder at the ever-new creativity of God. People who pray from the heart inject new life into traditional formulas. Despite the fact that they have used the Lord's Prayer a thousand times, they say the words reverently, letting them find the cadence on the tongue proper for this day, and make their proper solicitation to unharden our hearts right now.

That God is *our* Father is not something we can take for granted. That we should want to hallow God's name is obvious, but few of us do it perfectly, even well. How passionately do we want the kingdom of God to come, when we know that it will challenge our successes, our comforts, in the world? Will we want the will of God to be done if it leads us to the cross, as it led Jesus? Do we really believe in heaven, a realm where God's will thrives completely? We do need God to provide us the most crucial nourishment, bread for our bodies and bread for our souls, so we ought to pray for it ardently.

Just as much, we do need the forgiveness of God, the possibility of confessing our sins and making a new start. Otherwise, we may despair over our moral mediocrity. But to receive the forgiveness of God, we have to forgive other people, those who have sinned against us. The terribly demanding command of Jesus that we love our enemies and do good to those who persecute us rings in the background. Vengeance belongs only to God. Similarly, God must protect us against temptation if we are not to fall ignominiously. God must deliver us from evil if we are not to be corrupted by sin.

These final verses of the Lord's Prayer are a confession of our complete need of God. Without divine grace, we cannot sustain any progress, economic or moral. When we are converted to the proposition that God is our creator and redeemer, we see that everything we treasure is a free gift of God, nothing of our own doing. Everything significant in creation is grace.

Work for social justice aims at fair-dealing for all our neighbors, labors to make sure that everyone gets a proper chance, an equal opportunity, a level playing field. Contrary to ideologues of any stripe, mature Christians committed to social justice do not indulge in political correctness, waste no time on *a priori* judgments. They deal with cases one at a time, knowing that bias and sin infect all social classes. Right may lie with this group in one situation and with that group in another. Women may enjoy the support of the angels now but be the devil's advocates later. No group has a guarantee of virtue, an establishment in the right. The saints know this most acutely and account themselves the worst sinners.

Social justice as a pursuit is a many-sided effort, trying to match a many-sided reality. The natural, economic, political, sexual, racial, educational, medical, artistic, scientific, and other zones of a high culture all beg purification, so that people can find themselves judged by their talent and goodness rather than any extrinsic qualities. In the churches, perceptive people weep to find such causes of injustice to women and others as fundamentalism, clericalism, and other species of closure to the Spirit of God, who moves where she will. Any service of institutional self-preservation, rather than the glory of God, is idolatry and sin. Once I watched an ambitious Roman Catholic cleric led down the garden path to a public confession that he made no distinction between God and the church. He was performing in front of his conservative bishop and a powerful cardinal visiting from Rome. He flunked Catechism 1 because his mind was bent on showing his great loyalty to the institutional church. To the astonishment of most in attendance, he made a public sale of his birthright for a mess of pottage.

O God, the first objective of social justice, and the best guarantee of its even-handedness, is our dedication to worshipping only you, our knowing that worshipping anything other than you brings us to a practical idolatry. The church, the community of us rag-tag sinners called out of our mediocrity to be the people of God, is never more than the bride of Christ, blushing because of her unworthiness. Not to see that only you are fully holy, only you are never in need of blushing, is to miss the simple reality of our human situation. The best gift we have to offer other people is a practical love rooted in your priority, free of the cant and stultifying convention that an unmystical life tends to spawn. Such cant and convention can thrive in the church as well as in the university or the business conglomerate. It prospers wherever people are not deep enough, mature enough religiously, to see that virtually nothing is certain, guaranteed. All flesh is grass, and the splendor thereof.

Social justice ought to flow from the church in great freedom. The venerable maxims that (a) we need insist on uniformity only in the few things necessary for orthodox Christian faith such as the Creed (*In necessariis unitas*), that (b) in all things not necessary, not certain, not crucial, the rule ought to be to leave people free to express themselves as, under the Spirit, they find best (*In dubiis libertas*), and (c) that in all matters, whether necessary or doubtful, the love that Jesus promoted ought to reign (*Et in omnibus caritas*) can go a long way toward articulating how members of even a large church can live together peacefully. Pope John XXIII championed these venerable maxims, exemplifying them in his good humor and warmth toward all.

Few things are necessary, certain. Whether democracy is the best form of government, outside the church or inside, is certainly debatable. Whether Jesus would approve the ordination of women is something we can never know with empirical certainty. That the early Christians found Jesus to be fully human and fully divine is certain, as the classical creeds show. That one cannot hold the faith long handed down and not confess that the Father raised Jesus from the dead is equally certain. But apart from a few constituent parts of Christian faith, most conventions are open for reconsideration. How people ought to pray, what forms the liturgy ought to take, how much theft constitutes mortal sin, what obligations a Christian has to employ mechanical means to prolong life – we ought to debate these important matters, with freedom and respect. In all things, we should assume the good will of people who disagree with us, until we have to admit that they are ideologues who hate the light, will not discuss faith openly.

Feminists can champion this threefold program because it squares well with their own instincts and needs. Too often women have been held to standards of thought and conduct based more on patriarchal conventions than anything essential to the gospel or required by the creeds. Too often social justice has not come to term, has been aborted in the womb, because women have not been as free to exercise their talents, express their minds, contribute the fruits of their experience, as men.

When women are not as free to do these things as men, humanity is not the full image of God that it ought to be, which curtails the liberty of the children of God. I believe that women should simply go ahead and act on their instincts, seize their proper liberty, unless to do so would cause more harm than good. It is right and fun to make mischief as well as merriment before the Lord, but we ought not to scandalize the weak or ruin the concord of the Christian community. Discretion must be the golden rule every day, the better part of valor, whether we are working in the chancery or the ghetto. But we women ought to be as free as men to learn discretion by making honest mistakes. Under the Spirit of God, we ought to enjoy the liberty to make work for social justice, for a society based on fair-dealing, from the convictions that we develop day by day though honest assessment of what happens to us on the job, around the dinner table, in the bedroom, at church, in recreation.

Study Questions

1 What are the rightful sources for a Christian feminist ethics?
2 Sketch a feminist Christian view of the common good.
3 What is the proper place of love in a feminist Christian ethics?
4 How ought the feminization of poverty to orient our analyses of social justice?
5 How central ought abortion to be to a Christian feminist sexual ethics?
6 What are the main spiritual lessons that you find in eco-feminism?
7 How important ought prayer to be in Christian ethics?

Notes

1 See Denise Lardner Carmody, *Virtuous Woman* (Orbis, Maryknoll, NY, 1992); also Denise Lardner Carmody and John Tully Carmody, *Christian Ethics* (Prentice-Hall, Englewood Cliffs, NJ, 1993). On Christian feminist

ethics, see Barbara Hilkeit Andolsen et al. (eds), *Women's Consciousness, Women's Conscience* (Harper and Row, San Francisco, 1985).

2   "Why?," *Commonweal*, cxxi, no. 8 (22 April 1994), pp. 3, 4, referring to John Carmody, *Cancer and Faith* (Twenty-Third Publications, Mystic, CT, 1994).

3   See *The World's Women: 1970–1990* (United Nations, New York, 1991).

4   For one (controversial) estimate of ecological trends, see *Vital Signs* (Worldwatch Institute, Washington, DC, 1994).

5   See Rosemary Radford Ruether, *Gaia and God* (Harper San Francisco, San Francisco, 1992).

6   See Emilie Griffin, *Turning* (Doubleday, New York, 1981).

Chapter 9

CONCLUSION

The Harmony of "Christian" and "Feminist"

The adjective "Christian" applies to what follows from a confession that Jesus is the Messiah, the Christ of God, the uniquely authenticated spokesman and "bringer of salvation." In my usage, the adjective "feminist" applies to what follows from a thoroughgoing commitment to realizing the full equality of women with men in the possession and exercise of human nature, human dignity. The issue in this first section of our retrospective conclusion is how these two adjectives relate positively, their harmony. In the next section we discuss the challenges that Christians put to feminists and feminists put to Christians – the tensions in any marriage the two groups attempt.

A traditional yet free interpretation of Christianity such as the one that I have attempted to construct takes seriously, orientationally, the goodness, the encouragement, of the news attributed to the advent and victory of Jesus. I believe that the gospel stems from a perception, indeed an experience, that where sin had abounded, grace abounds the more. I find my heart lift when I read implicit interpretations of the gospel such as Irenaeus's dictum that God's glory is human beings fully alive. Similar "short formulas" of Christian faith such as Karl Rahner's sayings that "God gives himself" and that "God is our absolute future" convince me that at all points where hope squares off against discouragement an authentic Christian faith chooses hope. I believe that the Christian story, the dramatic interpretation of human existence stemming from the evangelical accounts of the life, teaching, death, and resurrection of Jesus, fit our biographies to the frame of comedy rather than tragedy. In the final analysis, I believe that we can hand over to the God revealed through Jesus a blank check, trusting that this parental God will take better care of us than we could ever take of ourselves alone, on our own.

From such a hopeful horizon in faith in Jesus the Christ, I look upon feminism as a blessing from God, a heavenly sign of the good future times that God is brooding nowadays. The emancipation of women from the distortions of patriarchal cultures that effectively denied their equality with men in the possession of human nature and dignity strikes me as a liberation from an old regime of sin to a new dispensation of grace. Even though the Christian church, along with all the other major religious establishments, has through virtually all of its history been a patriarchal institution needing radical reform, the good news of Christ sanctions, makes valid, an interpretation of Galatians 5:1 ("For freedom Christ has set us free") that justifies, perhaps even requires nowadays, a feminist struggle to free women from the sexism that has ravaged the Christian millennia of history.

Working from the side of feminist convictions, the harmony of struggling to realize the full equality of women with Christian faith may seem problematic, because the Christian faith that many feminists think they have met has not been hopeful, open, positive in the ways that I have indicated I want mine to be. All the major families of Christian churches – Eastern Orthodox, Roman Catholic, mainstream Protestant, and now Evangelical/Fundamentalist – have worked, must work, with a Bible formed in patriarchal cultures.

Both the Hebrew Bible and the New Testament reflect worlds – Israelite, Jewish-Christian, Hellenistic – in which men and women were not cultural equals. Men could not do without women, but seldom were women welcome in the precincts of "higher," "upper," culture, where were created most of public history – such overt matters as war, trade, shifts in agricultural technology, the education of the elites, worship, and ideology (usually in the sense of the theological rationale for the ethos and mores of the group, whether tribe or nation). Few women could study Torah with leading rabbis

(Jesus was an innovator). Few Christian women could avoid the limitations implicit in the Pauline injunction (1 Timothy 2) that women were not to teach or have authority over men but were to keep silent.

From these beginnings, the Christian church, both Greek and Latin, often assumed that women were the second sex, Adam's rib, the one who had led the father of the race to the Fall. When celibacy started to become statutory for the upper Christian clergy in the Latin church (beginning with the Council of Elivra in Spain in about 306), and the monastic movement gained force, women started to appear as primary obstacles to the sanctification, the spiritual fulfillment, of men. Church fathers such as Augustine, Tertullian, Chrysostom, and Jerome spewed considerable bile at women, and Aquinas, following his philosophical master Aristotle, could write of the female as a misbegotten male.

The classical Protestant reformers repudiated Aristotle and went back to scripture, but this meant renewing the patriarchal views of women operating in Genesis, the Prophets, the Pauline literature, and even, on occasion, the gospels. While the reformers' rejection of celibacy and endorsement of marriage as the normal Christian vocation (both holy and worldly) brought some liberation from the prudishness that monastic views of sex could inculcate (Luther was quite earthy at points, as well as quite scatological), a Reformed view of marriage often made husbands "heads" of their wives in ways that inhibited a full friendship between the two.

The so-called "free" Protestant churches began to allow women to exercise ministerial power in the church, eventually granting qualified women access to ordination, and some utopian groups, such as the Shakers and the Christian Scientists, could look back to female founders. Overall, however, women cannot strike present-day feminists as having found in Christian history much support for their equality with men.[1] Perhaps Western history, with its many debts to Christian views of the equal access of all human beings to salvation, does show a greater appreciation of the individual, female as well as male, than we find in traditional non-Christian Asian and African cultures, but such individualism has rarely meant welcoming women into full social, cultural, economic, and political equality with men. Only relatively recently have most democratic Western countries enfranchised women, giving them the vote, and women still struggle for equal representation in the congresses, parliaments, and diets of even the most advanced industrial nations.

From their equality as children of God, conjoined images of God, and candidates for salvation, Christian women and men ought to construct a political equality that would lay before the world a model of how the sexes can relate for the fullest flowering of both. Inasmuch as the Christian church ought to be a great city lifted up on a hill, showing all people what healthy community life, sociability, can be, the quality of the relations between the sexes that obtain in the Christian church is of crucial importance.

No relationship is more fundamental than that between men and women. Those who argue that race or socio-economic class is just as fundamental as sex forget that human life itself depends on the interactions between men and women. In purely biological terms, we are constituted heterosexually. The psychological and other cultural consequences of this biology have created the tragi-comic plotline of large portions of human history. Men have not been able to do without women, and women have not been able to do without men, even though both sexes have often wanted to (even have tried on occasion). For procreation, but also for much of the erotic desire and consummation, much of the drive for beauty and romance that gives life its spice, the majority of human beings have found it good to interact with the other sex. Indeed, the majority of human beings have found that falling in love with a member of the other sex has furnished them their keenest indication of human fulfillment, the place where they were most themselves. Thus the Song of Songs in the Hebrew Bible became one of the major sources for believers' imagining their intercourse with divinity, while Paul and all the evangelists, but especially John, made love the best characterization of the peak of the Christian virtues and the nature of the Christian God.

Secular feminists can only be truly secular, limiting human destiny and potential to this-world of space and time, at the price of largely avoiding the far reaches of the phenomenology of erotic (and also agapeic, self-spending) love. They have to curtail the mysteries of erotic love (homosexual as well as heterosexual), lest these mysteries start to suggest how creation itself came into being, how desire for union may be the great code running many of our atoms and genes.

In contrast, a religious existential philosopher such as Gabriel

Marcel can interpret human love as a confession that the beloved will never die. Something eternal, deathless, emerges at the heart of a profound human love, making it a claim on the deathlessness of God, its source. This implies that God gives us our decent, holy loves, through the Spirit's moving in our spirits as our paraclete. The Spirit washes what is dirtied, waters what is dry, heals what is diseased, making us worthy to join the saints in heaven.

Equally, the incarnation of the divine Word grounds a fully embodied approach to human love, a completely sacramental use of food, sex, music, incense, walks through nature, hugging of little children, anointing of the dying. An incarnational faith even says that the sacrament that God has made most central, most revelatory of her own nature, is the human flesh we know so well, suffer from so radically and fully. What Jesus took from Mary became for an incarnational (that is, a traditionally creedal) Christian faith the axis of history and through the resurrection the first-fruits of a new creation, where death no longer holds ultimate sway.

Since the flesh that Jesus took from Mary is fully human, we find it in women as much as men. The woman Mary was human enough to become the source of the humanity of God. *De facto* if not *de necessitate*, without Mary we would not have the historical Christianity that we have had. We would not have the comedic history of salvation that began at the Annunciation and came to climax through the Cross, beneath which Mary stood sorrowing and where she received the broken body of her Son, becoming once and for all the *Pietà*.

Can feminists identify with Mary, the unwed mother, the prime symbol for the Christian church through her complete dedication to Jesus, the paramount faith she showed? If they cannot, they miss something of immense historical and sapiential import.

Historically, it is hard to overestimate the significance of Mary in Byzantine and European (and so Western) culture during the past two thousand years. Developing the stories about Mary in the New Testament, Eastern Orthodox theologians such as Ephrem the Syrian, along with the main makers of medieval European Christianity, and even with some Reformed thinkers, have seen in the Virgin Mother an epitome of Christian femininity. The icons of Mary, the Gothic churches dedicated to Mary, the place of Mary in any Christian imagining of the family life that formed the child Jesus – all this ensured that this Jewish Christian woman would become the Second Eve, the mother of a new human line. Marian piety sometimes got out of hand, in effect treating Mary in the little tradition as a Christian goddess, but when it kept relations between Jesus and Mary healthy, insisting that only he was the Word incarnate and absolute savior, Mary could serve as a beautiful focus of the sacramentality stemming from the incarnation and a historical anchor without whom a fully Christian view of time and destiny was unthinkable.

The Mutual Challenge of "Christian" and "Feminist"

We have noted some of the points at which Christians and secular feminists might clash about (a) the history of women's experience in patriarchal cultures indebted to Christian faith and (b) the proper view of women's destiny. Here let us focus on the heart of such a clash, asking why secular feminism strikes the Christian as a truncated view of human nature, a humanism *manqué*, and also asking why secular feminists assume as a matter of course that religion is their enemy.

To take the second matter first, the principal answer is the classical Marxist one: secular feminists think of religion as alienating. In their view, religion has syphoned away energies that ought to have gone into the reform of ordinary culture and history so as to make women the political equals of men. The religious institutions, Jewish, Christian, Muslim, and other, have seduced women into acquiescence with the patriarchal dominance of men by telling them that cultural inferiority means little, compared to the judgments of God, the rewards of heaven.

In Christianity, women have been the majority of churchgoers, even though in most churches they could not lead the liturgical ceremonies that they attended. Women have been the mainstay of the institutional churches, the sex more pious, religious, inclined to prayer and social service. In part this has been because, until recently, women seldom worked outside the home. They had some leisure for churchgoing, despite their shouldering most of the care for the children, the meals, the clothing – everything domestic, including the religious health of their family. Men might be the supposed heads of the families, for matters economic and theological, but women were the hearts. It was mothers who tended to rise in the middle of the night, when a child took sick, mothers who tended to pray passionately to God for the child's wellbeing, in times when human medicine was primitive. Wastrel children could be surer of indulgence from mothers than from fathers. Mother-love became famous for its unconditional character. Seldom would a mother turn her back on the child she had carried in her womb, no matter how galling or trying that child became.

In the view of the most negative secular feminist critics, the Christian church turned all of this to patriarchal account, giving women great praise as mothers but virtually no access to institutional power. Similarly, the Orthodox and Roman Catholic churches encouraged girls to join convents, where they might pray for the wellbeing of the community at large or spend themselves in practical works of teaching or nursing, but these churches did not admit even consecrated, virginal women to the inner precincts of institutional power. A few unusually strong women, such as Catherine of Siena, became reformers, wagging their fingers at sinful popes, but most saintly women bowed their heads in obedience to male authorities, who regulated their lives even in the cloister.

Summarily, then, the case of secular feminists against the institutional Christian church, and the theology of gender on which that church drew, has been that both have repressed women, shrewdly keeping them silent as Pauline theology desired. On such currently boiling political issues as abortion, feminists still see the Catholic church, along with some evangelical and Orthodox churches, as their major enemy. Among secular feminists for whom an untrammeled right to an abortion is a shibboleth of emancipation, Christian right-to-lifers are the troglodytes, the primitives, still trying to keep women down.

The counter-case of Christians, as of the adherents of many other religious traditions, is that a secular horizon is a prison. Indeed, Mircea Eliade, the dean of the past generation of historians of religion, has written extensively of the opposition between the sacred and the profane, equating the sacred with the human quest to transcend this-worldliness and the profane with a flattened secular horizon. For the person seeking full emancipation, a flattened secular horizon, one that does not go beyond the grave, that allows no lift of the spirit toward "heaven" or "God," is a prison. Only with dread does the refined human spirit contemplate a life without a third dimension of holiness, an escape from the flatlands of a continuum limited to space-time.

Shamans have sought to escape from profanity by ecstatic flights to the gods. Yogins have gone within, in enstasis, seeking freedom below the flux of the mind and will, in the untroubled peace of *samadhi*. Through their myths and rituals, their mysticisms and theologies, the world religions have made transcendence, the sacred, available as something mediated by consecrated bread and wine, by privileged biblical words, by music and silence that focus the heart on the mystery at the center of all being, on the no-thing-ness hinted at the foundation of all things.

Behaving and thinking in these ways, religious people, both archaic and modern, have argued that they were enriching the lives of those they formed, those they served. They have argued that theirs was the true emancipation, the one that went to the very roots of the human condition and showed how intercourse with its Creator could transform it – take it outside itself, into the very deathlessness of the Creator herself. Compared to such a fulfillment, what secular activists could achieve through political victories, or secular theorists could achieve through explanations of how women became subjected to men, were only thin beer.

The resolution of this conflict, of course, beckons as an agreement that liberation is not a matter of either political progress in space and time or ultimate transcendence for fulfillment outside of space and time, in heaven. Liberation is a matter of both/and. The best of the Christian liberation theologians (for example, Gustavo Gutierrez[2]) who have arisen lately in Latin America, Asia, and Africa have made this point cogently. Not surprisingly, many of them have been strongly influenced by the Marxist thought that was the rage, the regnant horizon, of European intellectuals in the 1950s, 1960s, and 1970s. The collapse of Soviet communism in particular, and the revelation of the poverty of Marxist economic and philosophical analysis in general, have changed the intellectual atmosphere dramatically, but they have not ousted secularism from its predominance among Western intellectuals, British and American as well as

European. Certainly, religion has made a comeback in some circles, more of them American than British or European, but the pace-setters, the milieu-makers, in virtually all Western universities continue to be secularists leery of religion.

Christian intellectuals who know the implications of the Incarnation can agree with most of the importance that secularists accord to economics, politics, cultural analysis, and natural science. Following the Roman poet Terence, they can say gladly, proudly, that they want to count nothing human foreign to them or their faith. Song and dance, astrophysics and molecular biology, social work and medicine all strike them as worthy occupations, good ways of being in the world with faith that serving the expansion of truth or the welfare of their fellow human beings, even their fellow non-human creatures, pleases their Creator immensely.

What Christian humanists cannot do, however, is default on their further conviction that the full outreach of such a humanism takes honest people into great mysteries. Where do the stars come from? Why do we have poor people, generation after generation? Is death something that we shall ever remove from the human condition? Would such a removal of death be desirable, or would living for vast periods in space and time be the ultimate frustration?

For religious people, these questions tend to bring the mind to a halt, inviting it to contemplate the mystery of human existence simply, holistically. In the course of such a contemplation, which might focus the mind on the sea, or on the whorl of a baby's ear, or on the flickering of a candle in a dark church, the spirit of the person can come into a collectedness, a peace, that seems unearthly. Death and disappointment can lose much of their sting. Hope can emerge shyly, humbly, letting the person think it good to keep going on, anticipating tomorrow, assuming that life may turn out well, that the ultimate news may be good – may even be, as Paul promised, what eye has not seen, ear has not heard, it has not entered the human heart to conceive (1 Corinthians 2:9).

Inasmuch as they cling to different evaluations of the ultimate nature of reality, Christian feminists and secular feminists will always have bones to pick with one another. However, this need not prevent them from cooperating on agendas for the improvement of women's lives in such areas as economics, health care, and political power. It need not keep them from working together to improve the image of women in the culture at large, from diminishing the ways in which advertising degrades women as sex objects or cinema and television portray women as weak, or superhuman, or anything else that continues the tradition of not letting women seem as median, as normal, as men, either by overestimating the virtue of women (woman as holy virgin) or by overestimating the vice (woman as whore).

Last, it would be well for Christian feminists to keep talking to secular feminists, because secular feminists can help Christians stay honest. Christians have to blush when they look at the sexism still defacing their churches, and often they ought to turn down the volume of their cultural criticism. Most churches still have a spotty record concerning women, much of which to be ashamed. Sexism lingers in many Christian theologies, even appears in the practical policies of many churches regarding worship and social action. The reluctance of secular feminists to consider Christians full allies in the fight for women's liberation from patriarchal oppressions, the fight to make Third World women full partners in the economic and political revolutions that many poor, violent nations of Africa and Latin America need, ought to keep Christians sober.

Similarly, the best, the most honest, secular feminists will take to heart the critique of mature Christians and other religious people who say that limiting one's estimate of women's destiny to this-worldly fulfillments short changes them badly. The contemplative life, whether undertaken as a response to our drive for meaning, or our flight from pain, or our ecstatic pursuit of beauty, or our desire to shed our moral shabbiness and deal with something fully holy, real without spot or wrinkle, moves us human beings, women and men virtually indiscriminately, out into what the Canadian novelist Robertson Davies has called "a world of wonders." Natural scientists can enjoy this world, as can artists, lovers, people who pray regularly. Their common report is that visiting it makes them more human, not less. Visiting it is not a journey of alienation but a journey of both homecoming and promise. In fact, many secular people do visit this world, because many are susceptible to the calls of poetry, music, even political enthusiasm, where the world that might be, the world that is – powerful in our souls as an ideal for which to strive – welcomes us as a homeland, a *Heimat*, a utopia that tells us volumes about who we are, what we are for.

Theology as a Lyrical Calling

There is place for "scientific" theology that pores over biblical texts philologically, over conciliar texts with all the literary-critical skills and hermeneutical sophistication available nowadays. Such science helps theology to refine its logic by studying analytical philosophy, to broaden its historical appreciations by learning how anthropologists and sociologists approach the construction of meaning in ordinary human communities. Studies of myths and rituals in other religions can stimulate Christian theologians to rethink Christian doctrine and liturgy. Feminist critical theories can open stimulating new horizons for evaluating the impact of patriarchal cultures in the history of Christian thought and practice.

Nonetheless, were Christian theology to think of itself as only scientific, only academic, it would lose something precious, indeed something arguably intrinsic to its nature as faith seeking understanding. For want of a better image, I have named this something a "lyrical calling." The source of this image may be Augustine's saying, "*Bis orat qui cantat*" – she who sings prays twice. Theology ought to sing about the good news of Christ. The faith that it labors to understanding ought to raise music in the soul, as John Climacus said of laughter in prayer. In fact, a lyrical Christian theology is never but a step removed from prayer. Even when it is doing its best to think clearly, lay out the Christian doctrines logically, it draws much of its motivation from the beauty that such thinking brings to mind.

Faith is not blind, but it is prejudiced positively. The traditional Christian theologian is not neutral about God, does not sit back with her hand under her chin like a dispassionate judge. The traditional Christian theologian is a sinner, a petitioner, someone amazed that God should have offered her forgiveness, salvation, sanctification, the prospect of divine life now, endless glory with God after death. This is "good news" with a vengeance, a clout sufficient to wash every sadness from her soul. Yes, pursuing God, through penance and prayer, hard thought and social action, can become a daunting vocation. True, God turns out to be hidden, the flesh of Christ does not remove the intrinsic mysteriousness of salvation and grace. As we come to see how deeply sin has thrown human existence off balance, both outside us in the general culture and inside us in the vices mottling our own souls, we have to fight discouragement. Asking the Spirit of Christ to wash what is soiled in us, to defend us against the *nosos*, the madness, of the secular world, can become no luxury, simply part of our daily petition for forgiveness and bread.

However, all this can remain musical, if not lyrical. All this, even when we moan it as a lament, keen it as a dirge over the deadliness threatening the human prospect, can flow out to a God we have known in peak experiences to be surpassingly good and can hope will return soon, to lift our hearts again. If we center our spiritual lives where we should, in the eucharistic liturgy and the Bible, we shall meet regularly paradigms supporting the view that God is constant, true to the covenant he has struck, a liberator from the time of the Exodus, a Father powerful enough to raise Jesus from the dead. As the prophet Ezekiel discovered, God wants the life of the sinner, not her death. As the disciples of Jesus discovered, the Son of God came to heal the sick, not the healthy who had little need.

We are sick, though also healthy. Catholics can admit the stark statement of the Westminster Confession that "there is no health in us" without denying their own Tridentine position that sin has not made human nature intrinsically corrupt. The health in us has always come from God, as have our being and grace. However darkened, our minds continue to allow us to find traces of God in nature, other people, works of art. However weakened, our wills continue to allow us to get behind programs of health reform, the reform of welfare, the goal of keeping kids out of trouble. We continue to be responsible for the fate of the earth, the control of nuclear weapons, the reduction of the sufferings caused by epidemics such as AIDS. On our heads continues to lie guilt from the manifest decline of (American) public education, the ongoing depredations of criminals and drug addicts, the persistent messiness of our dealings with immigrants, both legal and illegal.

How responsible we human beings are for all this disorder is never clear, but certainly we are responsible enough to give us pause, require us to examine our consciences daily, and keep us at the task of political reform without surcease. The inefficiencies, if not outright injustices, that our bureaucracies create, along with the irrationalities in our legislatures and judicatories, lay giant claims on all our consciences to improve common life, put down the splintering of politics into a hundred ventures in the aggrandizement of private interest groups, and affirm again, make practical again, the priority of the common good.

Theologians can speak about these things prophetically in their own names, and they can inspire others, who often will have more practical expertise, to speak more precisely, pragmatically, programmatically. A prophetic speaking is not so much a venture in predicting the future as a report on what the Word of God, the judgment of God, says about current times. Prophets call their constituents to moral account. They pass judgment on the quality of justice and mercy they see prevailing in their places and times. For taking the trouble to do this they usually reap resentment, if not hatred. Many of the biblical prophets complained about this harvest bitterly. Jeremiah did not like his vocation, and Jonah fled from the task of preaching to Nineveh, strangely enough because he was afraid that he would succeed (he did not want Nineveh to repent).

The genuine prophet tends to move into poetic, lyrical, parabolic speech, even into dramatic symbolic action. It was no accident that Jesus taught in parables, posed riddles to his hearers, pondered the mysteries of the human heart, offered cures and miracles, washed the feet of his disciples. It was characteristic that Jesus grew sad at the irrationality of sin, coming to wonder with Isaiah why God seemed to have hardened some, so that though they had ears they could not hear, though they had eyes they would not see. The irony so sharp in John stems from this sadness, this frustration at dealing with people who seemed to flee the truth, because of the claims it would make upon them, the requirements that they grow out of the comfortable, self-serving mental habits they had formed. To many of the Johannine Pharisees Jesus was a blasphemer, his "I am" statements amounting to a claim that he was equal to the Mosaic God. To Johannine Christians, the blasphemers were those Pharisees who would not admit the obvious implications of the signs that Jesus had worked, the indubitable character of his credentials to speak for God, present himself as the privileged revelation of God.

Theologians sing about these things, which focus the gripping drama of the interactions between divine holiness, bent on trying to save us from ourselves, and human weakness, fear, sin, which make us run from divine holiness like scared rabbits, lemmings driven by secular contagions. The better educated such theologians are, the more they appreciate the universal outreach and operation of dynamics such as these, how the same forces work powerfully in Buddhist cultures, among Chinese trying to understand the ways of the *Tao*, for Jews puzzling about the tragedies of their history.

A truly incarnational Christian theology is profoundly humanistic, sympathetic to the full sweep of humanity's grand effort to survive evolutionarily and grow culturally. Like the French existentialist writer Albert Camus, it finds more to admire in humanity than to condemn. Despite all our stupidity, selfishness, even malice and outright evil, we have mustered the energy, the courage, the wit to survive for hundreds of thousands of years. At our best, we have turned out people truly holy and wise, genuine saints and sages. We have nourished artists to dazzle our minds, hearts, and souls with beauty. We have educated scientists to uncover a natural world to boggle the mind, intrigue the imagination, and empower engineers to overturn much of our servitude to nature, eliminate much of our fear and make our lives much more enjoyable.

The same Augustine quoted earlier, one of the most lyrical of all the Christian theologians, a rhetorician by both temperament and training, also said that God has made us for himself and our hearts are restless until they rest in God. This may express the inmost melody of our human spirits, the song always playing in our depths. If we ask why, generation after generation, people have kept pursuing meaning, pushing ahead in search of truly ultimate reality, of clearer understanding of the natural world and the ability to make more beautiful cultures, the best answer may well be that the most human thing about us is our spiritual desire, an *eros* for something always beyond us, Plato's *epekeina*.

The Christian equivalent is the confession that God is intrinsically mysterious, and that this is precisely what we need, a beyondness that never fails to challenge us to keep moving ahead. Even in heaven, we shall not understand God, get our minds around divinity. God is limitless, and even in heaven we shall be limited, if we continue to be human. The Christian doctrine of the general resurrection implies that in heaven we shall have bodies, however much changed, and all embodiment entails limitation, though a Pauline spiritualized body (1 Corinthians 15) may be much less limited than the earthly ones we inhabit now.

All imagination of heaven is speculative, to say the least, and not overly profitable. Sufficient for earthly days are the evils thereof – the tasks of prayer and social service incumbent on us patently most weeks. Theology can be the lyrical confession that these are good tasks, fitting and uplifting. Even the sufferings that they bring, or the occasional opprobrium, can serve our purification and good. Just as illness can make us more mature (though this is not inevitable), as misfortune can, so the opposition of people who hate the light, because their deeds are evil, can increase our proper, judicious sobriety. If we are to follow Jesus closely, we have to try to love such people, do good to them even when they make themselves our enemies.

When this work is difficult, our songs may be labored, like the songs of the exiles sitting along the banks of the rivers in Babylon, feeling they could not sing their real songs, because those required their return to Sion. The blues and spirituals that kept American slaves going prior to the Civil War were similar songs of exile.[3] Often any honest theology is going to speak, pray, sing from a psychology of exile, a realization that we have here no lasting city. We have been made for God. Any earthly city is going to leave us restless. Our songs will reflect this, our spiritualities make it constitutive.

Last, if our spiritualities, our passionate pursuits of meaning and holiness, make a restlessness with secular values and horizons constitutive, our religion, the exercise of our Christian faith, is bound to be counter-cultural. No matter how deep and peaceful our humanism, we shall always be aliens, *Auslanders*, tourists and pilgrims. In the best of cases, we shall live gracefully now, with our eyes lifted toward glory later. Grace is the life of God giving deeper beauty and pathos to the spark in our clod right now. Glory is the life of God unveiled, shining in the domain where God's will suffers no resistance, where human sin has been scrubbed away.

In ordinary times, we shall probably slug along, sometimes gracefully, sometimes awkwardly, even sinfully. Still, theologians rejoice to sing about all times under God, all things, trying to hand on the wonderful visions they have received. Grateful to join the great cloud of witnesses who have kept so lovely a faith living, faithful theologians want only to sing in chorus, harmoniously, as part of the 144,000 ceaselessly praising the Lamb. To hope that they are doing this can be reward enough now, a claim upon God for a kindly verdict then, on Judgment Day.

Holiness as a Realistic Goal

The French spiritual writer Leon Bloy said once that the only significant failure is not to become a saint. In contrast, we tend to think of sanctity as something rare, and we tend to characterize it as moral perfection. We are not completely wrong to think this way (the number of people who so realize their human potential that they shine with light and love seems always to be small), but often we defend ourselves against the holocaustal claims of God (who "jealously" wants us to love him with whole mind, heart, soul, and strength) by trying to make saints into nerds, hopeless idealists, people whose virtues (spiritual strengths) are superhuman, due to either an extraordinary biological inheritance or extraordinary helps from God, who dispenses grace as she chooses. This sort of self-defense can be the result of bad faith – less a matter of honesty and humility than of laziness and fear. A better approach to sanctity, holiness, equates it less with moral perfection than with utter realism, wisdom about what we ought to love, passion to let God bring such wisdom to fruition.

As a careful reading shows, the Christian desert fathers and mothers sought nothing less than the remaking of human nature – that was the reason for their preoccupation, indeed their obsession, with the principal virtues and vices. Living in the solitary wastes of the Thebaid, the upper Nile that became the cradle of Egyptian monasticism, they could see the deformations of the human soul clearly, undistracted by cultural overlays. But when they went to work on remaking human nature, the fathers and mothers of the desert found that they were not equal to the task. Willful as they might be, they succumbed again and again, until they surrendered themselves to the grace of God. Just as they had not made themselves in the womb, so they could not remake themselves outside the womb into full likenesses to Christ. Certainly, Christ was, like them, fully human, but with one enormously significant difference: "save sin." The sinlessness of Christ meant his complete trust in God and a related gracefulness (balance, wisdom, courage), that they could only approximate after years of intense openness to the Spirit in prayer and fasting.

The lesson of the desert, which became canonical for all later

Christian monasticism and orthodox spirituality, was that the shift involved in the process of sanctification, of being made holy by the Spirit of Christ and the Father, takes the person from selfishness to preoccupation with God. Supreme Christian wisdom is the realization that there is almost only God. Human reality is paper thin. When God is realer to us than the world, so that both nature and history repose in God, contained by the divine limitlessness, we have verged upon a proper sense of creation, an ordering of our minds and hearts that is right, fitted to the way that things actually are.

Until we gain such a proper sense of creation, such a right order, at least in germ, we swim against the stream, move against the grain. This is the great Taoist insight, made into scripture in the *Lao Tzu* (*Tao te Ching*). The Way (*Tao*) runs things, whether we like it or not. Our only sane choice is to acknowledge this priority of the *Tao*, take it to heart, and adapt our actions to it. The Way is always greater. We are always lesser. For the lesser to try to dictate to the greater is absurd, both grotesque and humorous.

What the Way is in traditional Chinese culture God is in traditional Christianity. God is always greater. Compared to God, both nature and we ourselves are minuscule, barely blips on the screen. A few of the mystics have seen this so vividly that they have feared annihilation. Most of the saints have experienced it as a great liberation, cause for endless joy. The seraphim and cherubim do not sing endlessly because they fear the lash if they should stop. They sing endlessly because they are overwhelmed by the majesty of God. The majesty of God is not the artificial pomp of a human sovereign. It is the outflow, the ruling glory, of what God simply is. God simply is utterly real, utterly without flaw, entirely without end. To be God, God has to be completely good, blazing with light and love. For our limited minds and hearts, this utterness (what Buddhists call "suchness") must often seem dark, even threatening. It defeats us from the start, throughout the process, at the end. The only way that we can "win" is to admit it, be honest enough to become good "Muslims" and submit to it, bowing low in awe.

Holiness of this ontological sort is a realistic goal, because all our experiences turn us in its direction. All our experiences take their shape from our finitude: ignorance, mortality, moral imperfection. We do nothing with complete awareness, without at least subterranean fear of getting hurt badly and so being brought close to death of some sort, or with completely pure motivation. We do nothing as God does. And we know this, though only dimly, with an ache. The more carefully we contemplate Jesus, whom traditional Christians consider to be the only adequate icon of God, revealing as much of the divine holiness as flesh can, the more exactly we see the difference between God and ourselves. By the time we contemplate Jesus dying on the cross, we sense that God's ways are as distant from our spontaneous, unregenerate human ways as the heavens are from the earth.

However, God can take over our hearts and change our ways. We can surrender much of our egocentricity, even much of our sinfulness. We can repent and believe in the gospel. By the grace of God, we can live outside of ourselves more and more, moving into the capacious limitlessness of God. Ideally, we shall do this while keeping our feet on the ground, remembering that we come from dust and unto dust we all return. Ideally, our realism, our growing holiness, will be sacramental and good-humored. The life of God in us is not grim. God made the world in delight. To sustain this delight, God was willing to suffer for us human beings and our salvation. But the suffering was not an end in itself. The sobriety of the Christian saints is not God's last word. While the bridegroom is in their midst, the most mature Christian saints rejoice – drink, sing, dance. In heaven the bridegroom is in their midst constantly. Death is no more, so no more is there lamentation or weeping.

The realism that is the hallmark of Christian maturity, significant sanctity, brims with hope. We may distinguish hope from optimism. Hope results from contemplating God and receiving the grace to see that God is always greater. Hope knows what it means to call God the absolute future and say that the only worthy response to God is to hand over a blank check. Optimism stems from a good digestion, the good fortune of not yet having been mugged. Optimism is hard-pressed to stand against random violence, a diagnosis of terminal cancer, the arrival of a child with Down's syndrome. People who previously have been shallow, sunbeams with little experience of shadows, can change from optimism to hope, but often they do not. So Christian spiritualities ought to make sure that they focus on hope, the expectation that God will be good mysteriously, just as God chooses, rather than on any tacit, optimistic expectations that life will always go onward and upward, always get better and better.

Life can devolve. Entropy can run us down, break us apart. Like Jesus, we can end up on the cross, a complete failure in the eyes of the world. Are we willing to imagine joining Jesus on the cross, learning about the power and wisdom of God through suffering? We can be, if our Christian formation has made us hopeful. Jesus on the cross, in the first, agonizing phase of his passover from death to life, expresses the starkest sort of realism. Here is how God's best creature, God's most fully authenticated emissary, ended up. Here is the way that the *Christos*, the one anointed by God to bring in God's reign, did his best work. He let God take everything. He let sin and death do their worst. Opening his arms wide, his heart, he broke the cycle of hurt for hurt, sin for sin, proving that love is stronger.

Love comes from God. In its purest forms, love is unearthly, the one power that can create being from nothingness, perhaps most dramatically through forgiveness. Through the love of Christ, God forgave the world masses of sin it could barely recognize. Augustine, who seems sometimes to have declined from hope to pessimism, once called the human race a *massa damnata*. The most realistic message stemming from the death and resurrection of Jesus is that God has changed such a designation, taken away its propriety. The fall of Adam has become a *felix culpa*, a happy fault, because it stimulated the appearance of so great a savior. There is no parity between the sin that was committed and the grace with which God responded. God not only forgave whatever outrages sin involved, she went on to raise human potential to the point where we might become partakers of the divine nature (2 Peter 1:4), sharers in eternal life.

This potential may have shaped human nature from the beginning, the time when reflective spirit first began to quicken our animality with reason. Christians are bound to say, however, that only with the life, death, and resurrection of Jesus the Christ did this potential become clear. The resurrection of Christ, as the declaration of our human justification and elevation by God, was a new thing in history, a *hapax legomenon* (unique word). Because of the resurrection, which it found completely fitting as the denouement of the drama of Christ's compelling life, the early Christian community sensed that Jesus was as much divine as human.

Only one who had come from God, who took his inmost identity from God, could have placed such goodness and power in the world.

Certainly, he was fully human. Had the disciples not seen him face to face, broken bread with him, placed their fingers in the holes made by the nails in his side? But humanity could not contain or explain the full reality of Jesus. He must have been with God in the beginning. What he enfleshed must have been the Word of God, the eternal self-expression (a concept partially available in the Hebrew Bible, as we have seen, and also influential in the Hellenistic culture that shaped John).

The realism of precisely Christian holiness is a wisdom focused by this lens of the Incarnation. To the theses we can fashion from experience of the constant majority of God, the certain priority of the divine in all times and places, it adds what happens when divinity takes flesh, walks in our midst, submits itself to our handling. The history of God in our midst as one of us, like us in all things save sin, intensifies the distance between creation and the Creator. God is beyond us morally as well as ontologically. The love of God, the patient goodness, matches the limitless divine fecundity. God is as skillful in means to save us (another Buddhist sentiment) as to bring forth new creatures from the divine storehouse. God is as great a physician for our spirits as she is a designer of our sinews and nerves.

A realistic holiness is simply an absorption with these wonders, a lyrical appreciation of the marvels making possible the natural world that sustains us, the mental worlds we can travel without end. Theology can be simply the most ultimately based humanism, the one that loves best the silence at the beginning, the silence at the end. If it has an advantage over other humanisms, other ways of appreciating the human condition, that advantage comes from faith. Theologians take to heart the witness of past sages, and the testimony of their own experience, that life is always greater, the ultimate always abides in darkness, God is never a mere problem, is always a genuine mystery.

The proper response to this situation, this plain reality, is faith, the knowledge born from loving it. Go to reality honestly, lovingly, and you will hear a still small voice telling you to put aside your arrogance, let the majority of reality make its full say, have its full way. You have not made yourself, nor any other living being in the world. You should admire what you have not made, what you cannot make, and take to heart its lessons. Doing that, you may become realistic, and so holy, in the sense of real yourself. You may become a success story, a person who realizes that we become saints by saying to God, "Yes!"

Study Questions

1 Is it possible to harmonize a traditional understanding of "Christian" and a critical understanding of "feminist"?
2 What are the most valid challenges that Christian faith presents to radical feminists?
3 What is the validity of a purely academic, non-lyrical theology?
4 Why should we bother about holiness?
5 Write a paragraph giving your concluding understanding of the phrase "a constructive Christian feminist theology."

Notes

1 See Gerda Lerner, *The Creation of Feminist Consciousness* (Oxford University Press, New York, 1993).
2 See Gustavo Guttierez, *We Drink from Our Own Well* (Orbis, Maryknoll, NY, 1985).
3 See James Cone, *The Spirituals and the Blues* (Seabury, New York, 1972).

INDEX

abortion   212, 213, 227, 248
adoption   227
aesthetics   22
agape   145
alienation, religion causing, in secular
    feminist thought   247
altruism   14
anchorites   134
annunciation   42–4, 134
anointing (last rites)   121–2
Aquinas, Thomas   54, 67, 194, 196,
    244
Arians   58
Aristotle   7, 142, 168, 194, 244
arts, search for beauty in   22
Athanasius   58
Augustine, St   30, 48, 51–2, 53, 54,
    67, 153–4, 178, 181, 194, 244,
    252, 255, 260
Aung San Sun Kyi, Mrs   12–13, 14,
    15, 16, 21, 30

baptism   58, 120
Bahai   62
beauty, search for   21–5
Bernard of Clairvaux   147
Bible   45–9, 119, 148, 183, 217, 229,
    243–4
  and creation/nature   78–82, 87,
    92–3

images of justice   17
patriarchal/subversive of patriarchy
    48–9, 74, 76, 82
  see also New Testament; Old
    Testament; scripture
bishops   58
Bloy, Leon   257
Buddhism   29, 61, 62, 63, 95, 118,
    125, 150, 174, 180, 255, 258
  scriptures   45, 217
  and suffering   13, 15–16, 166

Calvin, John   67
Catherine of Siena   248
Chalcedon, council of (AD 451)   58,
    60, 121, 188
children, women's involvement in
    care and socialization of   50,
    155, 156–8
Christian belief, early formulation
    57–8, 239
Christian community
  early   42, 102–7, 260
  vision of   102–7, 126
  see also church
Christian feminism, constructive
    1–6, 65
Christian/feminist
  mutual challenge of   247–51
  relationship   208, 242–7

Christian feminist theology   9–11,
    66–9
Christos   217–18, 260
    see also Jesus Christ
Chrysostom, John   51, 244
church
    function and mission   64, 127–8
    growth of   199–200
    scripture in mainstream churches
        46–8
    women in *see under* women
    see also Christian community
church councils   58, 60, 121, 188,
    244
church fathers   6, 9, 51, 117, 174,
    182, 221, 244
church history   55–61, 103
circumincessio   200
class
    in the church   61
    socio-economic   59, 224
clericalism   238
colonialism   93
common good, priority of   221, 224,
    254
communicatio idiomatum   187–8
communion of saints   148
communities, and search for meaning
    19
community, as ethical touchstone
    211–16
    see also Christian community
Confucianism   61, 62, 63, 141, 142,
    217
connatural knowledge   210–11, 236
Conroy, Frank, finding oneself
    through work in *Body and Soul*
    139–44
Constantine, Emperor   59
Constantinople, council of   121
constructive Christian feminism   1–6,
    65
constructive Christian feminist
    theology   9–11, 66–9
contemplation   20–1, 204
    see also prayer
conversion   16, 22–3, 164

centrality of prayer and social justice
    234–40
counter-cultural quality of Christianity
    187, 256
covenant   98, 177
creation   10, 29, 41, 72–101, 105,
    117, 175–6, 178, 183, 200,
    231–4
    see also ecology; nature
creation myths   74
creeds   239–40
culture
    counter-cultural quality of
        Christianity   187, 256
    "higher" culture and "little
        tradition"   49–50, 62, 156,
        243–4
Cyril of Alexandria   58

Daly, Mary   101n7
Dante Alighieri   145, 153
death   32–4, 250
democracy   239
desert fathers/mothers 58, 143, 257
despair   9
    choice between hope and   30–4
dialogue, as strategy for dealing with
        human sin   115–19
Dinnerstein, Dorothy   154–5
diversity   3
divorce   228
doubt   3

Eastern Orthodoxy *see* Orthodox
    church
ecclesiology   10, 102–38
    see also Christian community;
        church
ecocide   17
eco-feminism   91, 234
ecological spirituality   234
    development of   95–100
ecology
    as example of overlap of ethics and
        spirituality   230–4

as religious issue 67, 91–5, 118, 178
and human search for meaning 17–21
see also creation; nature
egalitarianism
  of early church and its diminution 48, 57, 58–60, 106
  of Jesus 48, 54–5, 58, 59, 80, 117, 187, 193
Eiseley, Loren 232
Eliade, Mircea 62, 248
Elvira, council of (*c.* ad 306) 244
Emerson, Ralph Waldo 125
Enlightenment 2, 3
environmental movement/issues 149, 223
  see also ecology
equal opportunity 55, 245
  see also egalitarianism
equality, sexual 5, 6, 10, 12, 35–6, 48, 54–5, 186, 209, 226, 242, 244–5
  see also patriarchy; sexism
Erikson, Erik 231
ethics 10, 55, 206–41
  Christian feminist view of 206–11
  community as ethical touchstone 211–16
  conversion 234–40
  love as the power of persuasion 216–20
  sexual 212–13, 225–9
  and spirituality 230–4
  women and poverty 220–5
eucharist 58, 104, 105, 106, 107, 117, 120, 135, 169
euthanasia 213
Eve 51–2, 53, 108–9, 133, 135
evil, problem of 113, 175, 190–1
existentialism 150, 245–6
experience 40, 68–9, 160
Ezekiel 183

faith
  church as stumbling block to 128

related to theology 6–7, 252, 261
rand life-cycle of women 159–66
  sole requirement for communion 106
  traditional orthodox, as basis of constructive Christian feminism 1–2
fall, the 108–11, 153, 260
  see also original sin
family planning 212–13, 227
feminity/masculinity
  of God 36–8, 67, 75, 76, 192–8
  of Holy Spirit 202–3
feminism, moderate 1, 4–6, 12
feminist/Christian
  mutual challenge of 247–51
  relationship between 208, 242–7
feminist critical theory 252
feminist theology 9–11, 66–9, 82
Feuerbach, Ludwig Andreas 192
finitude 84, 107
Fiorenza, Elisabeth Schüssler 69
flood, Noah's 111
folk religion 62
forgiveness 130–1, 260
Francis of Assisi 94
free will 180
Freud, Sigmund 140–1
fundamentalism 238

Gandhi, Mohandas, Mahatma 14, 15, 129, 130
Gilchrist, Ellen, love in *The Anna Papers* 144–7
Gimbutas, Marija 63
Gnosticism 135
God 6–9, 10, 67, 117, 258
  beauty of 22–5
  constancy 253
  as creator 72–6, 173–4, 175–6, 231, 232; *see also* creation
  as Father/Mother 36–8, 192–8, 202
femininity/masculinity of 36–8, 67, 75, 76, 192–8
  and finding oneself 139–44
  generosity 175–6, 219–20

glory   175–6, 201–2, 256
graciousness   165
holiness   8
immanence   177, 178–82
and justice   14–17
as love   27–30, 79, 176, 210–11,
        219–20, 260
as mystery   6–8, 255
patience of   191
providence of   29, 76, 78, 85
search for, in prayer   166–70
and search for meaning   19–21
self tied to   150–1
signs of, in nature   82–6
and sinners   112, 193
suffering of, in Jesus   187–92
supereminent nature of   36–8
transcendence of   82, 173–7, 186,
        249
wisdom of 87–91, 98–9, 100, 200–1
wisdom of, Jesus as   182–7
see also Word of God
grace   3, 10, 63–5, 118, 127, 136–7,
        199, 203, 219, 243, 252, 259
related to glory   201–2, 256
grace, materialization of
in creation   93, 94–5, 96, 99–100
in Incarnation   134, 168
in sacraments   126
gratitude   170
Greek culture, female life-cycle in
        161–3
Greek thought   54, 182, 192
Gregory of Nyssa   174
Gutierrez, Gustavo   249

Hartman, David   131
heaven   174–5, 255–6
Hebrew Bible   45, 183, 189–90, 243
see also Old Testament
Heidegger, Martin   125
Hellwig, Monika   133
heresy   4, 58, 60
hierarchy   67
Hildegaarde of Bingen   94
Hinduism   29, 36, 61, 63, 160–1,
        162, 180

scriptures   45, 217
holiness   63, 64, 181, 199
as a realistic goal   257–62
Holy Spirit   106–7, 120–1, 176, 183,
        199–204, 246, 253
hope   6, 9, 117, 242–3, 250, 259
choice between despair and   30–4
for women   34–8
human autonomy   152, 181, 213
human dominion over nature
        89–91, 92–3
diminishing   95–100
human nature/spirit   117, 149
foundational issues   10, 12–39
transcendence of   21, 166–7
human rights   117–18, 223
humanity
heterosexuality/homosexuality   5,
        226, 245
place in creation   86–91
responsibility for creation   86, 92–5

idealism   125
ideology   28
Ignatius of Loyola   97, 233
immanence   177, 178–82
immortality   33
Incarnation   95, 105, 134, 168,
        186–7, 207, 219, 246, 255, 261
Jesus as Word of God incarnate *see*
        Word of God
individualism   244
see also egalitarianism
institutions, loyalty to   238
Irenaeus   193, 242
Isaiah   97
Islam   44, 61, 63, 181, 192
Muslim–Jewish–Christian trialogue
        128–31
scriptures   41, 45, 178, 217
Israel
history of, as revelation   42
Jewish–Palestinian relations
        128–31

Jainism 62
Jerome 244
Jesus Christ 9, 16, 41, 67, 211, 235, 242
  attitude towards women xi, 48, 54, 55, 80, 187, 193
  in Christian church history 56–61
  death and resurrection of 80–2, 192, 207–8, 246, 260
  egalitarianism of 48, 54–5, 58, 59, 80, 117, 187, 193
  ethics as imitation of *see* ethics
  and goodness of God as creator 85–6
  humanity/divinity 3, 58, 60, 61, 187–8, 260–1
  love and kingdom of God 217–19
  Messiah 41, 57, 77, 105, 188, 194, 218, 242
  and poverty/wealth 48, 117–18, 221, 223–4
  relationship with God, 7, 151, 193–4, 197
  role in maintenance of creation 76–82
  sacraments as acts of Christ's body 119–26
  and sinners 59, 112–13, 151, 254
  Son of Man 185, 190
  and suffering of God 187–92
  Suffering Servant 190
  transfiguration 124
  wisdom of God in flesh 182–7
  Word of God incarnate *see* Word of God
  see also Incarnation
Jewish *see* Judaism
Johannine theology/material 27, 45, 46, 57, 60, 105, 120, 121, 184–5, 188, 201, 202, 203, 236, 245, 254
  imagery 9, 176, 185
  reconception of creation in light of Christ 77–80, 87
  see also under New Testament *for individual references*
John, of the Cross 95, 132, 147

John XXIII, Pope 239
John, the Baptist 112, 146
John Paul I, Pope 198
Johnson, Elizabeth xi, 17–18, 21, 30, 66–8, 69
Judaism 59, 61, 63, 176, 192, 255
  Jewish–Christian–Muslim trialogue 128–31
  scriptures 45, 49, 183, 189–90, 217, 243
  tradition 2, 49–50, 147, 175
  see also Old Testament
Jung, C. G. 123, 125
justice 6, 107, 118, 234–40
  search for 12–17, 250–1
justification 199

kairos 121, 127, 235
karma 29, 180
Keegan, John 113–14
Kierkegaard, Søren 150
King, Martin Luther, Jr 14, 15, 129
kingdom of God 56, 135–6, 217–19
Kingsolver, Barbara, search for love in *Pigs in Heaven* 25–9
koinonia (common life) 102, 104, 106, 121
  see also Christian community; church
Koran 41, 45, 178, 217

LaCugna, Catherine xi
lectio divinia (divine reading) 47–8
Leninism 224
Lerner, Gerda 101n7
liberation theology 249
Lonergan, Bernard 189
Lord's Prayer 237–8
Lord's Supper 104
  see also eucharist
love 140, 142, 144–8, 210–11, 226, 245–6, 260
  as the power of persuasion in ethics 216–20
  human search for 25–30

see also under God
Luther, Martin   67

McFague, Sallie   xi, 66, 68–9, 101n6
machismo   228
Marcel, Gabriel   246
martyrs, for social justice   14
Marx, Marxism   19, 192, 224, 249
Mary   79, 183
    annunciation   42–4, 134
    in Christian theology and tradition
        51, 52, 125, 133–4, 135, 219,
        246–7
    Magnificat   48
Mary Magdalene   48
meaning, search for and creation of
        3, 6, 7–8, 17–21, 30, 63, 255
medical ethics   212–15
    see also sexual ethics
Meier, John   190
Menchu, Rigoberta   14, 15, 16
Mendes-Flohr, Paul   131
men's movement   123
Messiah *see under* Jesus Christ
modernity   2–3
monastic life   50, 58, 59, 148, 244,
        248
    see also desert fathers/mothers
Monophysites   58
monotheism   85, 177, 192
Moore, Thomas   123, 142
moral dimension of self   143
mother   162, 248
    church as   121–2
    God as   36–8, 192–8, 202
    and warfare   114–15
Muslims *see* Islam
Myanmar, Daw Aung San Sun Kyi
    and search for justice in   12–13
mystery religions   57
mysticism, mystics   23, 132, 147,
        165, 167, 178, 229, 258
mythological thinking   123

narcissism   123, 154
nature   223

relationship of self to   148–9
signs of God in   82–6
negotiation, as strategy for dealing
    with human sin   115–19
Nestorians   58
New Testament   45–6, 57, 169, 190,
        207, 243
    gospels   123–4
    synoptic materials   45, 46, 188,
        190
    Matthew *6:25–31*   85–6; *7–16*
        212; *13:31–3*   136; *17*   124
    Mark *1:14*   234; *9*   124; *15:39*
        189
    Luke 43; *1:26–38*   42; *1:46–55*   48;
        3:38   43; *4:18–19*   218; *15*
        191; *16*   221; *24*   104
    John   *1–12*   79; *1:1–18*   194;
        1:1–14   183; *1: 1–5*   77–9;
        1:14–18   201; *3:14*   188; *4*
        54; *9*   184; *10:30*   201; *14–17*
        121, 188; *14:8–14*   201
    Acts *2:43–7*   102–7, 221; *9*   206;
        10:34–5, 44–8   64–5
    Romans: *5:5* 27; *7*   108; *8:26*   142,
        199
    1 Corinthians *1:23*   131; *1:24*   184;
        2:9   17, 250; *11:1*   206; *12:31*
        223; *15*   255
    Galatians *3:28*   38, 48, 106, 216; *5:1*
        229, 243
    Philippians *4:8*   64
    Colossians *1:15–20*   80–2, 183, 194
    pastoral epistles   59
    1 Timothy   *2*   244
    Hebrews   *4:12*   185
    James *1:17*   23, 232
    1/2 Peter   59
    2 Peter *1:4*   260
    I John *4:8*   27, 210
    Revelation   166, 176, 185, 192,
        194; *1:13–16*   185; *5:12*   185;
        8:1   22; *19:13*   185

Nicaea, council of (AD 325)   58, 60,
        121
Niebuhr, Rainhold   31

Nietzsche, Friedrich Wilhelm 128,
154
nirvana 15
nuns 50, 248
see also desert fathers/mothers;
monastic life

Old Testament/Hebrew Bible 45, 46,
183, 189–90, 243
Genesis *1–11* 111; *1:1–5* 73–4,
77; *1:26–8* 89–90; *1:27* 5, 88;
3:1–7 108–11, 117, 133
Exodus *3* 98
Leviticus *25* 218
I Kings *19:9–14* 23
Job 87
Psalms 170; *1* 98; *148:3–12* 83
Proverbs *8:22–31* 87–9; *9:1* 98,
184
Song of Songs 229, 245; *3:1–5*
147–8
Isaiah *40:6–8* 173; *45:12, 18–19*
75, 88
Daniel *10:5–9* 185
Oosterhuis, Huub 64
optimism, distinguished from hope
259
Origen 67
original sin 31, 51, 107–13, 165, 191
Orthodox church 47, 50, 65, 120,
183, 202, 246, 248
orthodoxy 4, 59–60

panentheism 180
pantheism 179–80
paraclete *see* Holy Spirit
patriarchy 5–6, 35, 155–9, 191, 215,
221, 222, 225, 228, 240
in Bible 48–9, 74, 76, 82
in Christianity xi, 38, 50, 51–5,
59, 60–1, 66, 67, 69, 135,
243–4, 252
in world religions 63, 65
see also sexism
patripassianism 189

patristic era *see* church fathers
Pauline theology/material 45, 46,
96, 105, 120, 121, 137, 245, 248
imagery 9, 229
see also under New Testament *for
individual references*
perichoresis 200, 201, 219
pilgrimage 96
Planned Parenthood 212
Plato/Platonism 125, 135, 166, 216,
255
pluralism 3
poor, moral rights of 48, 117–18,
221
see also poverty
post-modern 3, 61
poverty, women and 220–5
see also poor
power
Christian feminism and 113–19,
222–3
male will to 18, 126, 154
marginality of women 133, 135,
136, 156, 248
praise 170
prayer 141, 142, 148
centrality of 234–40
as ultimate freedom 166–70
pride 133, 153—4
priesthood, exclusion of women from
125–6, 135, 187
prophets 97, 254
Protestant Reformation 2, 3, 49, 50
Protestantism 10, 47, 120, 125, 186,
199, 244
providence 29, 76, 78, 85
psychoanalytic reading of human
development 156–8
psychology, archetypal 123, 124

racism 224
Rahner, Karl 55, 67, 199, 219, 242
rape 228
reason 7, 19, 89
reconciliation 130–1
redemption 27, 52, 113

social location of 126–33
women's role 133–7
Reformation 2, 3, 49, 50
reign of God 56, 135–6, 217–19
relationship
　social, of self 148–52
　with God 150–1, 181–2
　women and 67, 152
relativity 61
Renaissance 2, 3
repentance 112, 164, 234–6
resurrection
　general 255
　of Jesus 80–2, 192, 207–8, 246,
　　260
　Jewish stories 33
revelation 10, 40–4, 45
rights, Christians and 117–18, 223
Rilke, Rainer Maria 125
Roman Catholicism 47, 50, 52, 65,
　119, 186, 187, 213, 248, 253

sacraments 58, 104, 119–26, 246,
　259
　see also eucharist
sacred
　and profane 248–9
　scripture as 45
saints
　activist 14, 16
　Christian 147, 170, 177, 181, 220,
　　233, 238, 258
　communion of 148
salvation 41, 43, 104–5, 127, 132,
　200, 252
sanctification 199
　see also holiness
scepticism 3
schism 4
science
　and beauty 24–5
　and search for meaning 19, 21
scripture 42–9, 67, 68, 69, 104, 119
　canon 45, 46, 58
　necessity for reading in the round
　　53

see also Bible; Koran
sectarianism 4
self, sick and healthy 139–72
sex, Augustine on 51–2, 53
sexism 6, 54–5, 65, 67, 69, 224, 243,
　251
　see also patriarchy
sexual equality see equality
sexual ethics 212–13, 225–9
shamans 62, 249
Sikhism 62
sin 3, 19, 117, 186, 252–3
　original/structural 31, 51, 107–13,
　　165, 191
　and self 153–9
　stereotypes of 113–14, 153, 154–5
skepticism 3
social justice see justice
social relationship of self 148–52
socialism 223
society, Christian, vision of 102–7,
　126
Socrates 145
spiritual life-cycle 164–6
spirituality
　and the elderly 163
　overlap with ethics 230–4
　see also prayer
Starhawk (Miriam Simos) 101n7
suffering 13, 15–16, 30, 34, 132–3,
　175, 256, 260
　of God in Jesus 187–92
suicide 213
synoptic scriptures 45, 46, 188, 190

Taoism 61, 62, 63, 167, 255, 258
　scriptures 45, 217
Teresa of Avila 147
Teresa of Lisieux 147
Tertullian 30, 51, 244
theodicy 99
　see also evil, problem of; suffering
theology 6–11, 173–205
　as a lyrical calling 252–6
　constructive Christian feminist
　　9–11, 66–9

early formulation   57–8
scientific   252
see also individual subjects
Theos (God)   6, 7
theosis (divinization)   160, 201
   see also grace
theotokos   52, 125, 134, 219
Tillich, Paul   125
Tower of Babel   111
tradition   2, 10, 49–55, 68, 211
traditional Christian faith, theology
      1–4, 9, 10
traditional cultures   2
   femininity/masculinity of God   36
   hunting and gathering cultures and
      creation   94
   and life-cycle   160–1, 162, 163
   sexual dualism and power   115
   tribal peoples and religion   62
transcendence *see under* God *and*
      human spirit
Trible, Phyllis   69
Trinity   3, 60, 77, 120–1, 176, 177,
      182, 192, 204
   see also God; Holy Spirit; Jesus Christ

utopian groups   244

warfare   113–19, 222–3
Westminster Confession   253
Whitehead, Alfred North   101n5
wicca   94, 162–3
wisdom   86, 98, 142, 162–3, 168,
      258
   divine *see under* God
Wittgenstein, Ludwig   6
women

in Bible   48, 69, 79–80
in Christian tradition/history
      xi–xii, 50–61, 133–7, 243–8,
      251
in church community   106, 245
dominion over creation   89–91
in "higher" culture and "little
      tradition"   49–50, 156, 243–4
hope for   34–8
identification with church   121–2
Jesus Christ and   xi, 48, 54, 55, 80,
      187, 193
life-cycle and faith   159–66
ordination to and exclusion from
      priesthood   125–6, 135, 187,
      239
and poverty   220–5
and power   113–19, 133, 135, 136,
      156, 222–3, 248
relational thinking   67, 152
in world religions   63–5
women's movement   60
wonder   168, 261
   and nature   92–5, 96, 234
Word of God   44, 77–82, 87, 125,
      176, 183, 184–5, 187, 189, 192,
      219, 246
   scripture as   46–7
work   140–4, 148
world religions   61–5, 249, 252
   and nature   97
   see also individual religions
worship   46, 203

yogins   249
Yugoslavia, former   128–9, 130–1

Zoroastrianism (Parsis)   62